exploring

Adobe
Illustrator CS6

exploring

Adobe
Illustrator CS6

Toni Toland/Annesa Hartman

DELMAR
CENGAGE Learning·

Australia • Brazil • Japan • Korea • Mexico • Singapore • Spain • United Kingdom • United States

DELMAR
CENGAGE Learning·

Title: Exploring Illustrator CS6
Author(s): Toni Toland, Annesa Hartman

Vice President, Careers & Professional
  Editorial: Dave Garza

Director of Learning Solutions: Sandy Clark

Senior Acquisitions Editor: Jim Gish

Managing Editor: Larry Main

Product Manager: Meaghan Tomaso

Editorial Assistant: Sarah Timm

Vice President Marketing, Career and
Professional: Jennifer Baker

Executive Marketing Manager:
Deborah S. Yarnell

Associate Marketing Coordinator:
  Erin DeAngelo

Senior Production Director: Wendy Troeger

Production Manager: Andrew Crouth

Senior Content Project Manager: Glenn Castle

Senior Art Director: Jack Pendleton

Technology Project Manager: Chris Catalina

Media Editor: Debbie Bordeaux

Adobe® Illustrator is a trademark or registered trademark of Adobe Systems, Inc. in the United States and/or other countries. Third party products, services, company names, logos, design, titles, words, or phrases within these materials may be trademarks of their respective owners. Adobe product screenshot(s) reprinted with permission from Adobe Systems Incorporated.

Library of Congress Control Number: 2012941802
ISBN-13: 9781133693253
ISBN-10: 1133693253

Delmar
5 Maxwell Drive
Clifton Park, NY 12065-2919
USA

Cengage Learning is a leading provider of customized learning solutions with office locations around the globe, including Singapore, the United Kingdom, Australia, Mexico, Brazil, and Japan. Locate your local office at: **international. cengage.com/region**

Cengage Learning products are represented in Canada by Nelson Education, Ltd.

To learn more about Delmar, visit **www.cengage.com/delmar**

Purchase any of our products at your local college store or at our preferred online store **www.cengagebrain.com**

Printed in Canada
1 2 3 4 5 6 7 16 15 14 13 12

For my husband, Hugh Phillips
—Toni Toland

For my father, Terry Hartman
—Annesa Hartman

| Contents |

Contents

| Contents |

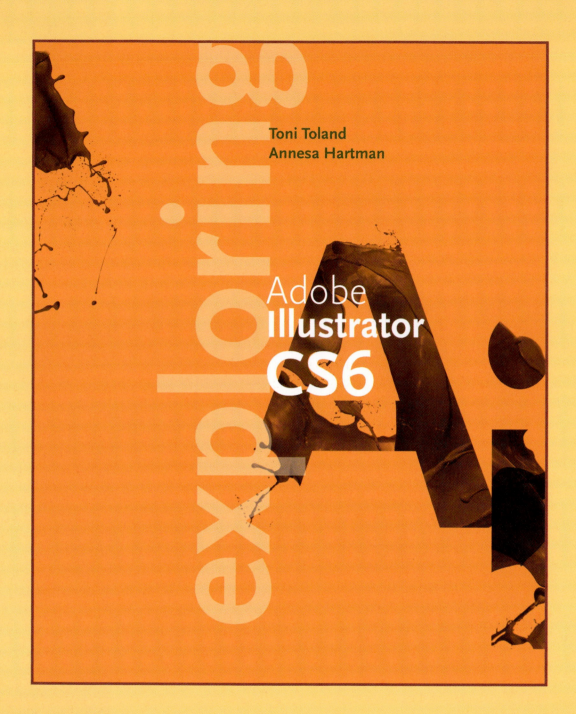

exploring

Toni Toland
Annesa Hartman

Adobe
Illustrator
CS6

| Preface |

intended audience

You are here. Destination, Adobe Illustrator. Your guide, this book. *Exploring Adobe Illustrator CS6*, like other books in the Cengage Delmar Learning Design Exploration series, takes an inventive approach to the introductory study and application of popular computer graphic software programs.

A new student to digital illustration, a computer graphics or arts educator, or a professional graphic artist looking for fresh ways to use Adobe Illustrator will find this book's content relevant, straightforward, and engagingly accessible. It speaks clearly to the artist in all of us, approaching what could be complex design concepts practically, visually, and in the context of the many tools, effects, and workflow features currently available for both print and Web artwork creation in Adobe Illustrator CS6.

background of this text

Pablo Picasso once exclaimed, "Computers are useless. They can only give you answers." True, perhaps. However, accompanied by the right questions, such answers can bring an enlightened perspective to mundane tasks, complicated procedures, and traditional methods of creative endeavor. Successful graphic artists realize the importance of having a foundation in design principles and knowing the tools, and also having the skills to communicate clearly and collaboratively with others in the innovation process. The artists highlighted in this book were asked, "What suggestions for success would you give to the emerging graphic artist?" All emphasized the need for one to be adaptable to change and alterations, to be professional, organized, and prompt in all matters of his/her business, and to be personable to others, and yet persistent in self-promotion. And finally, to keep learning, exploring, and engaging with all that this expansive world offers—such as this book!

This full-color book

- ► explores the questions that face today's illustrator/designer and provides some educated answers through the use of Adobe Illustrator's digital tools and features;

- ► offers process-oriented lessons developed from actual implementation in classrooms and production firms;

- ► develops an understanding of core concepts related to digital artwork creation through fundamental design elements (line, shape, value, texture, and color) and methods; and

- ► most importantly opens the door for continued, self-guided discovery.

As you will learn in the first chapter, Illustrator is a powerful program for the reworking, repurposing, and reproduction of artwork, as well as development of completely new digital imagery. Its fundamental way of making illustrations, which is explained and demonstrated step-by-step in this book, is through the use of vectors, making lines and shapes point by point. Yes, having taken a few traditional drawing and design classes can more quickly move along your understanding of how Illustrator works, however, that's not mandatory. This book addresses the fundamentals of using Illustrator, as well as the creation of digital artwork in general and within the context of established elements of art and design. All you really need to get started is some motivation to venture forth.

Textbook Organization

Like all books in Cengage Delmar Learning's Design Exploration series, the instructional design of this book—its organization and features—is the result of the collaborative efforts of dedicated authors and production staff. The first edition of this book began with two months of researching the content and layout of other Illustrator books and the writing styles of textbooks in general. Conversations with many digital artists and computer graphics instructors and students centered around their training needs, with both general design concepts and practical application. Learning the best practices for integrating design concepts with tool-based software programs is becoming increasingly complicated (so many tools, so little time) and clear instruction, practice, and practical application are essential. Just as critical is the need for learning experiences to be fun and exploratory, providing timely, innovative approaches to artwork creation.

Each chapter builds upon itself, and material is presented in a linear fashion, introducing design elements and Illustrator tools and features on a "need-to-know" basis. This streamlines the amount of information a reader must know to successfully render a task. However, jumping around to get certain facts when you need them, especially if you are already somewhat familiar with the program is encouraged. Additionally, to accommodate those who appreciate alternative methods of learning, both textually and visually succinct explanations of the important concepts are included in each chapter. For those who prefer structured, hands-on experiences, step-by-step lessons are provided; for those who prefer to wander around a bit, final project files, samples, and suggestions for further exploration are available for deconstruction.

The following is a brief overview of the concepts and skills covered in each chapter. Since this book is all about a design program, notice that the content in most chapters corresponds to the fundamental design elements of line, shape, value, texture, and color, and then finally composition and space.

Chapter 1:   A Discovery Tour Build a logo in Illustrator to discover its purpose right away.

Chapter 2:   The Lay of the Land Get comfortable with the Illustrator interface, and learn the important landmarks of the program to navigate with ease.

Chapter 3:   Survival Techniques Develop a general understanding of how digital graphics are constructed. Learn about design elements—line, shape, value, texture, and color—and then, with these design elements in mind, explore some of Illustrator's tools and features.

Chapter 4: Drawing Lines and Shapes Learn the process of creating illustrations in Illustrator by first creating basic lines and shapes, then more precise objects with the Pen tool.

Chapter 5: Using Color Uncover some fundamental concepts of using color in digital art and design, then play with the color features and tools in Illustrator.

Chapter 6: Value and Texture Create value and texture in your drawing by working with Illustrator brushes, filters, effects, graphic styles, and patterns.

Chapter 7: Working with Type Practice methods for creating, formatting, and importing type in Illustrator, and get an overview of design techniques when choosing and working with fonts and type layouts.

Chapter 8: Object Composition Go beyond the basic components of drawing in Illustrator and produce more complex paths, shapes, and complete illustrations. Apply the elements of design in the construction of organized graphic layouts.

Chapter 9: Spatial Illusions Move into the third dimension and learn the tools and techniques used to produce more spatial depth, organic form, and dimension in your drawing and design.

Chapter 10: Technically Speaking Spend time exploring Illustrator's 3D, Perspective Grid, and new pattern making features.

Chapter 11: Print Publishing Learn about the different types of printing processes and what it takes to prepare your artwork for print.

Chapter 12: Web Publishing Learn about image optimization and what it takes to prepare your artwork for the Web.

Features

The following list provides some of the salient features of the text:

▶ Learning goals are clearly stated at the beginning of each chapter.

▶ Instructional focus is on a visually oriented introduction to basic design elements and the function and tools of Illustrator, meeting the needs of design students and professionals alike.

▶ Client projects highlighted in the Adventures in Design sections share processes and techniques that a designer might encounter on the job.

▶ Explorer Pages sections provide an inside look at how artists working in the field come up with their ideas and inspirations.

▶ Exploring on Your Own sections offer suggestions and sample lessons for further study of content covered in each chapter.

▶ In Review sections are provided at the end of each chapter to test reader understanding and retention of the material covered.

▶ Visit cengagebrain.com to access support files to complete the book's exercises.

Instructor Resources

The Instructor Resources are Delmar's way of putting the resources and information needed to teach and learn effectively into your hands. All the resources are available for both Macintosh and Windows operating systems. These resources can be found online at: **http://login.cengage.com**. Once you login or create an account, search for the title under 'My Dashboard' using the ISBN. Then select the instructor companion site resources and click 'Add to my Bookshelf.'

File Setup

Located on www.cengagebrain.com are all files necessary to complete the lessons in this book. These lesson files are compatible with Illustrator CS6. For a trial version of Adobe Illustrator CS6, visit *http://www.adobe.com/downloads/*.

Before starting any of the lessons, create a folder on your local computer named **My Lessons** (or whatever name you prefer). From www.cengagebrain.com drag a copy of the lesson files to the folder. As you work on the lessons, open the lessons, assets, and sample files from this location. You can then also save your work in the same place.

Accessing Data Files for Students

To complete most of the chapters in this book, the students will need Lesson Files which are available online.

To access the Lesson Files for this book, take the following steps:

1. Open your browser and go to http://www.cengagebrain.com

2. Type the author, title, or ISBN of this book in the Search window. (The ISBN is listed on the back cover.)

3. Click the book title in the list of search results.

4. When the book's main page is displayed, click the Access button under Free Study Tools.

5. To download Lesson files, select a chapter number and then click on the Lesson Files tab on the left navigation bar to download the files.

6. To access additional materials, click the additional materials tab under Book.

About the Authors

Toni Toland is an accomplished designer, artist, writer, and educator. A full-time faculty member in the College of Visual and Performing Arts at Syracuse University since 1981, she served in administrative roles, including Chair of the Department of Visual Communication and Director of the School of Art + Design as well as Program Coordinator for Advertising Design. She earned her B.F.A and M.F.A. degrees in design with honors. Her career includes creative positions with design studios, advertising agencies, and at *Town & Country* magazine. She has earned design awards from *Advertising Age* and the Society for Publication Designers, among others. Ms. Toland has written two textbooks for Cengage: *Best Practice, the Pros on Adobe Illustrator* and *Best Practice, the Pros on Adobe Photoshop*. Her teaching expertise focuses on digital prepress and interactive design, and she has designed and maintains several websites. In her spare time, Toni enjoys knitting, sailing, and cooking.

Annesa Hartman holds a Masters in Teaching with Internet Technologies, focusing her attention on instructional design for online technologies, and Web and graphic design concepts and programs. Currently, she is a Content Developer for Kaplan University, where she designs and develops online courses for educators. For over 15 years she also has taught computer graphic courses and is a freelance graphic designer with clients from around the world. She is the author of *Exploring Adobe Photoshop CS5*, *Exploring Adobe Flash CS5*, *Exploring Illustrator CS4*, *Exploring Photoshop CS4*, and *Producing Interactive Television*. When she is not pushing pixels, she is performing in community theater and teaching yoga classes.

Acknowledgments

In writing a software book, the author faces many challenges. Chief among these is the short time frame in which to write the book and the creation and acquisition of the materials, lesson sources, and images for it. We find material (and inspiration) through close friends, family, students, and professional colleagues. A big thanks to those who contributed content for the book's lessons, visual examples, Adventures in Design and Explorer Pages, including Arthur Mount, Reggie Gilbert, Michael Fleishman, David Garcez, Kevin Hulsey, Michael Fleishman, Ann Paidrick, and Suzanne Staud. The staff of Cengage Delmar Learning, during the creation and marketing efforts of all editions of this book, has been utterly commendable—thanks for your patience and expertise.

Toni and Annesa are very grateful to Susan Whalen for ensuring the technical accuracy of this text.

Questions and Feedback

Cengage Delmar Learning and the author welcome your questions and feedback. If you have suggestions you think others would benefit from, please let us know and we will try to include them in the next edition.

To send us your questions and/or feedback, you can contact the publisher at:

Cengage Delmar Learning
Executive Woods
5 Maxwell Drive
Clifton Park, NY 12065
Attn: Media Arts & Design Team
800-998-7498

Or Toni Toland at: toni@tatoland.com

Or Annesa Hartman at:

Kaplan University
Content Developer
P.O. Box 83
Saxtons River, Vermont 05154
ahartman@kaplan.edu

How to Use This Text

The features discussed in the following sections are found in the book.

▶ ## Charting Your Course and Goals

The introduction and chapter objectives start off each chapter. They describe the competencies the reader should achieve upon understanding the chapter.

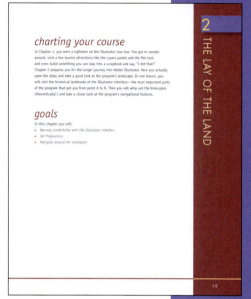

▶ ## Don't Go There

These boxes highlight common pitfalls and explain ways to avoid them.

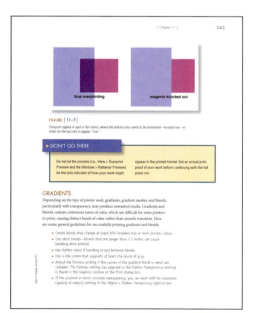

▶ ## Explorer Pages

These sections showcase the imagery, insights, and workflow processes of successful graphic artists.

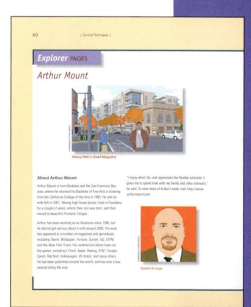

▶ In Review and Exploring on Your Own

Review questions are located at the end of each chapter and allow the reader to assess his or her understanding of the chapter. The section Exploring on Your Own contains exercises that reinforce chapter material through practical application.

▶ Adventures in Design

These spreads contain client projects showing readers how to approach a design project using the tools and design concepts taught in the book.

TULIP HILL CAFE

| A Discovery Tour |

1

charting your course

If you are the adventurous type with an inclination to jump into new experiences feet first, this chapter is for you. If you prefer to proceed with caution because you are more of a "stand-on-the-edge-and-dip-your-toes-into-the-water" type, this chapter is also for you. You will begin with a hands-on investigation of Adobe Illustrator, and depending on your learning style, you can choose to "do" the discovery tour or simply read through it. Perhaps you're ready to jump in with both feet and will choose both options. In this chapter, you will also discover the purpose and scope of this program, shedding some light on such impending questions as, "What's so great about Illustrator? What does it do? How can it help me?"

goals

In this chapter you will:

▶ *Get excited about Illustrator*

▶ *Build a logo*

▶ *Explore some of Illustrator's tools and features*

▶ *Discover the purpose of Illustrator, who uses it, and why*

JUMPING IN

You have a problem. It is your first day on the job, and the creative director arrives at your desk with a logo design cursorily sketched on a somewhat used dinner napkin. See Figure 1–1. She needs the sketch re-created on the computer right away, so it can be printed on business cards by the end of the week. What do you do?

a. Pack up your belongings and move to the mountains.

b. Politely explain that it is "just not possible."

c. Learn Adobe Illustrator.

FIGURE | 1–1 |

A logo sketched on a napkin.

The best answer is "c," of course! Without a doubt, learning Adobe Illustrator will solve your problem, and your future as a graphic designer will be greatly advanced. The clock is ticking, so let's get started.

LESSON: CONNECT-THE-DOTS LOGO TOUR

This lesson is an initial foray into what Illustrator can do. It is not meant to get into any great detail; that is coming soon enough in later chapters. Rather, it is an opportunity to experience how you might solve a common problem: re-creating a traditional drawing (a logo design) in a digital format using Illustrator. See Figure 1–2. Assuming that you have already scanned the dinner napkin sketch into your computer, follow these steps using Illustrator.

Importing the Sketch

1. Open Illustrator.

2. Click on the File menu and choose Open, and then browse for the Exploring Illustrator folder **chap01_ lessons**. Open the file **chap1L1.ai** (see Figure 1–3).

   In the middle of the document, you will see a blank artboard with a black border. This is your drawing space. To the left of the interface is the Tools panel. See Figure 1–4. You will use the Tools panel more than any other feature of Illustrator.

FIGURE | 1–2 |

Completed lesson: A logo redrawn using Illustrator.

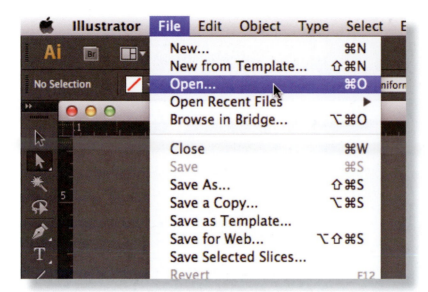

FIGURE | 1–3 |

Open **chap1L1.ai** from the
chap01_lessons folder.

3. Choose View > Actual Size. (Figure 1–5). Panels appear on the right in the interface, and
    they are used to monitor and modify your work. The Essentials Workspace is the default,
    where Illustrator panels are stacked in collapsed groups within docks (more details on
    panels and docks will be given in Chapter 2). Refer to Figure 1–4 again.

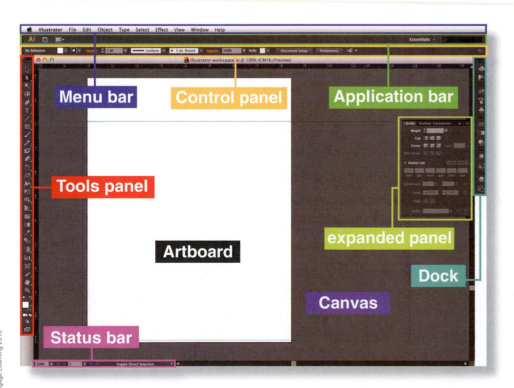

FIGURE | 1–4 |

The Illustrator interface (Mac). To view an image of the Windows interface, see Chapter 2.

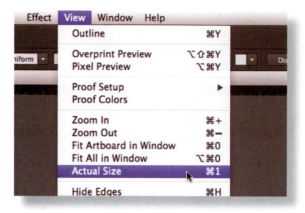

FIGURE | 1–5 |

Choose Actual Size from the View menu.

FIGURE | 1–6 |

The Layers panel with the napkin sketch layer selected.

FIGURE | 1–7 |

The Selection tool selects objects on the artboard.

4. Choose Window > Layers to open the Layers panel. Layers are a way of organizing parts of an image. You can add, delete, rearrange, hide/unhide, lock/unlock, and duplicate layers. In this lesson, the layers have already been created for you.

> Note: *If you prefer, you can detach a panel and place it elsewhere on the screen—simply click and drag the title tab of the panel you want to use (in this example, the Layers tab). Panels and docking are further explained in Chapter 2, "Lesson 1: Interface Highlights."*

5. Click once on the bottom layer—**napkin sketch**—to select it. See Figure 1–6. If you do not see all the layers, click on the lower-right corner of the Layers panel window; a double-headed arrow will appear on the border. Then drag down the arrow to expand the window.

6. Choose File > Place and browse for **chap01_lessons/ assets/logo.jpgpsd**. Click Place to import the image into Illustrator. This is the original scanned sketch, which will be used as a template to trace the new logo design.

7. Select the Selection tool (black arrow) in the Tools panel, if not already selected. See Figure 1–7.

8. If necessary, click and drag the imported image to center it over the artboard.

9. Click on the blank box to the left of the layer name—**napkin sketch**—to lock the layer. A little lock icon will appear. See Figure 1–8.

FIGURE | 1–8 |

Lock the napkin sketch layer, so it cannot be edited.

Figures © Cengage Learning 2013

10. Choose File > Save As to save your file. Rename it **chap1L1_ yourname.ai**, and save it in your lessons folder. If the Illustrator dialog box appears, leave the default settings as they are and click OK.

Drawing the Sky

1. Click on the blank box to the far left of the layer named **sky guide** to unhide the layer. A solid rectangle with an outline appears. See Figure 1–9.

   This icon indicates that a template object on this layer is visible. Objects on **template** layers are usually used as guides that you can trace over. Any elements on a **template** layer will not print. Other layers are visible when you see the eye icon in the visibility column of the Layers panel.

2. Look at the color options at the bottom of the Tools panel. Click on the Fill box to bring it forward if it isn't already in that position (see Figure 1–10).

3. Use Window > Swatches to open the Swatches panel. Separate it from the dock by clicking on the word Swatches and dragging it a bit to the left.

4. Choose a light lavender fill in the Swatches panel. See Figure 1–11.

> Note: *Illustrator panels are arranged in groups within the dock. For example, the Swatches panel is grouped with other related panels, such as Brushes and Symbols. To make things easier, click and drag the title tab of the panel you want to use (in this example, the Swatches panel) to another area of the screen to detach it.*

5. Click on the Stroke box at the bottom of the Tools panel to bring it forward. Click the None box below it to set the stroke color to none. See Figure 1–12.

FIGURE | 1–9 |

A rectangle with an outline indicates the layer is a template and will not print.

FIGURE | 1–10 |

The fill and stroke options at the bottom of the Toolbar.

FIGURE | 1–11 |

The Swatches panel.

FIGURE | 1–12 |

Set the stroke color to none.

FIGURE | 1–13 |

Highlight the **draw sky** layer.

FIGURE | 1–14 |

The Rectangle tool.

FIGURE | 1–16 |

Hide the guide and drawing layers.

6. Click on the layer named **draw sky** to highlight it. This is where you will draw the sky. See Figure 1–13.

7. Select the Rectangle tool (Figure 1–14) from the Tools panel, then click and drag from the upper-left corner of the sky guide diagonally down to the bottom right of the guide. See Figure 1–15.

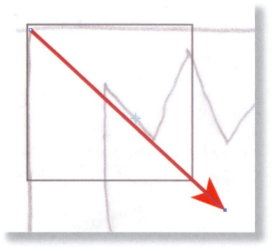

FIGURE | 1–15 |

Click and drag diagonally to draw a rectangle.

8. Click the empty box next to the eye icon in the **draw sky** layer to lock it, and then click on the template icon next to the **sky guide** layer to hide it.

9. Hide the sky guide and the **draw sky** layers. See Figure 1–16.

10. Save your file [File > Save, or Command S (Mac)/Ctrl S (Windows)].

Drawing the Sun

1. Click on the first empty box next to the **sun guide** layer to see the shape and size of the sun, and then click on the **draw sun** layer to highlight it. This is where you will draw the sun shape.

2. Click and hold on the Rectangle tool in the Tools panel to reveal additional shape tools, and then drag down to the Star tool. See Figure 1–17.

FIGURE | 1–17 |

Click and hold on the Rectangle tool to access the Star tool.

3. At the bottom of the Tools panel, set the Fill color back to white and leave the stroke color set to none. (Figure 1–18.)

4. Place the cursor in the middle of the sun, hold down the option key (Mac)/alt key (Windows), and click once.

    In the Star options box, set Radius 1 to 1.25 in and the Radius 2 to 0.65 in. Enter 15 in the Points field. See Figure 1–19. Click OK.

5. Select the Selection tool and adjust the position of the sun if necessary—don't worry if the points don't align exactly.

> Note: *Radius 1 refers to the outer dimension of the star, and Radius 2 refers to the inner points.*

6. Hide the **sun guide** and **draw sun** layers, then save your file.

Drawing the Grass

1. Click in the leftmost column next to the **grass guide** layer to show it, and then highlight the **draw grass** layer. This layer will contain your final drawing of the grass.

> Note: *If you do not see the Layers panel, choose Window > Layers from the main menu to reopen it.*

    A series of numbered dots appear on the document, strategically placed over the grass drawn in the sketch. You will create the logo as if you were drawing an image in a connect-the-dots activity book.

2. Click the Fill color box at the bottom of the Tools panel to bring it forward, if it is not already.

3. If the Swatches panel is not still open, select Window > Swatches, and then choose the lime green color swatch as the Fill color. The stroke color should still be set to none.

4. Select the Pen tool in the Tools panel. See Figure 1–20.

5. Position the Pen tool on point 1 on the document and click once. Then click on point 2 to create a straight path. You can guarantee that it's vertically straight by holding the Shift key when you click on point 2.

6. Continue to hold the Shift key as you click on points 3 and 4.

FIGURE | 1–18 |

Set the fill color to white, and leave the stroke set to none.

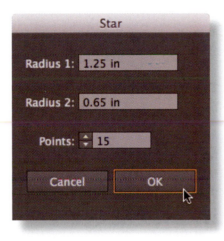

FIGURE | 1–19 |

Specify measurements in the Star options dialog box.

FIGURE | 1–20 |

The Pen tool.

▶ **DON'T GO THERE**

If you are unable to draw on your chosen layer even though the Pen tool is selected, this means the highlighted layer is either locked or hidden, or that you are on the wrong layer. In this case, an icon appears that looks like a pencil with a line through it.

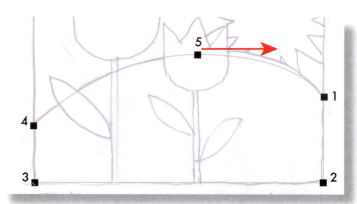

FIGURE | 1–21 |

Click and drag in one motion to create a curved path.

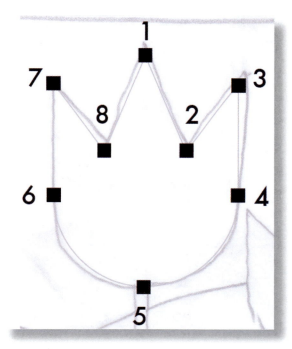

FIGURE | 1–22 |

Reveal the dots to guide your drawing of the tulip.

7. This step is a little tricky. At point 5, click and hold the mouse button down, and then drag the Pen tool to the right.

   Dragging when placing this point creates the curve to form the rounded grass shape. See Figure 1–21. The lines that extend from this point are called direction handles.

   Note: *If you make a mistake, choose Edit > Undo—Command-Z (Mac) or Ctrl-Z (Windows)—or hit Delete on your keyboard right away so you can try again. You can undo up to 20 previous steps.*

8. Close the shape by clicking on point 1 again. Illustrator will use the forward leading direction handle to complete the curved shape automatically.

   You now have a completed grass shape. Don't worry if the edges are not perfect. You will get a lot more practice as you learn Illustrator.

9. Hide the **grass guide** and the **draw grass** layers.

10. Save your file.

Drawing the Flowers

1. Unhide the **tulips guide** layer to see the dots that will guide your next drawing. See Figure 1–22.

2. Click the **draw tulips** layer. This is the layer you will draw on.

3. Click the Fill color box in the Tools panel to bring it forward, if it is not already.

4. In the Swatches panel, select the purple swatch. Make sure that the Stroke color in the Tools panel is still set to none.

5. With the Pen tool, start to connect the dots by clicking on points 1, 2, 3, and 4.

6. At point 5, click and hold, and then drag the Pen tool to the left to create the curve at the bottom of the tulip. This is the same motion you used to create the grass, just in the opposite direction.

7. Click (don't drag) on point 6, and continue to click on the rest of the points. Close the shape by clicking on point 1 again.

   Remember, if you make a mistake, Edit > Undo is always there for you—Command-Z (Mac) or Ctrl-Z (Windows).

8. Select the Selection tool and click on the tulip to highlight it. Select Edit > Copy, then Edit > Paste, to create the second tulip.

9. Select the Scale tool on the Tools panel (see Figure 1–23) and then, from the lower right, click and drag slowly up and to the left to resize the tulip. If you don't get it right the first time, you can continue to click and drag until you're satisfied, or Undo and start again.

> **Note:** *To keep the tulip in proportion, hold the Shift key as you drag.*

10. Use the Selection tool to position the new tulip, hide the **tulip guide** layer and the **draw tulip** layer, and then save your file.

Drawing the Stems and Leaves

1. Show the **stems + leaves guide** layer, and highlight the **draw stems + leaves** layer.

2. If the Swatches panel isn't visible, use Window > Swatches to open it again. In the Swatches panel, set the fill color to none, and the stroke color to the darker green.

FIGURE | 1–23 |

Hold the Shift key as you resize the tulip to retain the correct proportions.

Figures © Cengage Learning 2013

3. Select the Line tool from the Tools panel.

4. Use Window > Stroke to open the Stroke panel and set the stroke weight to 7 pt. See Figure 1–24.

> **Note:** *If you don't see all the Stroke panel's options, use the panel's submenu and select Show Options.*

5. Click and drag from the bottom of the tulip to the bottom of the grass, creating a tall, thin line for each tulip's stem. Deselect the stems by selecting the Selection tool and clicking anywhere outside the artboard.

6. Use the Tools panel to set the fill color to the same green you used for the stems, and the stroke color to none.

7. Click and hold the Rectangle tool to reveal the other shape tools, and then move your mouse to the Ellipse tool to select it. To draw the leaves, first draw a tall, thin oval.

8. Click and hold on the Pen tool on the Tools panel to select the Convert Anchor Point tool (Figure 1–25).

FIGURE | 1–24 |

Use the Stroke panel to set the thickness of the stems.

FIGURE | 1–25 |

The Convert Anchor Point tool.

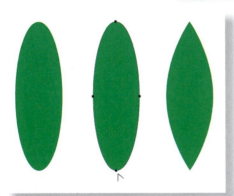

FIGURE | 1–26 |

Use the Convert tool to change curve points into corner points.

9. Click once on the bottom point of the ellipse, and then click once on the top point. The Convert Anchor Point tool changes the curve points to corner points by deleting the direction handles. See Figure 1–26.

10. With the Selection tool, click on the leaf to select it entirely (all the anchor points should be solid), then select the Rotate tool (see Figure 1–27) to adjust the angle of the leaf. Click and drag counterclockwise from the top point. Then use the Selection tool to adjust its position to match the scan.

11. While the leaf is still highlighted, use Edit > Copy and Edit > Paste to make a second leaf. Keep this new leaf highlighted and select the Reflect tool; click and hold the Rotate tool on the Tools panel to access it (refer back to Figure 1–27).

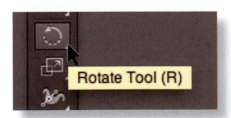

FIGURE | 1–27 |

The Rotate tool.

12. Hold down the Option (Mac)/Alt (Windows) key, and click once approximately in the middle of the tulip's stem. In the dialog box that opens, confirm that Vertical is selected, then click Copy (see Figure 1–28). Use the Selection tool to move the leaf into position.

13. Use Edit > Paste to create a third leaf; use the Selection tool to position it next to the second stem.

14. Use the Scale tool to adjust its size, and the Selection tool to adjust its position if necessary, just as you did with the tulip.

15. Hide the **stems + leaves guide** and the **draw stems + leaves** layers, and then save your file.

Creating the Text

1. Show the **text guide** layer, and click on the **draw text** layer to highlight it.

2. Select the Type tool. See Figure 1–29. On the **draw text** layer, click once near the letter *T*.

3. On the Options bar at the top of the window, to the right of the Character field (which should be automatically set to Myriad Pro), click the down arrow and select Black for the type style. In the field to the right of the type style, type 40 for the type size. See Figure 1–30.

FIGURE | 1–28 |

Use the Reflect tool to copy a flipped version of the smaller leaf.

FIGURE | 1–29 |

The Type tool.

FIGURE | 1–30 |

Select the typeface style, and size in the Options bar.

4. Type **TULIP HILL CAFE** in all caps. Make any adjustments in position and size that you think are necessary. See Figure 1–31.

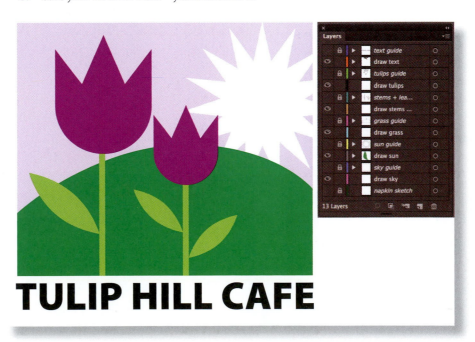

FIGURE | 1–31 |

Completed text.

5. Hide the **text guide** layer and the **draw text** layer.

6. Save your file.

> **Note:** *Creating beautiful typography is a true skill. You'll spend more time mastering that in Chapter 7.*

Unveiling the Final Logo

1. Set all the **drawing** layers to visible by clicking in the visibility column to reveal the eye icon. The layers are **draw sky, draw sun, draw grass, draw tulips, draw stems + leaves**, and **draw text**. Hide the **napkin sketch** layer. See Figure 1–32.

2. Your final image is revealed.

3. Save your file once more—you have done it!

FIGURE | 1–32 |

Reveal the finished drawing layers to see your final piece.

ABOUT ILLUSTRATOR

Adobe Illustrator is a great resource to reproduce, redo, revise, rework, and re-envision traditionally and digitally created artwork and imagery. Even if you are new to drawing or working digitally, Illustrator (along with this book) is a great place to start stirring up some creative energies. It also gets you out of many time-crunching, sticky, and unexpected situations that await you as a graphic designer. It offers a versatile new environment to draw, paint, and edit graphic images.

Lucky for you, each new version of Illustrator is significantly more sophisticated than the previous version. As the demand grows for more cross-product integration of digital content, new tools and effects are introduced and workflow techniques are added and improved, as is the product's ability to interact seamlessly with all types of graphic disciplines (i.e., interactive media, animation, print, the web, as well as mobile and touch devices). With all its capabilities, it is no wonder that Illustrator has been the most popular digital drawing program on the market since its inception—a necessary provision for print, Web, and interactive designers, architects, animators, and traditional artists.

Fundamentally, Illustrator has not changed that much. Its underlying magic lies in the use of vectors, a way in which computer-generated objects are drawn using points and lines. You got a taste of this in the logo design lesson; each shape you created was determined by the points you placed with the Pen tool. Alternatively, digital images created by pixels—square elements gathered in a grid—are mainly handled using Illustrator's companion product, Adobe Photoshop. Chapter 3 provides greater detail on the differences between these two ways of generating digital graphics, respectively known as vectors and bitmaps. For now, however, you should know Illustrator has the ability to

- ► create, color, edit, and add special effects to original or traced drawings;
- ► effectively format and render type and enhance typographic layout and design;
- ► produce objects and layouts that can be resized and reformatted for print, Web, and multimedia publication without losing their quality (resolution);
- ► export graphics to other vector-based formats, such as Adobe's Flash (SWF) and the Web vector standard SVG (Scalable Vector Graphics). I'll cover more of this in Chapter 11.

SUMMARY

As you have discovered, Illustrator is a powerful program for the reworking, repurposing, and reproduction of artwork, as well as the development of completely new digital imagery. Its fundamental way of making illustrations is through the use of vectors—making lines and shapes point-by-point. Without a doubt, Illustrator is a vital part of any graphic designer's repertoire.

▶ IN REVIEW

1. What is the purpose of a template image in Illustrator?

2. What are layers? How are they useful?

3. How do you know when a layer is hidden?

4. What does holding down the Option key (Mac)/Alt key (Windows) when clicking with a tool allow you to do?

5. Name at least two uses of Illustrator.

6. Who uses Illustrator?

▶ EXPLORING ON YOUR OWN

1. Visit the Illustrator Help and Support area of the Adobe site: *http://www.adobe.com/support/illustrator/*. The official Adobe site has a wealth of information on Illustrator, including developer resources, third-party plug-ins, inspirational customer, stories and examples using Illustrator.

2. Do a search for Illustrator artists on the Web and explore what other artists are creating using Illustrator. Many artists' sites have tutorials for further learning. Also, see the Explorer Pages in this book for more inspiration from others. Some example sites and resources include:

    ▶ *http://www.arthurmount.com*—Arthur Mount is a nonstop illustrator with a hefty client list.

    ▶ *http://www.ebypaidrick.com*—Ann Paidrick, of Eby-Paidrick Designs, creates beautiful, photorealistic designs—a feast for the eyes.

    ▶ *http://www.janetmcleod.com*—Janet McLeod is a Toronto artist with a lyrical, hand-drawn sense to her work. Her client list includes editorial, advertising, and educational publishing companies.

    ▶ *http://lifeinvector.com/vectors/*—Brook Nunez, illustrator, has an extensive gallery of her beautiful, diverse collection of work.

    ▶ *http://www.khulsey.com*—Kevin Hulsey, a master of cut-away technical illustrations, shares a site full of computer graphic illustration tutorials, tips, and tricks for students.

    ▶ *http://www.staudesign.com*—Suzanne Staud has a talent for creating fun and quirky illustrations that have been used in children's books, fabric designs, posters, and more.

    ▶ *Best Practice: The Pros On Adobe Illustrator*, by Toni Toland. Published by Cengage Delmar Learning, this book inspires readers to explore the creative process and technical skill behind the work of leading contemporary digital artists.

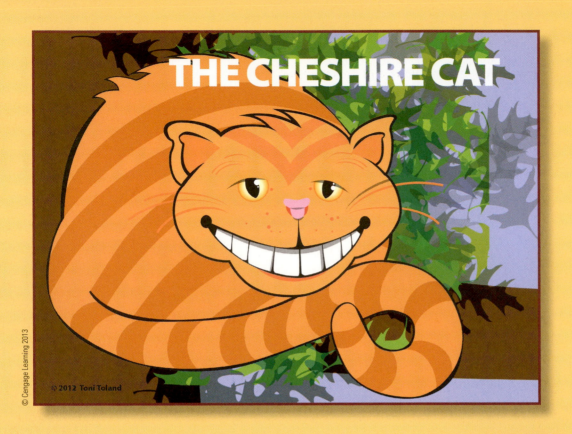

| The Lay of the Land |

charting your course

In Chapter 1, you were a sightseer on the Illustrator tour bus. You got to wander around, visit a few tourist attractions like the Layers panels and the Pen tool, and even build something you can slap into a scrapbook and say, "I did that!" Chapter 2 prepares you for the longer journey into Adobe Illustrator. Now you actually open the atlas and take a good look at the program's landscape. In one lesson, you will visit the historical landmarks of the Illustrator interface—the most important parts of the program that get you from point A to B. Then you will whip out the binoculars (theoretically!) and take a closer look at the program's navigational features.

goals

In this chapter you will:

► *Become comfortable with the Illustrator interface*

► *Set Preferences*

► *Navigate around the workspace*

HISTORICAL LANDMARKS

I live at the end of a long, winding dirt road in the backwoods of Vermont. The UPS guy gets lost every time he comes to deliver a package. I usually get a phone call from the dispatcher asking how to get to my house. Instead of giving street names already indicated on any map or sophisticated GPS (global positioning system), I mention a few notable landmarks: go across the covered bridge, stay to the left of the big pine tree, turn at the tilted mailbox, and go straight up the driveway to the end. In a matter of minutes, UPS is at my door. My point: You can be handed a detailed map of an unknown area, but that does not necessarily mean you can make your way to where you want to go, at least not as directly. You can memorize the map, but you will soon realize, after having talked to some of the locals, that a few historical landmarks can help you reach your destination much faster. You learn the shortcuts or discover there is more than one way to go, depending on your point of origin. The Illustrator interface or work area is no exception. For example, in Illustrator there are at least two ways to get to every tool: click on it in the Tools panel or use a keyboard shortcut (Edit > Keyboard Shortcuts). You will learn the secret routes over time, but for now let's get familiar with some tried-and-true historical landmarks, including the artboard, Tools panel, menu bar, panels, status bar, contextual menus, and preferences.

LESSON 1: INTERFACE HIGHLIGHTS

In this lesson, you identify the main interface elements of Illustrator.

Identifying Landmarks

1.   Launch Illustrator, and then choose File > New from the menu bar at the top of the interface.

2.   Type **myfile** for the document name in the New Document dialog box. Choose Print for Profile, and leave the other options set to their defaults for now. Select OK. See Figure 2–1.

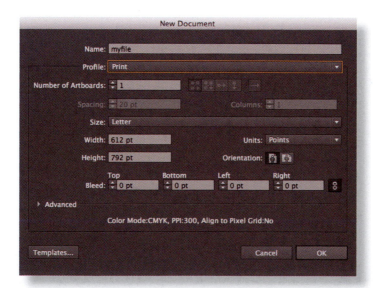

FIGURE | 2–1 |

The New Document dialog box.

3. Depending on whether you are using a Macintosh (see Figure 2–2) or Windows (see Figure 2–3) computer, the interface will look slightly different. In general, however, the landmarks are the same. Compare your open Illustrator interface with Figure 2–2 or Figure 2–3, and note where the various parts of the program are located.

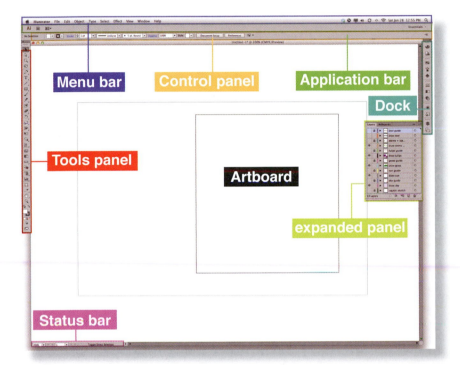

FIGURE | 2–2 |

The Illustrator interface (Mac).

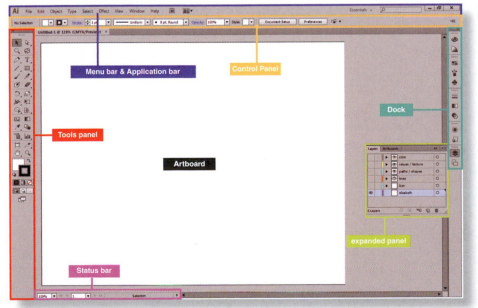

FIGURE | 2–3 |

The Illustrator interface (Windows).

▶ *Artboard:* The artboard is the big white space in the middle of the screen. When you chose File > New in Step 1 above, you created a specific size for the artboard. The area bounded by the solid line defines the area that contains your artwork. However, most printers cannot print right to the edge of this region. Therefore, a printable "safe" area is defined within the dotted line. (If the dotted line is not visible, go to View > Show Print Tiling in the menu bar at the top of the screen.) The area outside the artboard is called the "canvas." This is your doodling space, where you can create, edit, and store graphics that you may or may not use on the final artboard area. Keep in mind that anything in this space will not print.

▶ *Tools Panel/Toolbox:* On the left side of the screen is the Tools panel. It contains the tools necessary to select, create, edit, and manipulate objects. When you hover your cursor (pointer) over a tool, the name of the tool appears. This is called a "tool tip," and it is incredibly helpful when you're learning which tool is which. There are several more tools that are not initially visible in the Tools panel; some tools are hidden behind others. When you see a small triangle in the lower-right corner of a tool icon, click and hold on the icon, and more tools will be revealed. At the top of the Tools panel, click on the double arrow to toggle between the single-column (see Figure 2–4) and the classic two-column (see Figure 2–5) formats.

▶ *Menu Bar:* At the top of the screen is the menu bar, which contains drop-down lists of Illustrator's various features, tools, and commands. Don't bother memorizing everything in the menu bar; that knowledge will come on a need-to-know basis.

▶ *Application Bar:* The Application bar extends along the top of the program below the menus bar on the Macintosh interface and as part of the menus on the Windows interface. It contains universal commands found across the Creative Suite programs, such as the application's icon, a link to Bridge (more on that below), and Arrange Documents options. See Figure 2–6 on page 24. Also on the Application bar are workspace options. Workspaces are predefined panel sets for particular tasks in Illustrator. If you click the down-facing arrow on the right side of the Application bar, a drop-down list of preset workspaces appears (the Essentials workspace is the default). See Figure 2–7. A more detailed exploration of workspaces is covered in the Exploring on Your Own section at the end of this chapter. To the right of the Workspace submenu is a search bar, where you can enter in a search word or phrase (e.g., "Pen Tool"); a browser opens and help documents related to the search topic are provided. Refer to Figure 2–8 again.

Also on the Application bar is the option to access CS Live (indicated by a magnifying glass). CS Live provides online services and resources that you can access directly from Illustrator.

The Application bar also provides access to the Adobe Bridge program, a stand-alone application for file browsing and management across Adobe's Creative Suite programs. See Figure 2–8. You can also open the Bridge program by choosing File > Browse in Bridge. Among many features, Bridge allows you to quickly browse for a file on your local hard drive, and it even provides a visual thumbnail of the file for easy recognition. Check it out! See Figure 2–9.

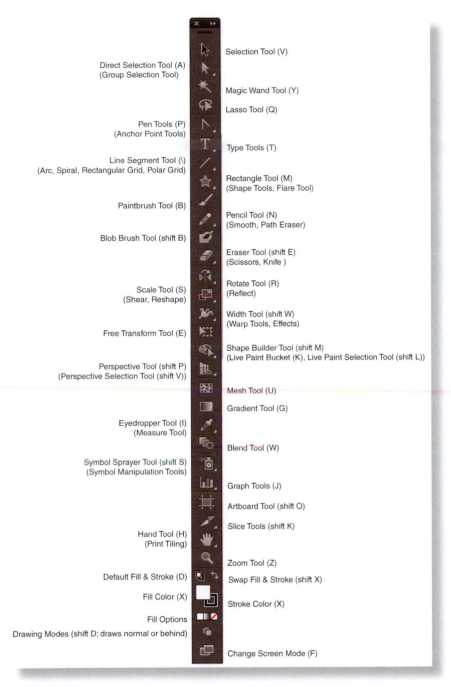

Selection Tool (V)

Direct Selection Tool (A)
(Group Selection Tool)

Magic Wand Tool (Y)

Lasso Tool (Q)

Pen Tools (P)
(Anchor Point Tools)

Type Tools (T)

Line Segment Tool (\)
(Arc, Spiral, Rectangular Grid, Polar Grid)

Rectangle Tool (M)
(Shape Tools, Flare Tool)

Paintbrush Tool (B)

Pencil Tool (N)
(Smooth, Path Eraser)

Blob Brush Tool (shift B)

Eraser Tool (shift E)
(Scissors, Knife)

Scale Tool (S)
(Shear, Reshape)

Rotate Tool (R)
(Reflect)

Width Tool (shift W)
(Warp Tools, Effects)

Free Transform Tool (E)

Shape Builder Tool (shift M)
(Live Paint Bucket (K), Live Paint Selection Tool (shift L))

Perspective Tool (shift P)
(Perspective Selection Tool (shift V))

Mesh Tool (U)

Gradient Tool (G)

Eyedropper Tool (I)
(Measure Tool)

Blend Tool (W)

Symbol Sprayer Tool (shift S)
(Symbol Manipulation Tools)

Graph Tools (J)

Artboard Tool (shift O)

Slice Tools (shift K)

Hand Tool (H)
(Print Tiling)

Zoom Tool (Z)

Default Fill & Stroke (D)

Swap Fill & Stroke (shift X)

Fill Color (X)

Stroke Color (X)

Fill Options

Drawing Modes (shift D; draws normal or behind)

Change Screen Mode (F)

FIGURE | 2–4 |

Single-column setting for the Tools panel. Figure identifies the name of each tool and its shortcut key.

FIGURE | 2–5 |

Classic two-column setting for the Tools panel.

Note: *For a useful visual of each tool and what it does, see Help > Illustrator Help > Workspace > Tools.*

Figures © Cengage Learning 2013

Mac Application bar

Windows Application bar

FIGURE | 2–6 |

The Application bar for Mac and Windows.

FIGURE | 2–8 |

Open Bridge from the Application bar.

FIGURE | 2–7 |

Choose workspace options from the Application bar.

FIGURE | 2–9 |

The Adobe Bridge program interface—a great resource to view and organize your images and files.

FIGURE |2–10|

Options in the Control panel change depending on the current tool or selected object.

▶ *Control Panel:* Near the top of the screen, below the Application bar, is the Control panel (Figure 2–10). This is similar to the Options bar in Adobe Photoshop. It offers quick access to options, commands, and other fields related to the current page item or objects you select, as well as tool options for the current tool. This type of panel is contextual; it displays different information depending on what artwork or tool is selected. Try it out. Open the logo lesson (**chap1L1_final.ai**) from Chapter 1. Using the Selection tool in the Tools panel, select objects on the artboard (paths or text) and watch the content for each selection change in the Control panel.

▶ *Panels:* Panels, usually located on the right side of the interface, allow you to monitor and modify your work. You can open panels using the Window menu. Panel windows come grouped together. To separate them, click on the panel name in the tab and drag it to another area of the screen. See Figure 2–11. Of course, you can dock any panel back into a group by dragging the separated panel's tab over the desired panel's group. You'll know it's about to become part of the group by the blue line that appears around the group. To close an unneeded panel or panel group, Ctrl-click (Mac) or right-click (Windows) the title bar and choose Close. This command closes either a panel or a panel group depending on which is open. See Figure 2–12. To bring a closed panel back, go to Window on the menu bar and select the panel name. Or, to temporarily hide all visible panels, press Shift-Tab. To restore them, press Shift-Tab again. (If you press just Tab, you hide or unhide all panels, including the Tools panel.)

FIGURE | 2–11 |

Click and drag on a panel's tab to undock it from other panels.

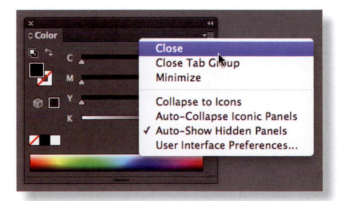

FIGURE | 2–12 |

Ctrl-click (Mac) or right-click(Windows) on the panel tab to access the Close option.

Figures © Cengage Learning 2013

▶ *Docks:* Docks are vertical bars comprised of panels/groups displayed in either an iconic or full-size format. By default, a dock is located on the right side of the screen in a single column. Docks, however, can occupy either the left or the right side of the screen in any number of columns. While a dock is collapsed (icons), clicking on any icon will expand the icon's whole panel/group. To view all panels at full size, click on the double arrow at the top of the dock to expand the dock. If you want to conserve valuable workspace, click the double arrow at the top of the panel/group or dock to collapse it to icons. See Figures 2–13 and 2–14.

FIGURE | 2–13 |

Click on the double triangles to expand panels.

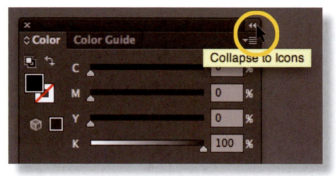

FIGURE | 2–14 |

Click again on the double triangles to collapse panels to icons.

To familiarize yourself with using the docks, try the following:

1. Be sure the Essentials workspace is selected in the Application bar (upper-right corner of the screen).

2. Click on the Color icon on the collapsed panels on the right side of the screen to open the panel. See Figure 2–15.

3. To undock the Color panel from the right side of the screen, click on the panel tab and drag it into the document area. See Figure 2–16.

FIGURE | 2–15 |

Click on an icon to open a panel.

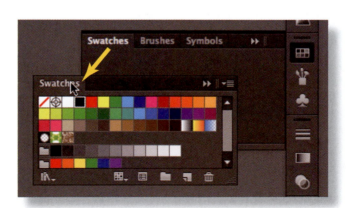

FIGURE | 2–16 |

Click and drag on a panel's tab to undock it from other panels.

4. Click on the double arrow to the left of the panel name to cycle through the various views of a panel. See Figure 2–17.

5. To close the Color panel, click on the Close icon on the left (Mac) or right (Windows) side of the title bar. See Figure 2–18.

6. Choose Window > Color to reopen the Color panel.

7. To redock the Color panel, click on the panel tab and drag it off the right side of the screen until you see the blue dock shadow appear. See Figure 2–19.

FIGURE | 2–17 |

Click on the up/down arrows next to the panel name to expand, condense, or collapse a panel.

FIGURE | 2–18 |

Close an undocked panel by clicking on the X at the top of the panel.

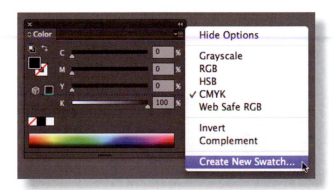

FIGURE | 2–19 |

Use the panel options menu to access additional options.

FIGURE | 2–20 |

Redocking a panel.

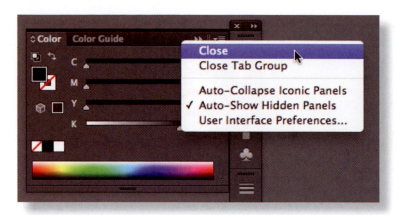

FIGURE | 2–21 |

Closing a panel.

▶ *Status Bar:* The status bar is located at the lower-left edge of the document window. It contains the Zoom pop-up, Status pop-up menu items, and Artboard Navigation. The Zoom pop-up allows you to change the magnification of the document window. The Status pop-up shows specific information, depending on which of the following items is checked under the Show menu: the Artboard name, current tool in use, date and time, number of undos and redos, or the document's color profile. Artboard Navigation allows you to quickly move between artboards (see more on artboards in Adventures in Design: Using Multiple Artboards).

▶ *Context Menus:* When you Ctrl-click (Mac) or right-click (Windows) your mouse, you will discover what are called context menus. These are submenus that give you quick access to various features of a tool you might be using. See Figure 2–22.

Marking the Territory

1. Hover the cursor (do not click!) over the Rectangle tool in the Tools panel. Notice that a text equivalent (a tool tip) of the tool name appears. Next to the tool name a shortcut key is indicated. See Figure 2–23.

FIGURE | 2–22 |

Ctrl-click (Mac) or right-click (Windows) to get to the context menus.

FIGURE | 2–23 |

The tool tip for the Rectangle tool is revealed.

2. Click and hold on the Rectangle tool to reveal more Shape tool options. See Figure 2–24.

3. Select the Star tool.

4. Click and drag on your artboard to create a star shape. Make three or four.

5. Place the cursor over one of your stars, and hold down Command (Mac) or Ctrl (Windows) to toggle the cursor to the Selection tool.

6. Keeping Command/Ctrl pressed, click and move the star to a different location on the artboard. By selecting or releasing Command/Ctrl, you can toggle between the highlighted tool and the Selection tool. This is a nifty trick to make, select, and move objects quickly.

7. Hold down Option-Command (Mac) or Alt-Ctrl (Windows) while you click, and move one of the stars. Be sure to release the mouse button first to make a duplicate of the star. The Option/Alt key makes duplicates of selected objects. (Or, you can take the longer route and choose Edit > Copy, then Edit > Paste.) See Figure 2–25.

FIGURE | 2–24 |

Click and hold on the Rectangle tool to reveal more Shape tool options.

Note: *If you make a mistake, choose Edit > Undo, or Command-Z (Mac) or Ctrl-Z (Windows).*

FIGURE | 2–25 |

Make stars.

Here are a few things you should know about Undo.

▶ Repeatedly choose Edit > Undo, or Command-Z (Mac), or Ctrl-Z (Windows), to undo, in reverse order, the previous operations you performed. To redo, choose Edit > Redo, or Command-Shift-Z (Mac), or Ctrl-Shift-Z (Windows).

▶ Depending on the amount of memory available on your computer, you can undo an unlimited number of the last operations you performed.

▶ You can use Undo even after you have chosen the Save command, as long as you have not closed and reopened the file.

▶ If an operation cannot be undone, the Undo option is dimmed.

8. We are done working with this file and identifying interface landmarks, so choose File > Save. For Format, make sure Adobe Illustrator (ai) is selected. Save **myfile.ai** in your lessons folder; you will use it again in the next lesson. Click OK to accept the default Illustrator Options.

> Note: *The ".ai" at the end of your filename is the native file extension for all Illustrator files. Any file with this extension was created in Adobe Illustrator.*

LESSON 2: GETTING PERSONAL

Every time you open Illustrator and begin to open panels, set import options, determine ruler units, and set grid and guide colors (basically customizing things to your liking), Illustrator creates a file on your hard drive that preserves these preferences. This is really great when you want to reopen the program and have everything preset your way. Let's set some preferences and see how this works.

Setting Preferences

1. Open Illustrator if it isn't already running. Make sure your workspace is set to Essentials in the Applications bar. Refer to Figure 2–7.

2. Choose File > Open and look for **myfile.ai**.

3. Select the Paintbrush tool in the Tools panel. Notice that the cursor changes to look like the tool selected. See Figure 2–26.

> Note: *If you do not have a **myfile. ai**, choose **chap2L2.ai** in the **chap02_lessons** folder.*

FIGURE | 2–26 |

The selected Brush tool changes the mouse cursor to a brush icon.

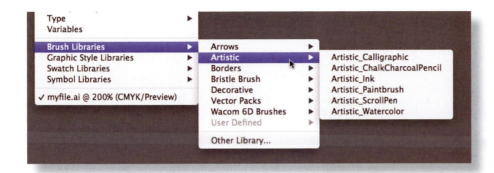

Figures © Cengage Learning 2013

FIGURE |2–27|

Use the Window menu to access additional brush styles—toward the very bottom.

4. Choose Window > Brush Libraries and select the Artistic > Artistic_ ChalkCharcoalPencil option. See Figure 2–27. Pick one of the artistic brushes in the library panel and paint some strokes on the artboard. See Figure 2–28.

5. Let's change some preferences. Choose Illustrator > Preferences > General (Mac) or Edit > Preferences > General (Windows). Any change you make in this box will be recorded in a Preferences file for the next time you open the program. There are a lot of Preference options; we will only tinker with a few, and it is a good idea to look through all of them.

6. Under the General option, select Use Precise Cursors and deselect Show Tool Tips. See Figure 2–29. Tool tips come up by default when you place your cursor over a tool in the Tools panel, and the tool name is revealed, along with the keystroke shortcut for selecting it.

7. Look at the list to the left in the Preferences window and select Guides and Grid. Change the Grid Color to Magenta.

8. Click OK to close the Preferences window.

9. Test your preference choices. First, hover your cursor over a tool in the Tools panel and notice that the tool tip is no longer available.

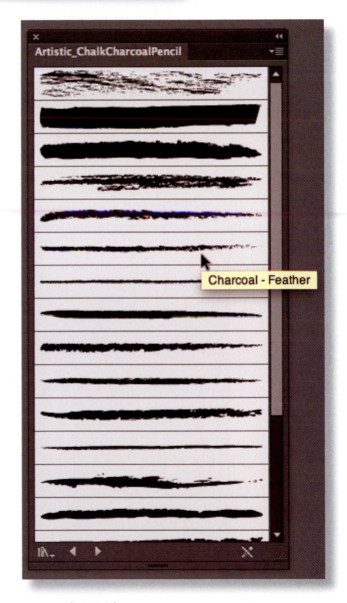

FIGURE | 2–28 |

Choose an artistic brush to paint with.

10. If it isn't already selected, choose the Paintbrush tool and notice that the cursor icon has changed. It is no longer in the shape of the brush icon; rather, it is a cross mark. This cross mark indicates a precise cursor: the center of the cursor is the exact spot where you will draw, and it is much more accurate than the traditional icon cursor.

11. Choose View > Show Grid to see the magenta-colored grid.

12. Save your file. Name it **myfile2.ai**.

13. Choose Illustrator > Quit Illustrator (Mac) or File > Exit (Windows) to shut down the program.

14. Reopen the program and **myfile2.ai**.

15. Notice the Preferences you set are still in effect.

16. If you need to reset defaults, open Preferences and under the General option, deselect Use Precise Cursors and reselect Show Tool Tips. Then, under the Guides & Grids option, select Cyan as the guides color. See Figure 2–29.

Use the General and Guides & Grids panes in the Preferences panel to undo the changes you made.

> Note: *To reset Illustrator's preferences to the default settings, quit the program and then relaunch it. While it's opening, hold the Option, Command, and Shift keys on a Mac, or the Alt, Ctrl, and Shift keys on a Windows.*

FIGURE | 2–29 |

Selecting the Use Precise Cursors option and deselecting the Show Tool Tips option in the General Preferences.

A CLOSER LOOK

You now have a bird's-eye view of the Illustrator landscape. Next, you will take a closer look at some of the navigational features of the program, such as the Hand and Zoom tools, the Navigator panel, Screen and View modes, and the status bar.

LESSON 3: NAVIGATIONAL FEATURES

Magnification Tools

1. In Illustrator, open the file **chap2L3.ai** in the folder **chap02_lessons.**

> Note: *If you get a convert color mode warning window, choose CMYK.*

2. Choose View > Fit All in Window to magnify the file to fit in the window area.

3. The document title bar indicates the current magnification of the artwork. See Figure 2–30. Depending on the size of your document window, this number will vary.

FIGURE | 2–30 |

The document title bar indicates the current magnification of the artwork.

4. Choose View > Actual Size to set the document view to 100%. This shows you the actual size of the artwork if it were to be printed on paper.

5. Select the Zoom tool in the Tools panel. Refer to Figure 2–4. Click once on the artwork to zoom in. Click again to zoom even closer.

6. Hold down Option (Mac) or Alt (Windows) to reverse the Zoom tool (notice the minus sign in the Zoom tool cursor). Continue to hold down Option/Alt, as you click once on the artwork to zoom out. Click again to zoom even farther away.

7. Let's zoom into a particular area of the artwork. With the Zoom tool selected, click and drag from the upper left to the lower right a rectangular shape over the copyright notice in the lower-left corner of the document. See Figure 2–31. With this area marqueed, let go and notice how the area selected fills your monitor. Cool!

8. Select the Type tool (the "T") in the Tools panel and change the text from 2012 to 2013. To do this, click and drag through the last digit (2) and type "3" on the keyboard. See Figure 2–32.

FIGURE | 2–31 |

Select an area to zoom in close.

FIGURE | 2–32 |

Change the text with the Type tool.

9. Use View > Zoom Out to see more of the image, then select the Hand tool in the Tools panel (the tool above the Zoom tool). Click and drag with the Hand tool over the document, pushing it down and to the left a bit until you see the "THE CHESHIRE DOG" text at the top of the artwork.

10. Select the Type tool and change DOG to CAT. To exit the Type tool, choose the Selection tool and click anywhere in the canvas area (outside the artboard).

11. Select View > Actual Size to see the completed artwork. Or, double-click on the Zoom tool in the Tools panel. See Figure 2–33.

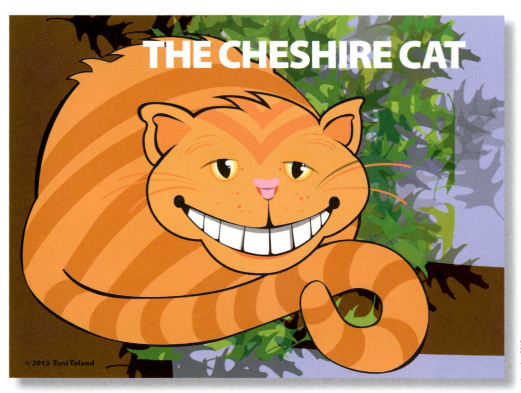

FIGURE | 2–33 |

The completed artwork.

The Navigator Panel

1. Another way to get a proper view of your artwork is to use the nifty Navigator panel. Choose Window > Navigator to open it. A small view of your artwork is shown in the Navigator window. See Figure 2–34.

2. In the Navigator panel, slide the small arrow in the lower part of the window to the right to magnify the document, and then to the left to reduce it. Notice the red border adjusts in the viewing window to indicate what area is viewable in the document. Zoom in to about 250%.

> Note: *Instead of moving the slider to zoom in and out, you can click on the mountain-like icons on each side of the slider. Also, you can type in a zoom percentage in the lower-left corner of the Navigator window.*

3. Locate a specific area of the graphic by placing the cursor over the red border area in the Navigator window (notice the cursor changes to the Hand tool). Click and drag the red border area until you locate the copyright (©) symbol in the lower-left corner of the document.

FIGURE | 2–34 |

The nifty Navigator panel.

FIGURE | 2–35 |

Edges, colored red in this figure, are visible for editing the artwork.

Other Viewing Modes

1. Choose View > Actual Size to see the completed artwork.

2. Select the Selection tool in the Tools panel. Marquee a selection of the cat's face by dragging from the upper left to the lower right. See Figure 2–35. Notice the edges (paths) of the artwork are visible for editing.

3. Hide these edges (paths) by choosing View > Hide Edges. (I don't like to hide the edges of my artwork because then I can't see the selected paths when editing, and sometimes I accidentally select View > Hide Edges. This feature might come in handy someday, so it is good to know it's there.)

4. Choose View > Show Edges.

5. Choose View > Show Artboards to view the outline of the document. Remember that the artboard is the region that contains your artwork.

6. To view the artwork in outlines, choose View > Outline. This option shows only the paths of the artwork, not the paint attributes. Viewing artwork without paint attributes speeds up the time it takes to redraw the screen when working with complex artwork. It also makes it easier to select items in a detailed illustration.

7. Choose View > Preview to see all the artwork attributes again.

Screen Modes and Status Bar

1. You can also view artwork at different screen sizes. In the Tools panel, you can choose Normal Screen Mode, Full Screen Mode with Menu Bar, or Full Screen Mode. See Figure 2–36 and try out all three options. Note: To get out of Full Screen Mode, press the ESC key on your keyboard.

2. In the Tools panel, choose Normal Screen Mode. Notice the status bar in the lower-left corner of the document window. It contains pop-up information for Zoom options and Document status options. See Figure 2–37.

3. From the pop-up menu near the magnification number, choose a new magnification for the artwork.

4. From the pop-up menu near the Artboard Navigation field, select Show from the pop-up menu and, explore each of the following options: Artboard Name, Current Tool, Date and Time, Number of Undos, and Document Color Profile.

5. Save the file, then close it. You are done with this lesson.

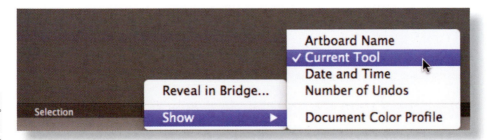

FIGURE | 2–37 |

Status bar options.

SUMMARY

After exploring this chapter, you should have a better command of the interface elements and navigational features of Illustrator. You will spend no more time wandering around dark alleys trying to find your way. With a little practice, you will be zooming in and out, selecting tools, and opening and closing panel windows with ease. Who needs a sophisticated GPS when you have historical landmarks and shortcut keys to aid you on your Illustrator journey?

▶ IN REVIEW

1. Explain the difference between the canvas and the artboard.

2. The nonprintable area of a document is indicated by what visual cue on the Illustrator artboard?

3. What does *.ai* at the end of a filename indicate?

4. What are tool tips? How can you turn them off?

5. What is a precise cursor?

6. Identify the shortcut key to undo a mistake.

7. What is the difference between View > Actual Size and View > Fit in Window?

▶ EXPLORING ON YOUR OWN

1. Create a new file and explore the different shape options available in the Tools panel: rectangle, rounded rectangle, ellipse, polygon, star, and flare. Use the Navigator panel to practice zooming in and out of the document window.

2. There are many ways to customize your experience in Illustrator. Explore the various options for how your workspace could be set up by choosing Window > Workspace or the down-facing arrow to the far right on the Application bar. See Figure 2–38 and also refer back to Figure 2–7. Keep in mind that you do not want to customize too much while you are doing the lessons in this book or things might get confusing; all lessons in this book are based on the Essentials workspace and keyboard shortcuts.

Some options for workspace setup include:

▶ *Essentials workspace:* Minimizes the workspace area into the most basic, docked versions of the panels.

▶ *Project-based workspaces (i.e., Painting, Printing and Proofing, Typography, Web):* Sets workspace with open panels used mostly for a specific project. For example, the Type workspace opens panels used most often for typographic creation and editing.

▶ *Save workspace:* Saves your favorite workspace setup (panels, menus, and keyboard shortcuts) for quick access every time you use the program.

▶ *Manage workspace:* View and delete any saved workspaces.

Also, in Illustrator, read the section "Workspace" under Help > Illustrator Help.

3. Once you get the hang of the general features of Illustrator, you can set personalized keyboard shortcuts under Edit > Keyboard Shortcuts.

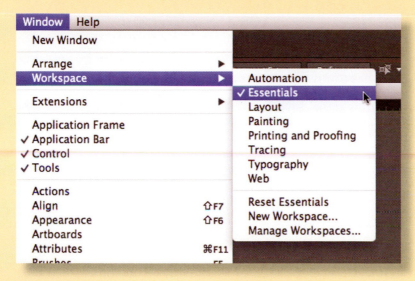

FIGURE | 2–38 |

Customize your workspace.

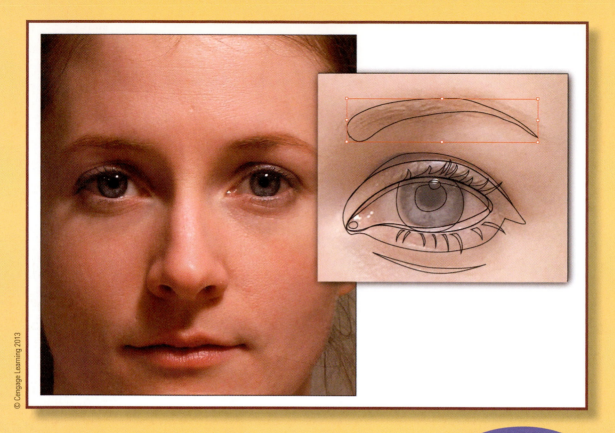

| Survival Techniques |

3

charting your course

Now that you have gotten your feet wet with Illustrator, you are ready to go in a little deeper. Chapter 3 is essential for aspiring graphic artists. If you can grasp this chapter, you will be well equipped for creative expeditions not only in Illustrator, but also in many other computer graphics programs.

In this chapter, you will discover that Illustrator, because it uses vector technology, opens up a world of possibilities for you, the artist. I will start with a brief explanation of what it takes to be an Illustrator artist, and then venture into the differences between vector and bitmap images, as well as image formats. In conclusion, I will guide you through a hands-on deconstruction of an Illustrator file with design elements in mind.

goals

In this chapter you will:

- ► *Discover that being an Illustrator artist is more than just knowing the tools*
- ► *Develop a basic understanding of the two types of digital images: bitmap (raster) and vector*
- ► *Learn about image formats and get an overview of common image format types*
- ► *Find out how an Illustrator user, well-versed in the program's fundamental design elements, can use Illustrator as an effective art medium*
- ► *Explore Illustrator's tools and features with design elements in mind*

IT'S MORE THAN COOL TOOLS

I'm going to give it to you straight: Being a graphic artist is not about knowing how to use the millions of tools in the hundreds of computer graphics software programs available. That would be like saying you must master all the tools at Home Depot before you build a house. Why learn how to use a miter saw before you need something cut?

Obviously, it helps to know what tools exist. And having some familiarity with a few common tools—such as a hammer if you are building a house, or the Pen tool if you are working in Illustrator (see Chapter 4)—does make things easier. Such knowledge allows you to better conceptualize how a project might come together. Truly mastering all the tools and features of a program comes when you have a real-life project with schedules and deadlines and picky clients. That kind of experience comes with time.

More important to comprehend than the tools themselves are the principles behind them. Understanding how digital images are created is key to your survival as a successful graphic artist. This includes knowing an image's distinguishing characteristics, its format, and (specific to Illustrator) how it is created in relation to fundamental design elements.

CHARACTERISTICS OF BITMAPS AND VECTORS

There are two ways digital images are created. One uses pixels, or small squares of color information, and are referred to as *bitmap* or *raster images*. See Figure 3-1. The quality of these images is directly related to the number of pixels in a square inch. The other method uses mathematical formulas to plot points—a lot like the graphs you may have created in Algebra—that are connected to form shapes. The quality of these images is unlimited; they can be enlarged or reduced without compromise. Understanding when to use which approach is important when developing graphics in Illustrator for either print or Web design.

ABOUT BITMAP IMAGES

A bitmap image is one where the content is described by thousands of small squares of color information, much like a mosaic. The smaller the squares, called *pixels* (short for picture elements), the more realistic the image. For this reason, bitmap images are perfect for reproducing photographs and continuous-tone images (paintings, and illustrations). Figure 3–2 is an exaggerated example of how a photo is broken down into these bits of color information.

The number of pixels in a square inch of an image is referred to as the image's *resolution*. Images with high resolutions generate more detailed

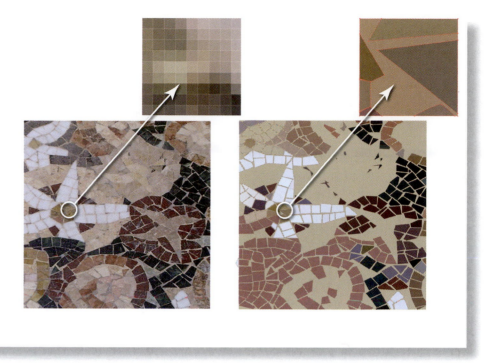

FIGURE | 3–1 |

On the left is an example photograph composed of pixels (small elements of data in a grid) that describe the image's color and quality. On the right is an illustration composed of vectors: specific points that define the object's outline using a mathematical coordinate system.

FIGURE | 3–2 |

Zooming in close to a bitmap image reveals its individual pixels.

images, and they have larger file sizes as well. Having fewer pixels per inch (ppi) reduces the quality and creates smaller file sizes.

For work that will appear on the Web, the number of pixels per square inch is usually around 72 because that is the typical resolution of a computer monitor. Keeping the file sizes smaller also ensures that images appear faster when loading on a Web page. For images that will be printed, the resolution should be anywhere between 150 ppi and 300 ppi. See Figure 3–3.

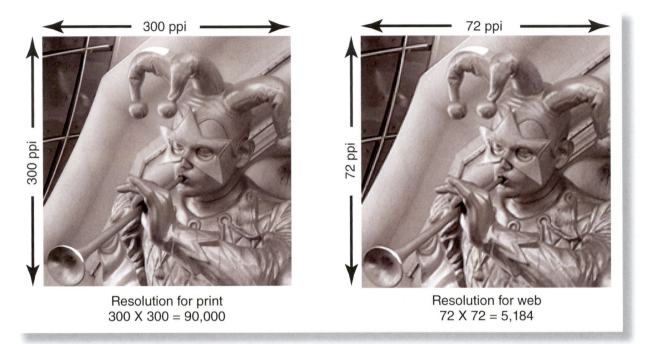

Resolution for print
300 X 300 = 90,000

Resolution for web
72 X 72 = 5,184

FIGURE | 3–3 |

A bitmap image of the same dimensions (for example, 1"-by-1") can have a different resolution (number of ppi) depending on its intended use.

> Note: *Because bitmap image quality is determined by the number of pixels per inch, enlarging them will seriously degrade the image; the pixels are being enlarged along with the dimensions of the image, and they will become big enough to be clearly visible. This phenomenon is referred to as* pixelation *and should be avoided at all costs.*

ABOUT VECTOR GRAPHICS

To visualize vectors, think of those activity books where connecting a series of dots revealed a complete image. You explored this in Chapter 1, when you created a logo. Each dot defines a particular point in space, with lines linking them together. These lines, called *paths*, determine the shape of the object.

Thanks to a French mathematician, Pierre Bezzier, vector objects can also have curves, unlike strict *x-y* axis point plotting. In Illustrator, the Direct Selection and Pen tools allow you to manipulate those paths to get exactly what you want.

Because bitmap images are dependent upon their resolution, manipulating them can get tricky—you can scale them smaller, but not larger. With vectors, this is not the case. In Illustrator, instead of trying to push pixels around, images are constructed with straight and curved paths, as defined by the position of the points (called *anchor points*). As a result, a vector image can be scaled large or small without compromising quality. Images created using vectors are usually bold and illustrative, with crisp lines and solid colors, and are ideal for things like text, logos, and graphic representations. See Figure 3–4.

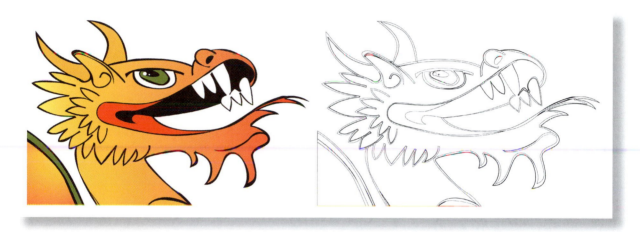

FIGURE | 3–4 |

On the left is an illustrative vector image. On the right are the editable lines (or paths) that comprise it.

CONVERGENCE OF IMAGE TYPES AND IMAGE FORMATS

Before moving on, I should mention a couple more vital points about vectors and bitmaps. Programs such as Adobe Photoshop, Adobe Fireworks, and GIMP are designed to work specifically with bitmap-constructed images. Adobe Illustrator, Adobe Flash, and CorelDRAW are designed to work with vector-based graphics. However, most programs—to some extent—have the ability to import and display both vector and bitmap graphics. Illustrator in particular has the option to convert vector objects into bitmap objects. This process is called *rasterization*. For example, by selecting Object > Rasterize in Illustrator, a basic shape can be converted from vector outlines to bitmapped pixels. You might do this if you want to apply a certain effect that can only be achieved using pixels. You can also convert bitmaps into vectors with Illustrator's Image Trace feature.

There also are different image formats for different types of images. A format is described by an extension at the end of the filename, like **image.jpg, mywork.tiff**, or **paper1.doc**. An image's file format helps you identify whether it is composed of bitmaps or vectors. A file format determines the file size, visual quality, and compression (if any) of the image. A highly compressed image has a smaller file size and less visual quality than an uncompressed or minimally compressed image. There are many image file formats to choose from, determined by where you are going to use the image (i.e., print, the Web, or exporting for use in another program). Most graphic programs support the use of the following:

Bitmap-based formats

- *BMP (short for "bitmap"):* A limited bitmap file format *not suitable for Web or print.*
- *GIF (Graphics Interchange Format):* A highly compressed format that supports transparency and is mainly used for Internet graphics with solid colors and crisp lines.
- *JPEG or JPG (Joint Photographic Experts Group):* A compressed format used for Internet graphics, particularly photographs and continuous-tone illustrations.
- *PNG (Portable Network Graphics):* A versatile bitmap compressed format used mainly for Internet graphics and photos.
- *TIFF (Tagged Image File Format):* Saves bitmap images in an uncompressed format, most popular for print and compatible with virtually all image editing and page layout applications.

> Note: *To maintain the highest quality, images are usually saved uncompressed in TIFF format. However, in Illustrator you can apply certain types of compression, such as LZW, on a TIFF, which compresses the file without discarding detail from the image.*

Vector- and bitmap-based formats

- *EPS (Encapsulated PostScript):* Flexible file format that can contain both bitmap and vector information. Most vector images are saved in this format.
- *PICT (Macintosh picture file):* Used on Mac computers and can contain both vector and bitmap data.
- *SWF (originally Shockwave Flash, and now also referred to as Small Web File):* The Flash™ file format. A common vector-based graphics file format for the creation of scalable, compact graphics and animations for the Web and handheld devices.
- *SVG (Scalable Vector Graphic):* An XML-based vector format for the creation of scalable, compact graphics for the Web and handheld devices.

IMPORTING AND EXPORTING

In Illustrator, you can import (place into the program) images and files saved in many types of formats. To import files into an existing document and view a list of all readable documents Illustrator supports, choose File > Place. See Figure 3–5. When placing an image or file into a document, you have an option to link it or embed it. See Figure 3–6. When the link check box is checked, the placed file uses the original image as an external reference to the document, reducing the document file size. When linking files, remember that they must not be discarded; without them, the document will not show your work properly.

If the link check box is unchecked, the placed file is embedded into the document. These embedded files become part of the document and, as a result, increase the document's file size. To import a file as a new document, choose File > Open.

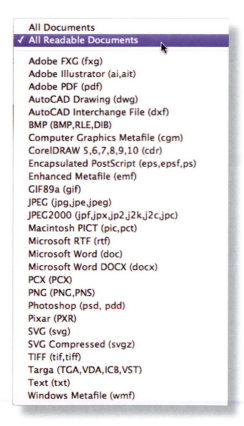

FIGURE | 3–5 |

Choose File > Place to import files into Illustrator.

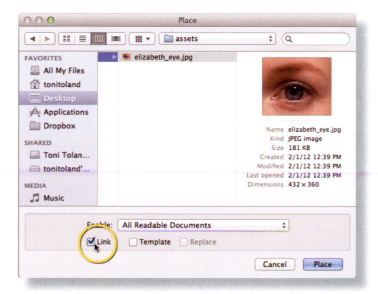

FIGURE | 3–6 |

The option to link rather than embed a file or image is available when you place the file or image into the program. Unchecking the Link option automatically embeds the image as part of the file.

Note: *If you decide to link images or files to your document, you always have the option to embed them later. Choose Window > Links or use the Control panel while the image is selected for options to embed and/or relink misplaced images. However, if you've deleted the linked image from your hard drive, it's permanently gone from your Illustrator file.*

You can also export (save) your Illustrator work in different formats, depending on where it will go next in the design process—print, the Web, or imported into another program. To export a file and view a list of file formats, choose File > Export. See Figure 3–7.

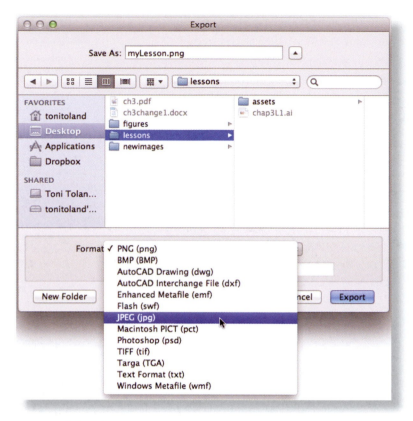

FIGURE | 3–7 |

Choose File > Export to save Illustrator artwork in a different format.

DESIGN ELEMENTS WITH ILLUSTRATOR

The approach to creating an illustration in Illustrator is not unlike traditional drawing and painting. Whether sketching by hand or with a computer mouse, the elements of design are essentially the same. With this in mind, you are ready to learn the tools and techniques of Illustrator as they apply to the fundamental building blocks of visual art.

"The corresponding structural elements of art are line, shape, value, texture, and color," according to the authors of *Art Fundamentals: Theory and Practice.* "In art the artist is not only the contractor but also the architect; he or she has the vision, which is given shape by the way the elements are brought together."

Each chapter of this book builds on the elements of art as they pertain to your growing understanding of Illustrator. With the elements of line, shape, value, texture, and color, a direct correlation can be made between how a vector illustration is constructed and the structural elements of art and design. As you will learn

objects

paths   **lines**   **points**

TEXTURE + VALUE + COLOR = spatial form   **PATHS + LINES + SHAPES = fundamental building blocks**

FIGURE | 3–8 |

Anatomy of an illustration with the elements of art and design in mind.

in Chapter 4, a digital illustration is composed of vector objects, each having one or more paths (shapes) made up of line segments having anchor points at each end. Each object's lines and shapes become unique, unified, and/or spatially whole by application of value, texture, and color. On a cursory level, you will explore this relationship in the next lesson, "Elizabeth's Eye." A visual diagram of this correlation might help. See Figure 3–8.

As an artist uses watercolors, charcoal sticks, or clay to bring a vision into form, the graphic designer uses Illustrator as a medium toward a creative end. See Figure 3–9. Its numerous tools and features are designed to support the elements inherent in visual artwork and beyond.

LESSON: ELIZABETH'S EYE

In this lesson, you take a guided tour of a previously created Illustrator file. Step-by-step, you import and place a bitmap image, add a warp effect, unlock layers, and explore the different stages of vector object construction, all the while keeping design elements in mind. See Figure 3–10 for the completed lesson.

Source: U.S. National Library of Medicine (NLM)

FIGURE | 3–9 |

Notice how line, shape, value, and texture make up the illustration of René Descartes, shown here. Value is indicated by the light and dark shapes in the drawing. Textural line effects bring out the subtle softness and depth of his hair and robe. Note: René Descartes can be considered one of the foremost fathers of vector illustration. A seventeenth-century mathematician and philosopher, he developed analytic geometry, in particular coordinate systems, which provide a foundation for describing the location and shape of objects in space.

Completed lesson: Elizabeth's Eye.

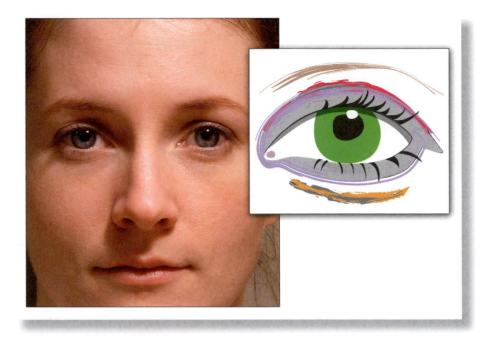

FIGURE | 3–11 |

The Layers panel.

FIGURE | 3–12 |

The Layers visibility option is indicated by an eye icon on the left of the Layers panel.

Setting Up the File

1. Launch Illustrator. Choose File > Open and, on your local hard drive, browse for the Exploring Illustrator folder **chap03_lessons**. Open the file **chap3L1.ai**.

2. Check that the Essentials workspace is selected in the upper-right corner of the Application bar.

> Note: *As mentioned in the File Set-up, to save your work, you must make a copy of the chapter lessons to your local hard drive, and select files from that location.*

3. Choose Window > Layers to open the Layers panel. See Figure 3–11. Layers organize the various elements of an Illustrator document. There are already several layers created for this document.

4. Unhide the **box** layer by turning on the visibility option in the Layers panel. See Figure 3–12 and Figure 3–13.

FIGURE | 3–13 |

Unhiding a layer reveals more of the illustration.

> **Note:** *If you don't see all the layers in the Layers panel, scroll down, or enlarge the panel by dragging the bottom-right corner of the panel down.*

Importing a Bitmap

1. Highlight the **box** layer by clicking on it in the Layers panel. See Figure 3–14.

2. Click the Create New Layer icon at the bottom of the Layers panel (next to the trash can icon) to make a new layer above the **box** layer. See Figure 3–15.

3. Double-click on the new layer (the blank area to the right of the name) to open the Layer Options. Alternatively, click on the options menu icon (an arrow with lines) in the upper-right corner of the Layers panel and select Options for "**Layer 7**." See Figure 3–16.

4. For the layer name, enter **eye_bitmap**, and click OK. See Figure 3–17.

5. With the **eye_bitmap** layer highlighted, choose File > Place from the menu bar.

6. Browse for **chap3_lessons/assets** and select **elizabeth_eye.jpg** and then click Place.

7. Be sure that **elizabeth_eye.jpg** is selected on the artboard. In the Control panel check to make sure the width and height options are

FIGURE | 3–14 |

Box layer is selected (highlighted).

FIGURE | 3–15 |

The Create New Layer option.

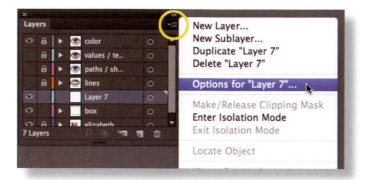

FIGURE | 3–16 |

Open the Layer options.

FIGURE | 3–17 |

Name the Layer.

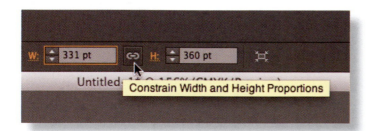

FIGURE | 3–18 |

Size the bitmap in proportion using the Control panel.

constrained; the chain will be unbroken. Then enter W: **331 pt** to reduce the bitmap's size. Hint: Hit Enter on the keyboard to execute the new size. See Figure 3–18.

> Note: *Illustrator might automatically convert the point (pt.) size—indicated in the Transform panel—to some other measurement. This happens if your default measurement is set to something other than points. See Illustrator > Preferences > Units (Mac) or Edit > Preferences > Units (Windows).*

8. Click and drag the bitmap image to fit into the box. For precise positioning, use the up/down and right/left arrow keys on the keyboard to move the image in small increments. See Figure 3–19.

9. In the Control panel at the top of the screen, click on the Embed button if it is available. See Figure 3–20. If you have inadvertently deselected the bitmap, select it again to show the Embed option. By embedding the image, you ensure the placed image will be saved with the document, and filters and effects can be applied to it.

> Note: *If the embed option is not available, it's because the "link" option was not checked when you placed the image, so it's been embedded automatically.*

10. For fun, choose Effect > Warp > Fisheye (be sure the bitmap is selected). In the Warp Options window, adjust the Bend option by moving the slider to 72%. Preview the effect on the bitmap by selecting the Preview option. See Figure 3–21. (Note: You might need to move the Warp Options window aside to see the eye bitmap effect on the document below.) Click Cancel to close the Warp Options window without altering the bitmap.

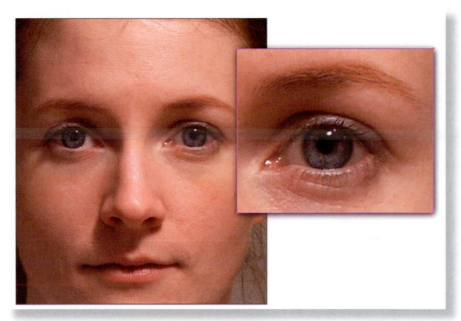

FIGURE | 3–19 |

Position the eye bitmap.

FIGURE | 3–20 |

Select the Embed button
on the Control panel.

11. Click on the **eye_bitmap** layer to highlight it, then use
the Layers panel options menu to choose Template.
This automatically dims the image and locks the layer
so you can't draw on it inadvertently. See Figure 3–22.

12. Choose File > Save As to save your file. Rename it
chap3L1_yourname.ai and save it in your lessons
folder. An Illustrator options box will come up—leave
the version set to Illustrator CS6 and all other settings
at the default. Choose OK.

Exploring Lines

1. Unhide and unlock the **lines** layer in the Layers panel.
Some lines, traced around the image of the eye, have
already been created. Constructing lines (or paths, as
they are called in Illustrator) is the first step in creating
an image in Illustrator.

2. Choose the Selection tool in the Tools panel. See
Figure 3–23.

FIGURE | 3–21 |

Preview the FishEye Warp settings.

FIGURE | 3–22 |

Turn the eye_bitmap layer into a template for tracing.

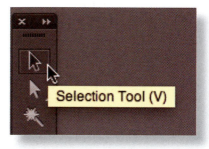

FIGURE | 3–23 |

The Selection tool is the black arrow that allows you to select objects in your document.

Note: *By default, your Tools panel should be open. If not, choose Window > Tools to open the panel.*

3. Explore selecting the different paths on the eye image by clicking on each one with the Selection tool. Notice how each line segment is composed of connected anchor points. See Figure 3–24.

4. Each line created is indicated in the **lines** layer. To see the list of lines (labeled <Path>) that have been drawn on this layer, click the small triangle next to the **lines** layer icon. To quickly select the various lines/paths in the document, click on the circle to the right of any of the sublayers. See Figure 3–25. To hide the layer's sublayers, click on the triangle again.

5. Let's make a new object by tracing the outline of the eyebrow. First, select the Zoom tool in the Tools panel (the magnifying glass icon toward the bottom), and then click once on the eyebrow to magnify the drawing area.

6. Select the lines layer and then use the panel's options menu to add a new layer above it. Double-click the layer name to rename it "eyebrow."

7. Select the Pencil tool in the Tools panel. See Figure 3–26.

8. With steady hand, click and drag a continuous line around the eyebrow, ending in the same place you started. See Figure 3–27. If you make a mistake, choose Edit > Undo Pencil, and try again.

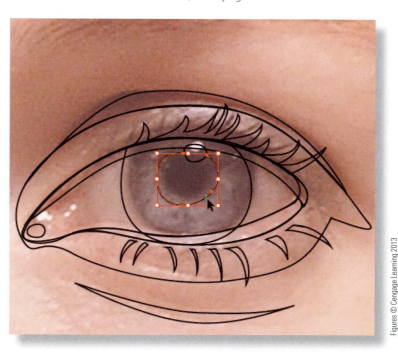

FIGURE | 3–24 |

Select lines and paths.

Note: *There are numerous ways to edit and reshape the line you created, which will be covered in later chapters. For now, just get a feel for what it is like to trace over an image.*

9. Save your file.

Filling a Shape

1. Unhide the **paths/shapes** layer. Notice the lines are filled with flat shading, creating distinct shapes.

2. Select the eyebrow. From the Control panel, click on the down arrow of the Fill option (first drop-down arrow). Select the 60% Black (C=0 M=0 Y=0 K=60) swatch to fill the eyebrow. See Figure 3–28.

3. From the Control panel, click on the down arrow of the Stroke option (second drop-down arrow). Select the Black swatch for the eyebrow's stroke. See Figure 3–29 and Figure 3–30.

Adding Value and Texture

1. In the Layers panel, unhide the **values/texture** layer. Notice the variations of line—width, intensity, and quality—that add value and texture to the illustration.

FIGURE | 3–25 |

To organize all the elements of an illustration, layers are further subdivided into sublayers—each sublayer contains one element or object.

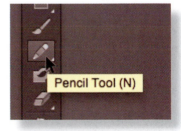

FIGURE | 3–26 |

The Pencil tool is just one of the tools used to create lines and paths.

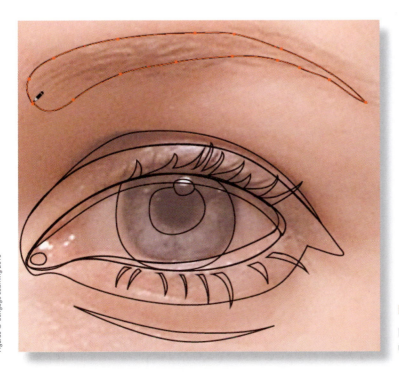

FIGURE | 3–27 |

Drawing an eyebrow with the Pencil tool using a mouse takes a steady hand.

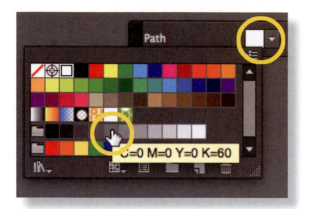

FIGURE | 3–28 |

The Swatches panel; available through the Control panel.

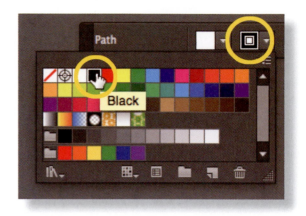

FIGURE | 3–29 |

Select a color for the stroke (outline) of the shape.

2. Choose the Selection tool in the Tools panel and select the eyebrow. From the Control panel, click on the down arrow for the Brush Definition options (or choose Window > Brushes). See Figure 3–31.

3. Choose the Dry Brush 2 art brush.

   A charcoal-like style is added to the stroke (outline) of the eyebrow. Explore the other available brushes by selecting them in the Brushes panel; the selected stroke is automatically updated each time you choose another brush. See Figure 3–31 and Figure 3–32.

FIGURE | 3–30 |

The filled eyebrow shape.

Adding Color

1. Unhide the **color** layer. As crazy as they are, colors have been added to the eye image, creating an illusionary effect and mood.

2. Select the eyebrow. Open the Color panel, and use the options menu to Show Options, if necessary, to see everything. See Figure 3–33.

3. In the Color panel, click anywhere in the color spectrum bar in the lower part of the window to select a fill color. See Figure 3–34.

FIGURE | 3–31 |

Select Dry Brush 2 brush from the Control panel.

FIGURE | 3–32 |

The eyebrow outline has texture and value.

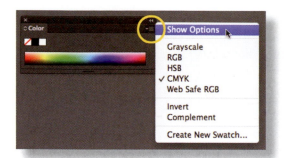

FIGURE | 3–33 |

Use the Color panel's options menu to expand the panel.

4. Change the stroke (outline) color of the eyebrow. First, click on the Stroke icon in the Color panel to bring the stroke option forward so you can edit it. See Figure 3–35.

5. In the Color panel, click on the color spectrum bar in the lower part of the window to select a color for the eyebrow's stroke.

6. Hide the **eye_bitmap** layer by toggling its visibility off in the Layers panel. If the Layers panel is closed, choose Window > Layers to open it again.

7. Choose View > Fit All In Window.

8. Save your file.

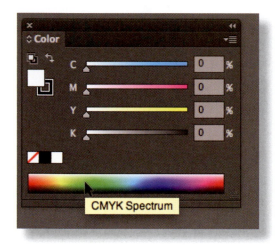

FIGURE | 3–34 |

Choose a color in the Color panel.

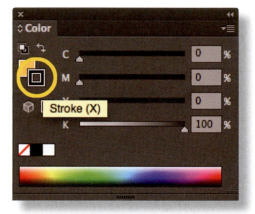

FIGURE | 3–35 |

Bring the Stroke option forward in the Color panel.

SUMMARY

Vital survival techniques for gung-ho graphic artists were revealed in this chapter. You learned that tools are cool, but knowing about digital image construction and design elements is what really keeps you alive in the Illustrator jungle. Briefly described were characteristics of bitmap and vector graphics, image formats, and resolution, all of which help prepare you for the idiosyncrasies of drawing digitally. Finally, you progressed through the creation of an illustration by using the elements of design, including line, shape, value, texture, and color.

▶ IN REVIEW

1.   Briefly describe the differences between bitmap and vector graphic types.

2.   Illustrator's underlying magic is its ability to work with what type of images?

3.   Bitmap images are most common for what type of images? Why?

4.   Text and logo treatments are created best as what type of graphic? Why?

5.   What is image resolution? Why is it important to know?

6.   What is an image file format?

7.   What are the five elements of art that can be explored in Illustrator?

▶ EXPLORING ON YOUR OWN

1.   Access the Help > Illustrator Help menu bar option. Under Using Adobe Illustrator CS6, in the section "Importing, exporting and saving," read the following topics: Importing bitmap images, Importing files, and Exporting artwork.

2.   Do an online search for "design elements" and/or "design principles," and read up on traditional design concepts and current trends.

Arthur Mount

Compliments of Arthur Mount.

Asbury Park for *Dwell Magazine*.

About Arthur Mount

Arthur Mount is from Berkeley and the San Francisco Bay area, where he received his Bachelor of Fine Arts in drawing from the California College of the Arts in 1995. He and his wife left in 2001, fleeing high house prices; lived in Pasadena for a couple of years, where their son was born; and then moved to beautiful Portland, Oregon.

Arthur has been working as an illustrator since 1996, but he did not get serious about it until around 2000. His work has appeared in a number of magazines and periodicals, including *Dwell*, *Wallpaper*, *Fortune*, *Sunset*, *GQ*, *ESPN*, and the *New York Times*. His commercial clients have run the gamut, including L'Oreal, Apple, Boeing, AT&T, Google, Sprint, Red Bull, Volkswagen, W Hotels, and many others. He has been published around the world, and has won a few awards along the way.

"I enjoy what I do, and appreciate the flexible schedule it gives me to spend time with my family and other interests," he said. To view more of Arthur's work, visit *http://www. arthurmount.com*.

Compliments of Arthur Mount.

Illustration for Google.

About the Work of Arthur Mount

"For the *Dwell Magazine* illustrations of Asbury Park, I worked closely with the designers at *Dwell,* as well as an architecture firm in New York that was developing blocks of downtown Asbury Park," Arthur said. "Working from photos of the existing site and architectural elevations and sketches, I was to render the finished development in place as well as add a street scene with people, cars, etc. Pulling everything together under a tight deadline was quite a task, particularly because at that time the building designs were not completed and only existed as flat, unfinished 2D drawings. In addition to the scene seen here, I also drew a scene from the other side of the development from across a small body of water as well as a cutaway, showing aspects of the development's interior. This was my first of many assignments with *Dwell*, and it's still one of my favorites. After completing the project, my wife and I took a trip to Asbury Park and its vicinity to see where the development was to be realized."

"Being a successful illustrator is a business," Arthur said. *"Do what you enjoy and be as creative as possible, but if you want to do it for any length of time and not have to find another job somewhere else, you must find a way to make it work for you."*

Learn more about this artist via an audio interview available on www.cengage.com

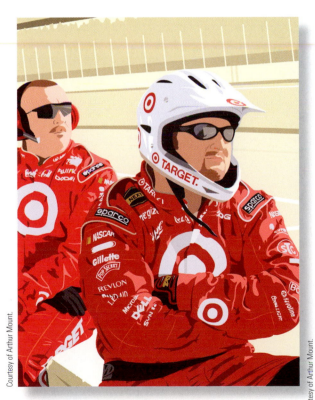

Courtesy of Arthur Mount.

Illustration that accompanied an article about NASCAR in America Airlines' in-flight magazine, *American Way*.

Courtesy of Arthur Mount.

Fire and Ice

Illustration for Celebrity Cruises.

| Drawing Lines and Shapes |

4

charting your course

Chapter 3 introduced you to the essential elements of visual imagery—line, shape, value, texture, and color. By focusing on the first two elements—line and shape—Chapter 4 further solidifies your understanding of how to draw in Illustrator. Illustrator has numerous tools to produce lines and shapes. Some of them create geometric shapes, others more freeform styles, and one in particular— the Pen tool—offers a more precise drawing experience. As you practice the methods for drawing lines and shapes, you will also encounter useful terminology for describing various shapes and the vector points, line segments, and paths from which they are made.

goals

In this chapter you will:

▶ *Review the process of creating illustrations in Illustrator*

▶ *Learn the difference between open paths and closed paths/shapes*

▶ *Draw and transform basic shapes, and describe shape types*

▶ *Explore the freeform drawing tools*

▶ *Discover the characteristics of Bezier lines and curves using the Pen tool*

▶ *Create, move, and edit straight and curved paths*

▶ *Combine straight and curved paths into object shapes*

▶ *Select and edit individual anchor points*

THE SIMPLICITY OF LINES AND SHAPES

Look closely at Figure 4–1. It's a candlestick, right? Look at it again. This time, squint your eyes and focus on its form—the outline and shapes that distinguish the object. It has a cylindrical shape at the top, some various shaped ellipses along the stem, each connected by smaller cylinders, and a cone-like base. What initially looks like an intricate candlestick is essentially a series of geometric shapes. See Figure 4–2.

As an artist, you need to develop the ability to visually break down objects into simple and familiar lines and shapes—to look at common objects as objective forms.

FIGURE | 4–1 |

An intricate candlestick.

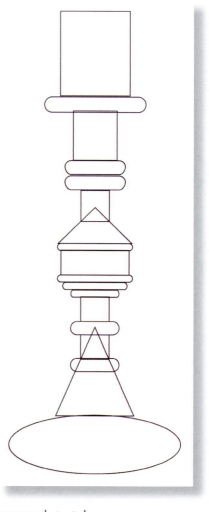

FIGURE | 4–2 |

On closer inspection, the candlestick is composed of basic geometric shapes.

Figures © Cengage Learning 2013

When looking at and drawing objects in this way, certain questions might arise: What is a line and what is a shape? A line, in drawing, is simply an edge or a boundary. In Illustrator, and most other graphic drawing programs, a line can have several different names. Generally speaking, a line can be referred to as a stroke, an outline, or a path. Lines can be either open or closed. A closed line is usually referred to as a shape. See Figure 4–3 through Figure 4–7 for clarification. Lines can also have different values (thicknesses) and colors, which are discussed in Chapter 5 and Chapter 6.

With an artist's eye, you will practice your design skills in the next series of lessons using basic shapes, freeform shapes, and precision drawing tools and techniques.

FIGURE | 4–3 |

A *shape* is defined as the outline of an area or a figure. In the study of design, shapes actually have specific definitions depending on what they look like, such as geometric, rectilinear, biomorphic, and irregular.

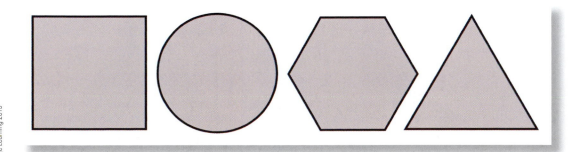

FIGURE | 4–4 |

Geometric: shapes are constructed mathematically.

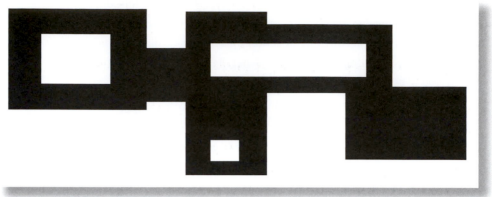

FIGURE | 4–5 |

Rectilinear: shapes are bound by straight lines that are not related to each other mathematically.

FIGURE | 4–6 |

Biomorphic (organic): shapes are bound by free-flowing curves, suggesting fluidity and growth.

FIGURE | 4–7 |

Irregular: shapes are bound by straight and curved lines that are not related to each other mathematically.

GEOMETRIC, FREEFORM, AND PRECISION DRAWING

Matching the visual image you have in your mind's eye with what actually materializes on the Illustrator artboard depends on three things: the tools you use, the methods you use, and the process by which you go about the endeavor. Take, for example, the idea to draw a giraffe. Should we make the giraffe look graphic or realistic? To draw the giraffe in a more graphic way, Toni traced over a photograph using the basic shape tools and then combined them. See Figure 4–8. To make it look more like the real thing, she traced over a photograph, using the Pen tool this time, which gave her the flexibility to draw more complex shapes. See Figure 4–9. Both methods produced an illustration of a giraffe, each with a different visual result depending on the process and tools used.

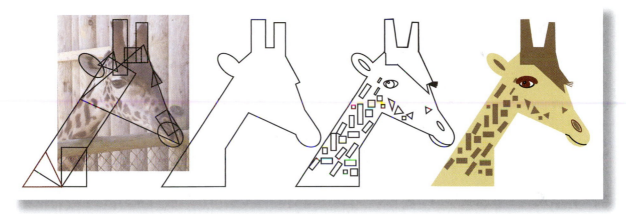

FIGURE | 4–8 |

A simple drawing of a giraffe using geometric shapes, then adding color and texture.

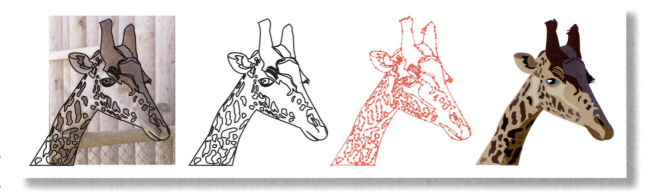

FIGURE | 4–9 |

A more complex drawing of a giraffe constructed using the Pen tool.

Now it's your turn to make lines and shapes using various tools and methods. You have had the opportunity to play with some of these shape-creation tools in Illustrator. In Chapter 1, you tackled the connect-the-dots logo design using the Pen tool, and in Chapter 3, you cursorily sketched an eyebrow in the lesson "Elizabeth's Eye" using the more freeform Pencil tool. As promised, I will now be more specific about these tools, starting with Illustrator's options for creating geometric and freeform shapes and then working with the more accurate Pen tool.

LESSON 1: BASIC LINES AND SHAPES

In this lesson you practice creating geometric and freeform shapes. To do this, you will use a template that defines the different shape types in art and design.

Setting Up the Stroke and Fill Attributes

1. In Illustrator, choose File > Open and open the file **chap4L1.ai** in the **chap04_lessons** folder.

2. Choose Shift Tab to temporarily hide any panels and give yourself more room to work.

3. Before you begin to draw, set up the fill and stroke (outline) color attributes. First, select the default Fill and Stroke option in the toolbox, making the fill area white and the stroke black. See Figure 4–10.

4. Click on the Fill box (the white one) to activate it. See Figure 4–11.

5. Choose the "None" option to indicate no color for the fill. See Figure 4–12.

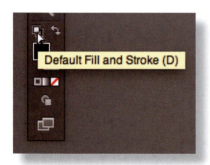

FIGURE | 4–10 |

Set the Fill and Stroke
to the default.

FIGURE | 4–11 |

Click the Fill box to activate it.

FIGURE | 4–12 |

Choose the "None" option to
indicate no color for the fill.

Making Geometric Shapes

1. Select the Zoom tool and zoom in close on the first quadrant of the file labeled **Geometric Shapes**. In the blank area below the row of geometric shapes, you will practice drawing the shapes. Let's call this the "drawing area."

2. Select the Rectangle tool in the toolbox.

3. Starting in the upper-left corner of the first quadrant drawing area, click and drag to create a rectangular shape. See Figure 4–13.

4. While it's still selected, practice moving the rectangle in different directions by tapping the up/down or right/left arrow keys several times. (Note: Hold down the Shift key with the arrow keys to move it in larger increments.) You can also use the Selection tool to move the shape, but remember that you must click directly on the stroke to select it (it will not select if you click in the fill area since there is no fill color).

5. While it's still selected, delete the rectangle by pressing Delete on the keyboard.

6. Choose Illustrator > Preferences > Units (Mac) or Edit > Preferences > Units (Windows). Under Units, make sure to check that General is set to Inches. See Figure 4–14.

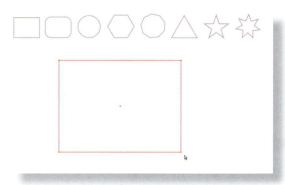

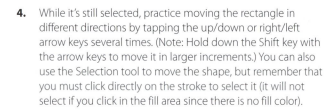

FIGURE | 4–13 |

Create a rectangle in the Geometric Shapes drawing area.

FIGURE | 4–14 |

Use Illustrator's General Preferences pane to adjust the distance the arrow keys move an object.

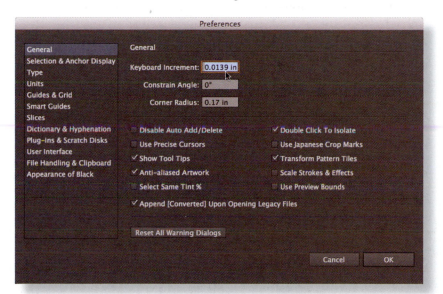

7. Select the Rectangle tool. Place your cursor anywhere over the drawing area and click once to open the Rectangle tool's options. Here, you can specify an exact width and height for the rectangle. To make a perfect square, enter 4 in by 4 in in the dialog box. Click OK to create the shape. See Figure 4–15.

8. Practice making a few more rectangles or squares, either by clicking and dragging with the Rectangle tool or by clicking on the drawing area and indicating exact dimensions in the dialog box.

> Note: *If the arrow keys don't seem to be doing anything, use Illustrator > Preferences > General (Mac) or Edit > Preferences > General (Windows) to set a larger Keyboard Increment.*

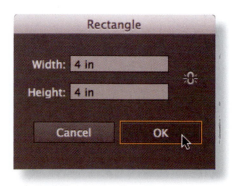

FIGURE | 4–15 |

Set a specific, numeric size for shapes.

9. Choose the Selection tool in the toolbox. Select one of the rectangle shapes you made, then hold down the Shift key and click on an edge of each of the other shapes to add them to the selection. See Figure 4–16.

10. Press Delete to delete the selected shapes and clear the drawing area.

FIGURE | 4–16 |

Select multiple shapes to delete them all at once.

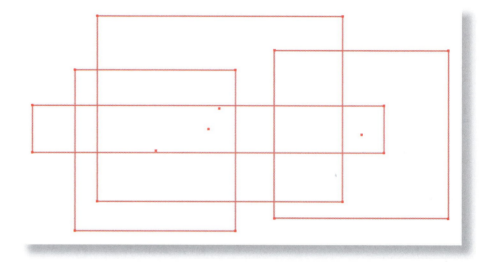

11. Click and hold the Rectangle tool in the toolbox to reveal the other Shape options. See Figure 4–17. Choose the Rounded Rectangle tool.

12. Click once on the drawing area to open the Rounded Rectangle options. Enter 1.5 in for Width, 2 in for Height, and 0.25 in for Corner Radius. See Figure 4–18. Click OK to see the result.

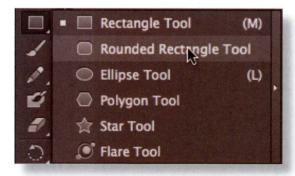

FIGURE | 4–17 |

Select the Rounded Rectangle tool option.

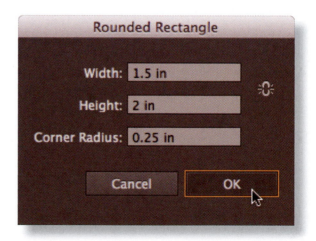

FIGURE | 4–18 |

Enter options for the Rounded Rectangle tool.

13. If you do not find it intuitive to put in a number for the corner radius, you can do it interactively. First, select the Rounded Rectangle tool.

14. After you click and drag to create the shape, keep the mouse button pressed down and then tap the up arrow key several times on the keyboard. The corner radius of the shape changes before your eyes!

15. With the mouse button pressed, tap the down arrow key several times. The corner radius goes in the opposite direction. What happens if you choose the right and left arrow keys?

16. Select all the rounded rectangles and delete them.

17. Click on and hold the Rounded Rectangle tool in the toolbox to reveal the other Shape tools again. Choose the Ellipse tool.

18. Click and drag to create an ellipse shape in the drawing area. As you draw the shape, notice how it is created from the point at which you first clicked.

19. To draw a shape from the center out, hold down Option (Mac) or Alt (Windows); the cursor changes to a cross surrounded by a circle.

20. Keeping Option/Alt pressed, click and drag to make an ellipse. Notice how it is being constructed from the center. This option is very helpful to create more accurately placed shapes.

> **Note:** *To create a perfectly symmetrical shape, press Option/Alt and Shift at the same time as you click and drag the circle.*

21. Delete all the ellipse and circle shapes.

22. Click and hold the Ellipse tool in the toolbox to reveal additional Shape tools. This time choose the Polygon tool.

23. Now that you have an idea of how shapes are drawn, create some polygonal shapes. Try clicking and dragging to create the shapes. Try clicking and dragging and then, while keeping your mouse button pressed, tap the up/down arrow keys to interactively add or subtract sides to the shape. This takes some coordination, but it is definitely a handy little trick. Using this method, see if you can make a triangle using the Polygon tool. How about a circle?

24. Select the Star tool. Practice the same method you learned in the last step to draw and adjust the star shape. Use the up arrow key to make more points on the star, or the down arrow key to make fewer.

Transforming Lines and Shapes

1. Select and delete (Edit > Clear or hit Delete) all the geometric shapes you created in the first quadrant of the lesson file.

2. Make a new star shape in the drawing area.

3. Choose the Selection tool (the solid arrow) in the toolbox and select the star shape. A Free Transform bounding box appears around the object—a box with positioning nodes (squares) on each corner and side. This bounding box is really a timesaver—it's a Move, Scale, and Rotate tool all in one. You will use it in the next steps and in later lessons.

Note: *If you do not see the bounding box around the object, go to View > Show Bounding Box to unhide this option.*

4. To move the star, click on its edge (the black outline) and drag it to a new position on the drawing area. See Figure 4–19.

FIGURE | 4–19 |

Move the star shape.

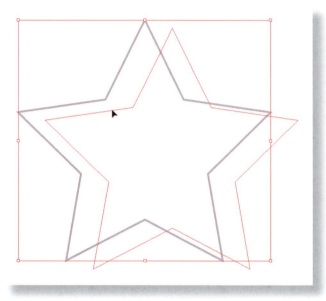

5. To scale the star, click on a corner of the bounding area and drag the shape to a new size. See Figure 4–20.

Note: *Hold down the Shift key as you scale the object to keep it in proportion.*

▶ DON'T GO THERE

In this particular lesson, you have been making shapes with a stroke (outline) color only, and no inside fill color. (If you recall, you played with strokes and fills somewhat in Chapter 1, and the topic is covered more in Chapter 5.) To be successful with selecting and moving an object, you must click on a part of the object that has color applied to it. If, for example, you click in the center of an object with no fill color, you end up deselecting the object—oops!

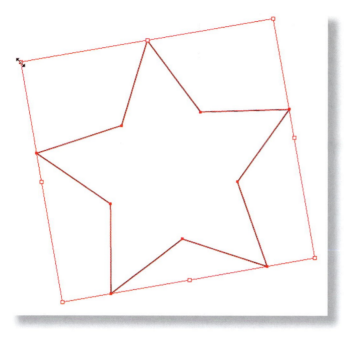

6. To rotate the object, first place the cursor slightly outside one corner of the bounding box. The cursor shifts to an icon of a curved line with an arrow at each end. See Figure 4–21. Click and drag to rotate the object.

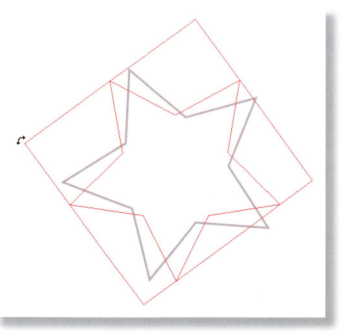

FIGURE | 4–21 |

Rotate the star shape.

Making Rectilinear Shapes

1. Still working on the file **chap4L1.ai**, choose View > Actual Size, and then use the Zoom tool to enlarge the second quadrant labeled **Rectilinear Shapes**. Two rectilinear shapes have already been created. You will trace over these shapes.

FIGURE | 4–22 |

Select the Line Segment tool.

Rectilinear Shapes

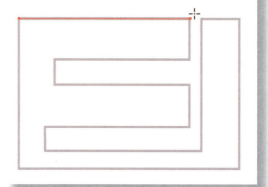

FIGURE | 4–23 |

Draw a line segment.

2. Select the Line Segment tool in the toolbox. The Line Segment tool allows you to create individual straight lines called line segments—how convenient! See Figure 4–22.

3. Place the cursor in the upper-left corner of the first rectilinear shape. Click and drag to the right, creating a line segment that defines the top left portion of the shape. See Figure 4–23.

4. Continue making line segments to construct the shape. To make a line limited to a 45-degree angle, constrain the line as you draw it by holding down the Shift key.

Note: *To move or transform a line, hold down Command (Mac) or Ctrl (Windows). The Line Segment tool will temporarily switch to the Selection tool.*

5. Go ahead and practice using the Line Segment tool to trace over the other rectilinear shape. Then make your own rectilinear shapes in the drawing area below the templates.

Making Biomorphic Shapes

1. Free yourself from the rigidity of the Line Segment tool and go organic. Select View > Actual Size and then use the Zoom tool to focus on the third quadrant—**Biomorphic Shapes**.

2. Select the Pencil tool in the toolbox. See Figure 4–24.

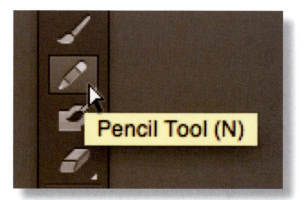

FIGURE | 4–24 |

Select the Pencil tool.

3. With a steady hand, draw a continuous line around the first biomorphic shape. Yeah, I know it's not easy; this is why you will learn the Pen tool later, which will give you more control. Nevertheless, try it again. Delete the shape or select Edit > Undo Pencil and then redraw it. See how close you can get.

4. Try tracing the other biomorphic shape.

5. Make your own organic shapes in the drawing area below the templates.

Making Irregular Shapes and Grouping Them

1. Finally, select View > Actual Size and then use the Zoom tool to enlarge the last quadrant—**Irregular Shapes**. These types of shapes have a combination of linear (straight) and biomorphic (curved) lines.

2. Select the Line Segment tool in the toolbox. Trace the straight lines of the first shape. (Hint: There are two of them.) See Figure 4–25.

3. Click and hold the Line Segment tool in the toolbox to reveal other options. Choose the Arc tool. See Figure 4–26.

4. Click where you want the arc to begin—in this case, the bottom-left corner—and drag up and to the right to create the arc. See Figure 4–27. If your curve doesn't exactly match the template, try tapping the up or down arrow key to adjust it. In any case, don't worry if it's not perfect.

> **Note:** *When drawing lines with the Line Segment and Arc tools, each line created is an individual element. Give it a test. Choose the Selection tool in the toolbox and, one at a time, select each line you created.*

5. To create the next arc, position the Arc tool cursor at the top of the right vertical stroke and drag up and to the left.

6. Continue from this point and drag once more to complete the shape, up and right just a bit. See Figure 4–28.

7. Let's group the individual lines of this irregular shape. With the Selection tool, click one of the lines in the object, then hold the Shift key and select each of the other four segments of the shape.

8. Choose Object > Group from the menu bar to group the selected line segments.

> **Note:** *Holding the Shift key while selecting objects adds each object to the selection.*

FIGURE | 4–25 |

Trace lines with the Line Segment tool.

FIGURE | 4–26 |

Select the Arc tool.

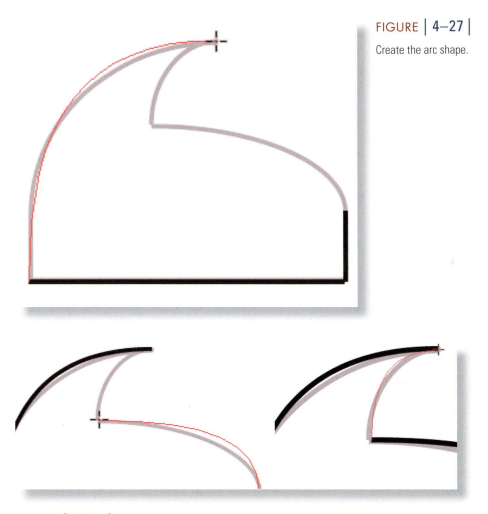

FIGURE | 4–27 |

Create the arc shape.

FIGURE | 4–28 |

Click and drag with the Arc tool to finish the irregular shape.

9. Using the Selection tool, move the irregular shape to see its grouped state. By grouping line segments and shapes, they become easier to move around, scale, and rotate.

> **Note:** *To undo a group, select the grouped object and choose Object > Ungroup.*

10. Use the Line Segment and Arc tools to trace the other irregular shape.

> **Note:** *To change the direction and degree of an arc, hold down the up/down arrow keys as you click and drag to draw the shape.*

11. Create your own irregular shapes in the drawing area below the templates. Select the individual lines and arcs and group them together.

12. Save your file in your lessons folder, if you wish.

Mastering the Precise Pen Tool

Most people's first attempt to use the Pen tool is mediocre at best, and no wonder; it's a lot like drawing with a bar of soap. However, it is worth learning how to use this tool well, as it is generally the tool of choice for most digital artists and designers. Think of the Pen tool as King Arthur's sword Excalibur (the one stuck in solid rock): unwieldy at first, but once mastered, mighty and faithful.

Like Illustrator's other drawing tools, the Pen tool creates vector-based paths and shapes. However, to be successful using the Pen tool, it helps to take a detailed look at a vector illustration's anatomy. See Figure 4–29. A vector illustration is composed of vector objects, such as the eye of the giraffe in Figure 4–29. Each object contains one or more paths (lines), which are composed of line segments. A line segment has an anchor point at each end. Anchor points are the most fundamental component of a vector illustration—they are the dots that define the shape of a path. Using direction lines and direction points (together called direction handles), anchor points define the position and curve attributes of each line segment. The curve attributes of a line segment are called Bezier (pronounced bez ee ay) curves. Pierre Bezier, a French mathematician, was the very smart fellow who developed the method for defining these curves mathematically. You will get to define your own curves—the Illustrator way—in the next lessons.

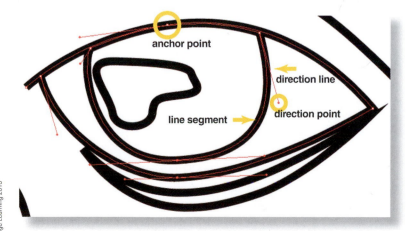

FIGURE | 4–29 |

The giraffe's eye illustrates the various parts of a vector's anatomy.

FIGURE | 4–30 |

Select the Pen tool.

LESSON 2: DRAWING PRECISE STRAIGHT AND CURVED PATHS

In this lesson, you will practice drawing with the Pen tool to create, move, and adjust straight and curved paths.

Setting Up the Stroke and Fill Attributes

1. In Illustrator, choose File > Open and open the file **chap4L2.ai** in the folder **chap04_ lessons**.

2. Press Shift Tab to temporarily hide any panels. You will need lots of space to work.

3. Select the default Fill and Stroke option in the Tools panel making the fill area white and the stroke black. Refer back to Figure 4–10.

4. Click on the Fill box (the white one) to activate it. See Figure 4–11.

5. Choose the "None" option to indicate no color for the fill. (Refer back to Figure 4–12.)

Starting with Straight Lines

1. Zoom in close on the first quadrant of the lesson template labeled **Straight Paths**. Hint: hold the Spacebar and Command key (Mac) or the Spacebar and Ctrl key (Windows) as a shortcut to selecting the Zoom tool.

2. Select the Pen tool in the toolbox. See Figure 4–30.

3. Click on—but do not drag—the red dot on the top straight line. This defines the first point.

4. Click—do not drag—at the end of the line to create the straight segment. See Figure 4–31.

FIGURE | 4–31 |

Click to make another anchor point at the end of the line segment.

Straight Paths

first click   second click

When using the Pen tool, there is a big difference between a "click" and a "click and drag" to define an anchor point. To create straight lines, click once to make each point. If direction lines appear, you have accidentally dragged with the Pen tool.

To fix this, choose Edit > Undo and click again. The click and drag action is used to make curves. Also, the first point you draw will not be visible until you click a second anchor point. It takes two anchor points to create a complete line segment.

Figures © Cengage Learning 2013

5. Prepare to start a new line segment by doing one of the following:

> ► Command click (Mac) or Ctrl click (Windows) anywhere away from all objects.

> ► Choose Select > Deselect.

> ► Click on the Pen tool icon in the Tools panel.

> **Note:** *When the cursor for the Pen tool has a little star next to it, that is a sign you are ready to make a new path. See Figure 4–32. If you don't see the pen icon as a cursor, but instead see a plus sign, go to Illustrator > Preferences > General (Mac) or Edit > Preferences > General (Windows) and uncheck the Use Precise Cursors option.*

FIGURE | 4–32 |

A star next to the Pen tool cursor indicates you are ready to start a new path.

6. Practice making another straight-line segment under the first one you created. To do this, click once at the left, then move the Pen tool to the right several inches and click again. Hold down the Shift key to keep the line perfectly horizontal.

7. Press and hold Command (Mac) or Ctrl (Windows) to toggle to the Selection tool. Click on the line and practice moving it. Remember, you can use the Free Transform bounding box to move, rotate, or scale any object, including open paths or lines.

> **Note:** *If you do not see the bounding box around the line, go to View > Show Bounding Box to unhide this option. You also won't see it unless the Selection tool is active.*

8. This time choose Select > Deselect to deselect all objects.

9. Select the Pen tool and click on the red dot at the left of the zigzag line.

10. Continue clicking points at each corner of the line until it's completed. See Figure 4–33.

11. Select (with the Selection tool) the zigzag path and practice moving, scaling, and rotating the line.

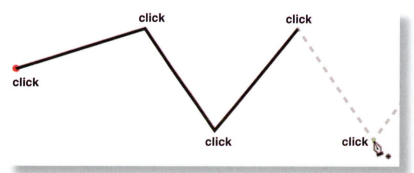

FIGURE | 4–33 |

Click to place the anchor points to create a zigzag line.

12. Now use the Pen tool on the third guide line; hold down the Shift key as you click on each point to ensure that the lines are perfectly straight.

13. In the first quadrant area of the lesson, practice creating your own straight and zigzag paths.

> **Note:** *If your lines end up connecting to one another, choose Edit > Undo, and make sure everything is deselected (see step 5 above).*

Making Closed Straight Paths/Shapes

1. Still working in **chap4L2.ai**, choose View > Actual Size.

2. Zoom in on the second quadrant labeled **Closed Straight Paths/Shapes**.

3. Select the Pen tool.

4. Click to place a point at the red dot of the triangle shape, then click at the next corner, and then the next.

5. To close the path, place the cursor over the starting point. Notice that the cursor has an open circle next to it. See Figure 4–34. This indicates you are ready to close this path. Click on the starting point to close the path.

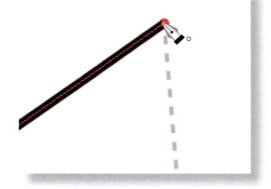

> **Note:** *Closing a path frees up the Pen tool to start creating something else, in contrast to ending an open path, where you have to click the Pen tool in the toolbox or hold Command (Mac) or Ctrl (Windows) and click away from the path, or Select > Deselect.*

6. On your own, practice drawing closed shapes using the snowflake shape on the template as a guide. Remember to watch for the circle next to the Pen tool to ensure that you are closing the path.

FIGURE | 4–34 |

Close a path.

Drawing Curved Paths

1. Still working in **chap4L2.ai**, choose View > Actual Size.

2. Zoom in on the third quadrant labeled **Curved Paths**. To make things easier, guides indicating the direction lines and/ or anchor points for the path are provided.

> **Note:** *Direction lines and anchor points do not print.*

3. Select the Pen tool.

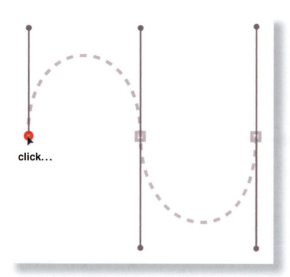

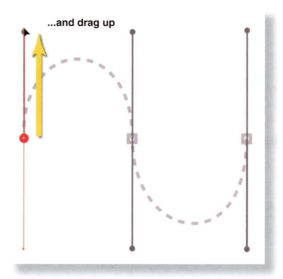

FIGURE | 4–35 | and FIGURE | 4–36 |

Start of the curve.

4. Click and hold on the red dot of the first curve. Without letting go of the mouse button, begin to drag up to create the direction handles. Extend the handles to the length indicated on the guide. See Figure 4–35 and Figure 4–36. If you make a mistake, Edit > Undo Pen and try again. Hint: hold down the Shift key as you drag for a more precise direction handle.

5. To continue the curved path, click on the center anchor point and drag down so that the handle's length matches the guide. Your first curve is formed. See Figure 4–37 and Figure 4–38.

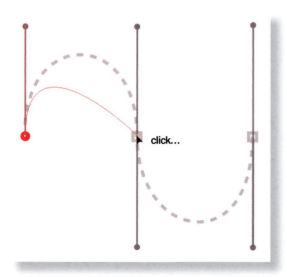

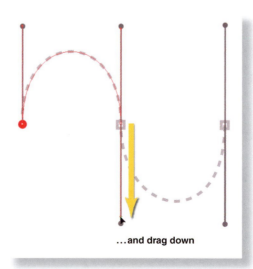

FIGURE | 4–37 | and FIGURE | 4–38 |

Complete the first curved segment.

6. To complete the curved path, click and drag up on the last anchor point. See Figure 4–39 and Figure 4–40.

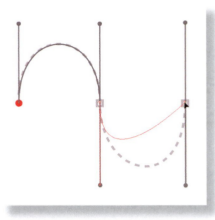 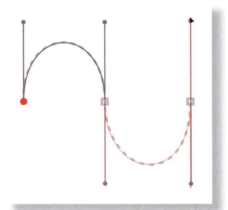

FIGURE | 4–39 | and FIGURE | 4–40 |

Finish the curved path.

▶ DON'T GO THERE

When first learning how to make curves, it is common to get "click happy." The tendency is to create lots of anchor points while drawing, thinking this will produce a more accurate shape. However, in this case, more is not necessarily better. Keep it simple! The trick is in the placement and adjustment of the anchor points and direction handles; if you place them with efficiency, you can create simpler, cleaner lines. For example, to achieve a more symmetrical path, place points at the ends of a curve, rather than at the high point of a curve. See Figure 4–41 and Figure 4–42.

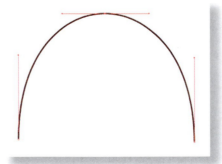 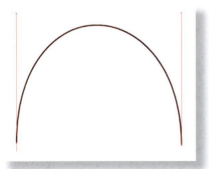

FIGURE | 4–41 |

Place a point at the high point of the curve—not very efficient when creating symmetrical shapes.

FIGURE | 4–42 |

Place points at the ends of a curve and adjust the handles—more efficient.

7. Practice your anchor point placement on the second curve in the **Curved Paths** quadrant. In this example, the direction handles are not provided for you, but the point placements are. Position each point and drag the handles out until you create each desired curve. (Hint: Drag your handles toward the next curve, rather than the one you just created.) See Figure 4–43.

8. See if you can re-create the third curved path with the Pen tool, then make some of your own curves in the drawing area of the Curved Paths quadrant.

Drawing Closed-Curved Paths-Shapes

1. Still in **chap4L2.ai**, choose View > Actual Size.

2. Zoom in on the last quadrant, labeled **Closed-Curved Paths-Shapes**.

3. Select the Pen tool.

4. Let's create a circle with only two points. Click on the red dot of the circle and drag up to match the handle in the guide. See Figure 4–44.

> **Note:** *Remember, if you hold down the Shift key as you drag, you can constrain the angle of the handles.*

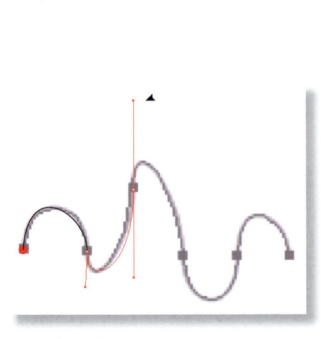

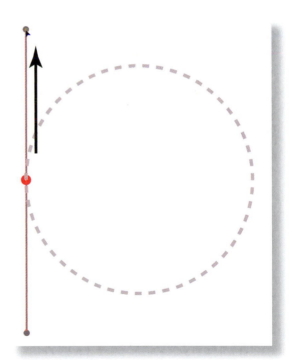

FIGURE | 4–43 |

Practice curves.

FIGURE | 4–44 |

Click on the red dot of the circle and drag up to create a handle.

5. Click on the point opposite the red dot and drag the handle down to form the top curve. See Figure 4–45 and Figure 4–46.

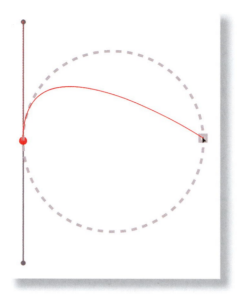 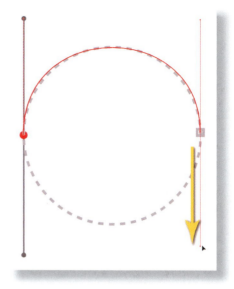

FIGURE | 4–45 | and FIGURE | 4–46 |

Click on the point opposite the red dot and drag the handle down.

6. Click on the first point again and drag the handle up to create the bottom curve and close the shape. See Figure 4–47 and Figure 4–48.

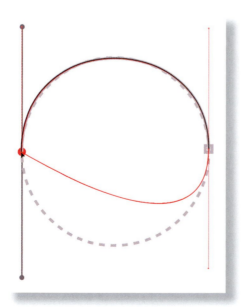 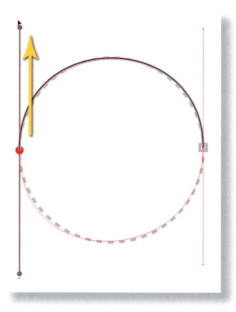

FIGURE | 4–47 | and FIGURE | 4–48 |

Click on the first point again and drag the handle up to complete the circle.

7. Practice your skill by combining corner points and curve points on the guide that looks like a flower. Click once at the inner points (don't drag), and then click and drag at the outer curves to create the rounded shape. Take a look at Figure 4–49 to get the idea.

8. On your own, practice making more closed-curve shapes. Can you make a butterfly shape? Some tree leaves?

9. Save this file **chap4L2_yourname.ai**, if you wish, and close it. We are done with this lesson.

Figures © Cengage Learning 2013

LESSON 3: COMBINING AND EDITING STRAIGHT AND CURVED PATHS

So far you have used the mighty Pen tool to draw straight and curved paths. Next you will use it to skillfully make and edit paths composed of both straight and curved segments.

Setting Up the Stroke and Fill Attributes

1. In Illustrator, open the file **chap4L3.ai** in the **chap4_lessons** folder.

2. Choose View > Actual Size.

3. Choose Shift Tab to temporarily hide any panels.

4. Select the default Fill and Stroke option in the Tools panel, making the fill area white and the stroke black.

5. Click on the Fill box (the white one) to activate it.

6. Choose the "None" option to indicate no color for the fill. Now you are ready to start drawing.

Putting Straight and Curved Lines Together

1. Zoom in on the gear-like object in the upper-left corner of the file.

2. Select the Pen tool.

3. Click once on the red dot to define the first anchor point.

4. Moving clockwise, click and drag on the other end of the first curve to make the curve segment. See Figure 4–50.

FIGURE | 4–49 |

Make a flower shape.

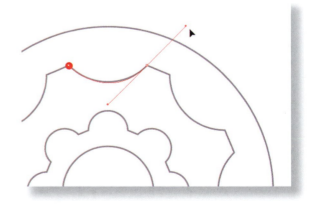

FIGURE | 4–50 |

Click and drag to make a curve.

5. Click on the top point of the next curve in the shape. See Figure 4–51. Oops—the curve is going in the wrong direction. This is because you are attempting to draw around a sharp corner in the shape. To change the direction of the curve, you must "break" the direction handle. See Figure 4–52 and Figure 4–53.

6. To delete the faulty anchor point, choose Edit > Undo Pen, or use the shortcut Command Z (Mac) or Ctrl Z (Windows).

FIGURE | 4–51 |

The curve goes in the wrong direction.

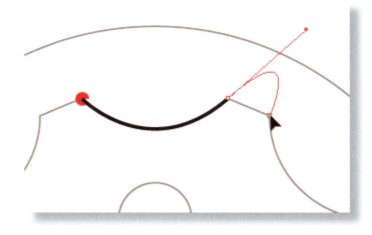

FIGURE | 4–52 |

An unbroken direction handle produces a continuous curve and works like a seesaw.

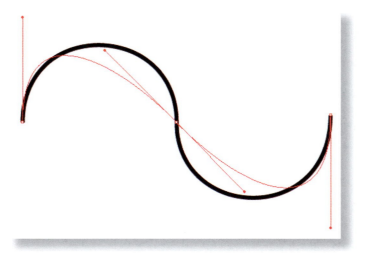

FIGURE | 4–53 |

A broken direction handle allows you to change the direction of the curve.

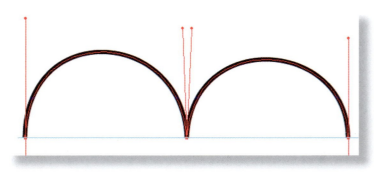

7. Place your cursor over the second anchor point. Notice the Pen tool has a little, upside-down V shape next to it. See Figure 4–54. This indicates that clicking again with the Pen tool will delete the leading direction handle. Click on the point to correct the path.

8. Click on the next point to create a straight path between the curved portions. See Figure 4–55.

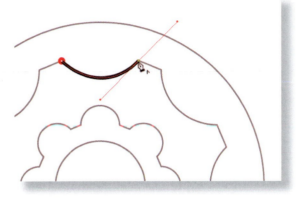

FIGURE | 4–54 |

Click on the anchor point again to convert the direction of the curve by deleting the forward direction handle.

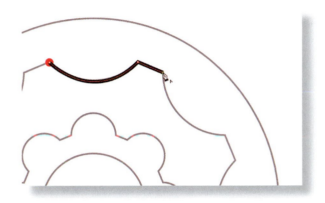

FIGURE | 4–55 |

Click once on the next corner to create a straight path between the curves.

9. Place your cursor over the point you just placed until you see the upside-down V-shaped icon. Click and drag to add a forward direction handle. See Figure 4–56.

10. Go to the ending point of this curve. Click and drag to make the curved path. See Figure 4–57.

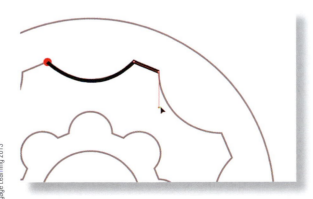

FIGURE | 4–56 |

Click and drag to add a new forward direction handle.

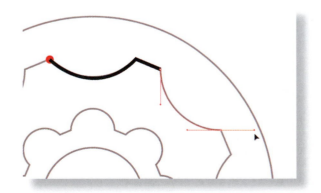

FIGURE | 4–57 |

Click and drag on the next point to finish the curve.

FIGURE | 4–58 |

Click once on the point to delete
the forward direction handle.

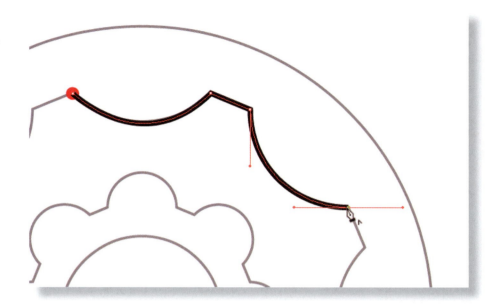

11. Click on that point again to delete the forward direction handle (Figure 4–58), and then click once on the next point to create the straight path.

12. Continue drawing around the shape, deleting and adding forward direction handles as you draw each straight and curved segment.

13. See if you can re-create the inner gear shape using the same technique. Remember to close the paths.

14. Two other template images have been provided to practice combining curved and line segments: a photograph of an oak leaf and an illustration of a dragonfly. Hone your pen coordination skills and trace over these objects. Try to be efficient with your point placement—less is better. Be sure to draw these outlines as one continuous line (i.e., close the paths). Once again, if you make a mistake, just undo it and try again. Now would be a good time to practice the Undo keystroke shortcut as well (Command Z (Mac) or Ctrl Z (Windows)).

▶ DON'T GO THERE

If at this point you are ready to give up using the Pen tool, please hang in there! Like any new skill, it takes practice. Once you get it, however, it will open up your Illustrator world.

If you find yourself getting stuck, it's often smarter (and sometimes faster) to delete everything and start over—practice makes perfect!

Converting and Editing Straight and Curved Paths

1. Still working in **chap4L3.ai**, choose View > Actual Size.

2. Zoom in on the lower section of the file labeled **Converting Straight and Curved Paths/Shapes**.

3. Choose the Direct Selection tool. See Figure 4–59.

> Note: *The Direct Selection tool lets you select individual anchor points or path segments by clicking on them. Any direction lines and direction points then appear on the selected part of the path for adjusting. Cool!*

4. Select the flower shape on the lesson file. Notice that all the points that comprise the shape are visible. Points that are hollow (white inside) are not selected. Points that are a solid color (in this case, red) are selected.

5. Select one of the points on the rounded part of one of the petals and move it up. See Figure 4–60. Notice how the unselected points stay fixed in position.

6. Select one of the direction points (the end of a direction handle) and drag it out to make the petal wider. See Figure 4–61. Extend the other direction point.

FIGURE | 4–59 |

Choose the Direct Selection tool.

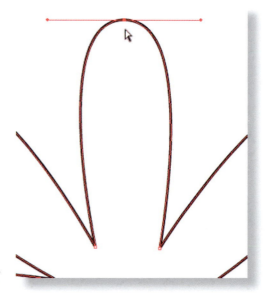

FIGURE | 4–60 |

Edit a petal with the Direct Selection tool.

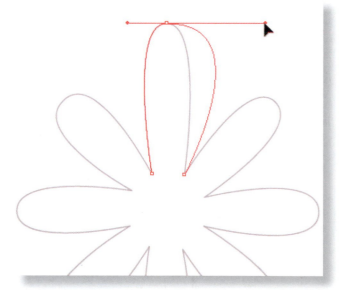

FIGURE | 4–61 |

Adjust the petal by clicking and pulling on the direction lines.

FIGURE | 4–62 |

Select the Convert Anchor Point tool.

7. Lengthen and expand each petal on the flower.

8. Let's convert the flower into a star. Place your cursor over the Pen tool and click and hold to reveal the other Pen tool options (yes, there are options!) and select the Convert Anchor Point tool. See Figure 4–62.

9. Place the Convert Anchor Point tool over one of the outer petal points and click to convert the curve point to a corner point. See Figure 4–63. Continue clicking on each point to turn the flower into a star.

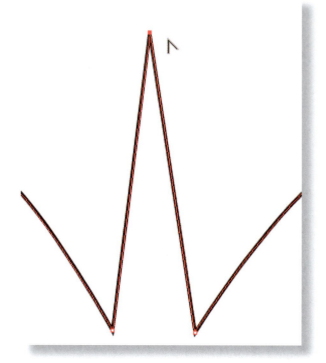

FIGURE | 4–63 |

Convert an anchor point.

Note: *If you get a warning that says, "Please use the convert anchor point tool on an anchor point of a path" (see Figure 4–64), don't panic. It usually pops up when you missed the anchor point you were attempting to click on with the Convert Anchor Point tool. Click on the anchor point again. If the points are difficult to see, zoom in on the area on which you are working.*

10. Change the star back to a flower. Use the Convert Anchor Point tool and click and drag the outer petal's anchor point to convert the corner points back into curved points. See Figure 4–65.

11. Let's change the flower into a circle. Place your cursor over the Convert Anchor Point tool in the toolbox and choose the Delete Anchor Point tool. See Figure 4–66. Notice, for future reference, that there is an Add Anchor Point tool as well.

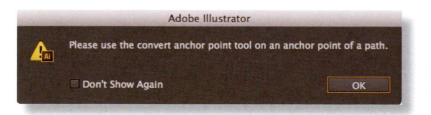

FIGURE | 4–64 |

Warning for Convert Anchor Point tool usage.

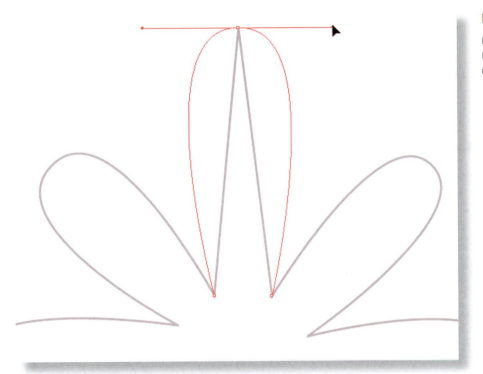

Figures © Cengage Learning 2013

FIGURE | 4–65 |

Click and drag with the Convert Anchor Point tool to convert corners to curves.

FIGURE | 4–66 |

The often-needed Delete Anchor Point tool. Right above it is the Add Anchor Point tool used to add points to a shape.

▶ DON'T GO THERE

As you drag new direction handles, you'll need to drag in the correct direction or the curve will get twisted. If that happens, just undo and drag again.

12.   Click on each of the innermost points of the flower shape to delete them and produce a circular shape.

13.   Select the Direct Selection tool in the toolbox (the hollow arrow). For fun, select the angular guitar shape (outlined in black) to the left of your mutated flower.

14. Use the Convert Anchor Point tool to reshape the angled lines so that they match the guitar shape. Don't forget that you can toggle to the Direct Selection tool by holding Command (Mac) or Ctrl (Windows) to make adjustments along the way. See Figure 4–67.

15. You have completed this lesson.

FIGURE | 4–67 |

Create the outline of a guitar.

SUMMARY

This chapter covered a lot of important stuff about lines and shapes: what they are, how they are constructed, and what tools and techniques are used to create, edit, and adjust them. You practiced making various types of shapes, developed your hand–eye coordination with the powerful Pen tool, and mastered some foundation skills for a more flexible and precise drawing experience.

▶ IN REVIEW

1.   What are some of the different names for a line in digital illustration?

2.   Name the four types of shapes in design.

3.   What keyboard command do you use to add objects to a selection?

4.   What keyboard command do you use to draw an ellipse or other shape from the center?

5.   What part of an object must you click on to select it?

6.   What is the purpose of a direction handle?

7.   What is a Bezier?

8.   What is the difference between a "click" and a "click and drag" when defining anchor points with the Pen tool?

9.   What tool do you use to select individual anchor points?

10.   How do you convert the direction of a curve?

▶ EXPLORING ON YOUR OWN

1.   Access the Help > Illustrator Help menu option and read the topic on Drawing.

2.   Practice your pen drawing skills by tracing over the sample images provided in the folder **chap04_lessons/practice**.

| Using Color |

5

charting your course

Color is an important aspect of illustrative work. I could easily fill 100 pages of this book discussing all the wonderful aspects of color in design. For now, however, let's start with the basics. This chapter covers some fundamental concepts of color, such as how color is reproduced, what color modes are, and an overview of some color theory you can't do without. You then get the chance to explore color in Illustrator, where a whole new aspect of your drawing can emerge.

goals

In this chapter you will:

▶ *Explore the concept of a color gamut*

▶ *Get acquainted with color models*

▶ *Learn what color mode to use*

▶ *Apply colors and patterns to strokes and fills*

▶ *Explore the color features and tools in Illustrator*

▶ *Make gradients*

▶ *Learn how to pick colors using color chords*

SEEING IS NOT NECESSARILY BELIEVING

Have you ever heard the saying "What you see is what you get"? Well, that is not always the case when working with color on a computer screen. Monitors can reproduce millions of colors, but even so, those are not all the colors available in our universe. Every device that has the capability to reproduce color has its own color range (or limits), which defines its color space or gamut (pronounced GAM-uht). The human color device—our eyes—can see many more colors than a computer can display or printer can reproduce. Take a good look at Figure 5–1. The chart indicates the visual (human), computer screen (RGB), and printer (CMYK) gamuts. (You will learn more about RGB and CMYK in the next section, Choosing a Color Model.) Notice the marked areas indicating the gamuts. All the gamuts overlap, and each is able to view like colors; however, the CMYK gamut has the fewest color possibilities.

So, if you pick a color for your digital image in Illustrator—which, by default, uses the RGB gamut to display your artwork, even if you have specified a CMYK document—you might find the color to be completely different when you print it. Most likely the color you picked in Illustrator is not available in the printer's gamut. Admittedly this predicament is very frustrating, but there are ways to achieve the result you want. I can't cover all the solutions in this chapter, but I will get you started with some explanation of color models and modes and provide you with additional reading in the section, Exploring on Your Own.

FIGURE | 5–1 |

The visual, screen, and print color gamut areas.

CHOOSING A COLOR MODEL

A color model is a system for describing color. You use color models when choosing and creating colors for your artwork. There are many different color models, but in computer graphics, and specifically in Illustrator, we will look at the following: Grayscale, RGB, Web Safe RGB, HSB, and CMYK.

GRAYSCALE

The Grayscale color model is used to select tints of black ranging in brightness from 0% (white) to 100% (black). In Illustrator, when you convert color artwork into grayscale, the luminosity (tonal level) of each color in the artwork

Figure © Cengage Learning 2013

becomes a shade of gray. To work in grayscale, select an object you are working on and choose Grayscale in the Color panel options. See Figure 5–2.

Note: *Converting an image to grayscale is a great way to visualize contrast in your image. Select your image and choose Edit > Edit Colors > Convert to Grayscale. Choose Edit > Undo to convert your image back to full color.*

FIGURE | 5–2 |

The Grayscale color model selected in the Color panel.

RGB AND WEB SAFE RGB

The RGB model represents the primary colors of light—red, green, and blue (RGB). The mixing of red, green, and blue light in various proportions and intensities produces a wide range of colors in our visual spectrum. RGB color is also referred to as additive color. When R, G, and B light are mixed, they create white—this is what occurs when all light is reflected back to the eye. (By the way, the absence of white light is black—what you get when you turn out the lights at night.) When R, G, or B overlap each other, they create the colors cyan, magenta, or yellow (CMY). See Figure 5–3. Devices that reproduce color with light are using the RGB color model, such as your TV or computer monitor.

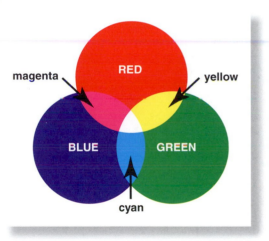

FIGURE | 5–3 |

The RGB color model.

Each component—red, green, and blue—in the RGB color model is labeled with a value ranging from 0 to 255. This means you can have a total of 256 shades of red, 256 shades of green, and 256 shades of blue, and any combination thereof (about 16.7 million colors!). For example, the most intense red color is represented as 255 (R), 0 (G), 0 (B), and a shade of deep purple is represented as 40 (R), 0 (G), 100 (B). See Figure 5–4 on the next page.

Illustrator also includes the Web Safe RGB, a modified RGB model that indicates the spectrum of colors most appropriate for use on the Web. The color components in

FIGURE | 5–4 |

The RGB model selected in the Color panel.

FIGURE | 5–5 |

The Web Safe RGB model selected in the Color panel.

FIGURE | 5–6 |

The HSB color model selected in the Color panel.

the Web Safe RGB space are measured using a hexadecimal system, a combination of numbers and letters, to represent a color rather than percentages. For example, a periwinkle blue in hexadecimal is indicated as #999EDD. See Figure 5–5.

Web Safe colors were originally established to ensure that everyone saw the same color on their monitors. At this point in time, however, about 95% of Web site users have monitors capable of displaying millions of colors, so it's much less of an issue.

Note that the colors specified in the Color panel for RGB (Figure 5–4) and Web Safe RGB (Figure 5–5) are the same, although the formula for defining them uses a different format.

HSB

Color can also be defined as levels of HSB—hue, saturation, and brightness. Hue identifies a main color property or name, such as "blue" or "orange." It is measured by a percentage from 0 to 360 degrees, as if picking colors from a standard color wheel. Saturation is the strength or purity of color. It is measured as an amount of gray in proportion to the hue, ranging from 0% (gray) to 100% (fully saturated). Brightness is the relative lightness or darkness of a hue, measured as a percentage from 0% (black) to 100% (white). See Figure 5–6.

The HSB color model can offer a more natural way to identify and modify related colors. Take a look at the section, Adventures in Design: The Moods of Color, at the end of this chapter.

CMYK

You learned that the RGB model reproduces color based on light. In contrast, the CMYK model reproduces color based on pigment or ink. The colors of CMYK are cyan (C), magenta (M), yellow (Y), and black (K, or key). The colors in this model are subtractive because when you add these pigments to a white page or canvas they subtract or absorb some of the light, reflecting what is left back to your eye. When the colors overlap, interestingly, they produce red, green, and blue (RGB). See Figure 5–7.

The "black" part of the CMYK color model is a bit elusive. To print a true black color on white, a higher percentage of cyan is mixed with magenta and yellow; it is not an equal amount of each color, as Figure 5–7 might lead you to believe. An equal mixing of just cyan, magenta, and yellow would actually result in muddy brown, not black, because of the absorption that occurs when ink hits paper. This is why black ink is used—in addition to the subtractive primaries cyan, magenta, and yellow—in four-color printing.

Each color component of the CMYK model is represented by a percentage ranging from 0% to 100%. To produce purple, for example, you mix 70% cyan, 100% magenta, 0% yellow, and 0% black. See Figure 5–8. In the print industry, this combining of the CMYK colors is appropriately called four-color process. And the individual colors produced by the mixing of any of these four colors are identified as process colors.

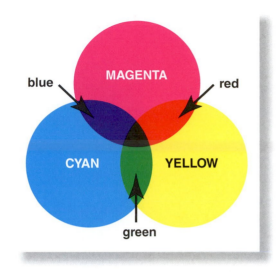

FIGURE | 5–7 |

The CMYK color model.

Note: *To get the color visually equivalent (or as close as you can) while working in Illustrator, read up on "Keeping colors consistent" under Color Management in the Illustrator Help files (Help > Illustrator Help).*

In addition to process colors, another color type used in printing is spot colors. These are special colors composed of premixed inks that require their own printing plates rather than the four used for four-color printing.

To help identify spot colors as they would look when printed, you can purchase color swatch books. Swatch books contain samples of colors printed on various types of paper. The colors are coded with specific names, such as Pantone®107C or TRUMATCH 23-a7. To see what we mean, go to Window > Swatch Libraries > Color Books > TRUMATCH or Window > Swatch Libraries > Color Books > PANTONE solid coated. Keep in mind, however, the issue of color viewed on screen versus print. Pantone 107C (a yellow color) will look slightly different on your monitor, which contains varying brightness and contrast

FIGURE | 5–8 |

The CMYK color model selected in the Color panel.

levels, than on the printed swatch. If you know that your artwork will go to print, trust the color you see on the printed swatch rather than the one on the screen.

You will run into process and spot colors as you work with colors in Illustrator, but don't worry about them right now. Preparing an image for a professional print job can easily become an advanced topic beyond the scope of this book. However, it is discussed in a bit more detail in Chapter 11, Print Publishing. For now, just remember, if your Illustrator artwork is going to print, choose colors within the CMYK model, or from spot color swatches.

GETTING IN THE MODE

Although you can select colors from various color models, ultimately you should set up your Illustrator project to a specific color mode depending on the intended purpose. A color mode determines the output of the artwork, either for display on screen (RGB) or for print (CMYK). When you create a new document in Illustrator, you can specify the color mode in the Advanced area of the New Document window. See Figure 5–9. However, you can change the color mode at any time without losing any information. To do so, choose File > Document Color Mode from the menu bar.

You may be wondering, "Why all this color mode business?" Well, remember, when it comes to color reproduction, what you see is not necessarily what you are going to get from print to screen and screen to print, so it's important to try every means possible to get it close. Setting the proper color mode is one of those means.

APPLYING COLOR

When adding color to vector-based illustrations, there are two possible parts of the drawing that you can affect: the stroke and the fill. The stroke is the path of an object—what defines its shape—and the fill is the area enclosed by the path. You have applied color to both parts in previous lessons. You can change the color of a selected stroke or fill in several places within the Illustrator workspace: the Color panel, the Color Picker (double-click the Stroke or Fill box in the Tools

Figure © Cengage Learning 2013

FIGURE | 5–9 |

Identify a color mode in the Advanced area of the New Document dialog box.

panel or Color panel), the Swatches panel, the Control panel, or by using the Eyedropper or Live Paint Bucket tool. You can also create color blends using the Gradient panel and Gradient tool. Each option is described and put in to practice in this chapter's lessons.

THE COLOR PANEL

The Color panel (see Figure 5–10) allows you to choose various color models for selecting and adjusting stroke and fill colors of a selected object.

THE COLOR PICKER

The Color Picker (double-click the Fill or Stroke box in the Tools panel or Color panel) is a somewhat more sophisticated version of the Color panel, offering the option to view, select, and adjust colors of all the available color models in one window. You can also access any open Swatch Libraries by clicking on the Color Swatches option. It can be overwhelming at first, so let's break it down. See Figure 5–11.

FIGURE | 5–10 |

No matter what color mode you've set for your document, you can use any color model to pick or mix stroke and fill colors.

The Color Picker is where you choose colors. The spectrum bar on the right of this area is where you pick the hue, such as red, blue, or green. The large box to the left allows you to adjust the hue's saturation (moving horizontally) and brightness (moving vertically).

Your current color selections are updated automatically in the top area of the color indicator box. The lower area indicates the original color of the selected object. Next to the color indicator are gamut warnings. They pop up when you have chosen a color that is outside either the Web Safe (the 3D box icon) or the CMYK (alert triangle icon) gamuts. When you click on the 3D box icon, the color shifts to the closest Web Safe color. Similarly, when you

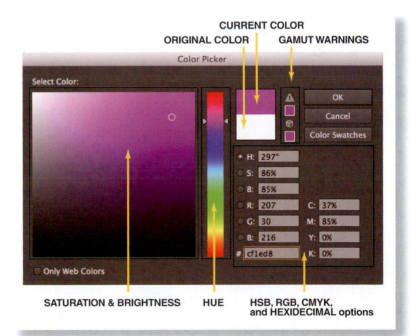

FIGURE | 5–11 |

The Color Picker.

FIGURE | 5–12 |

The Swatches panel.

click on the alert triangle, the color shifts to the closest CMYK color. This is a very handy feature!

The bottom-right area allows you to see and adjust colors in any of the four color models—HSB, RGB, CMYK, and Web Safe (hexidecimal) RGB.

THE SWATCHES PANEL

After spending hours picking your favorite colors, you should save them in the Swatches panel. See Figure 5–12. You can apply saved colors to selected objects by simply clicking on your saved swatches in the panel window. You can also save swatch libraries to reuse in other documents or use one of the many already provided for you. The Swatches panel saves solid color selections, gradients, and patterns.

THE CONTROL PANEL

To quickly change fill or stroke colors on a selected object, you can also access available swatches through the Control panel. This panel is usually located below the menu bar. If it's closed, choose Window > Control. At the top left, you'll see the Fill and Stroke icons. Just click on either one to access the Swatches panel. See Figure 5–13.

FIGURE | 5–13 |

Change fill and stroke colors in the Control panel.

THE EYEDROPPER

The Eyedropper—located in the Tools panel—is a tool common to many graphics programs. (See Figure 5–26, page 106.) With a click of the tool, the Eyedropper samples a color already used in a document (illustration or photograph) and applies it to a selected vector object. This is very useful when you need to match colors within the artwork.

THE LIVE PAINT BUCKET TOOL

The Live Paint Bucket tool (see Figure 5–14) is an improved version of Illustrator's previous paint bucket tool. And it is part of a more intuitive approach (feature) to painting in the program called "Live Paint." The Live Paint Bucket offers quick application of paint attributes,

FIGURE | 5–14 |

The Live Paint Bucket tool.

such as fill, stroke, and brush colors and patterns. See Figure 5–15. To execute, you create a selection (one or more objects) with the Selection tool. Select the Live Paint Bucket tool, and click on the selection to make it a Live Paint Group. Then place your cursor over a face (filled surface) or edge of the selection to highlight an area, and click to apply the defined attribute. Groups of faces and edges can be selected and updated with the Live Paint Selection tool (in the same tool set as the Live Paint Bucket tool in the Tools panel).

THE GRADIENT PANEL AND GRADIENT TOOL

Gradients are graduated color blends. They are useful to create smooth transitions of color in an object or across multiple objects to give them a more dimensional look. Gradients come in two types, linear and radial, both of which are explored in Lesson 2: Vegas Lady, Part 2. See Figure 5–16. Gradients are created using the Gradient panel, and their starting and end points are modified using the Gradient tool. See Figure 5–17 and Figure 5–18. You can also save your favorite gradients in the Swatches panel.

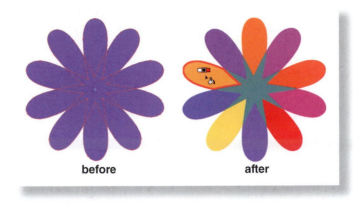

before   **after**

FIGURE | 5–15 |

Fill overlapping paths with color using the Live Paint Bucket tool.

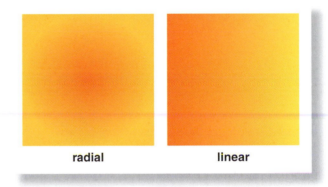

radial   **linear**

FIGURE | 5–16 |

Examples of linear and radial gradients.

FIGURE | 5–17 |

The Gradient panel is used to create gradient color blends.

Gradient Tool (G)

FIGURE | 5–18 |

Modify gradients with the Gradient tool.

Figures © Cengage Learning 2013

LESSON 1: VEGAS LADY, PART 1

In this lesson, you will apply solid colors to the strokes and fills of a pre-drawn image. You will choose colors from the Color Picker and Swatches panel, and create and save your own colors.

Setting Up the File

1. In Illustrator, open **chap5L1.ai** in the **chap05_lessons** folder.

2. Verify that your workspace is set to Essentials in the Application bar to ensure you are starting with the default panel layout.

3. Select View > Fit All in Window to see the original photo used as the drawing template.

4. Expand the Layers panel by clicking on its icon in the dock at the right side of the workspace. See Figure 5–19.

5. In the Layers panel, unhide the **lady layer** to view the drawing in grayscale. See Figure 5–20.

6. Choose View > Outline to see how the image is constructed with numerous paths and shapes.

7. Choose View > Preview to view the fills and strokes.

8. Save this file in your lessons folder. Name it **chap5L1_yourname.ai**.

Applying Color to Fills

1. In the Layers panel, expand the **lady layer**, if not already expanded. To do this, click on the arrow at the left of the layer name, so the arrow points down. The paths and shapes that comprise the image are organized in separate sublayers. See Figure 5–21. To collapse the **lady layer**, you could click on the arrow again to reduce the clutter in the Layers panel. For now, however, leave the **lady layer** expanded.

FIGURE | 5–19 |

Expand the Layers panel.

FIGURE | 5–20 |

Unhide the lady layer.

FIGURE | 5–21 |

The expanded layer.

Note: *You may not see all of the layers, paths, and shapes in the Layers panel. To see more, either use the scroll bar on the right side of the panel or resize the panel. To resize the panel, place your cursor over its bottom edge or its lower-right or left corner (a double-headed arrow will appear), then click and drag down. See Figure 5–22.*

FIGURE | 5–22 |

Expand the Layers panel.

2. If it is not already expanded, expand the **headband** layer to see the individual paths on sublayers.

3. Click the circle to the right of the **medallion** sublayer to select it. The selection column of the Layers panel is located along the right side next to the scroll bar; when an object is selected, a colored selection box appears in this column. See Figure 5–23. (If you can't see the full names of the objects, resize the panel: place your cursor over its left edge and click and drag to the left.)

4. Using the Color Picker, let's choose a new color for the medallion. Double-click on the Fill box in the Tools panel to open the Color Picker.

5. Select a purple color by choosing a purple hue from the spectrum and then adjusting the saturation and brightness levels of the color in the color box to the left. Alternatively, you can type the following in the CMYK fields: C: 40, M: 84, Y: 0, K: 0. Press Tab after each numeric entry. See Figure 5–24. Click OK.

FIGURE | 5–23 |

Select an object from the selection column in the Layers panel.

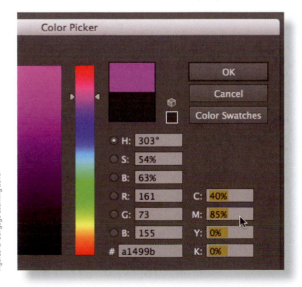

FIGURE | 5–24 |

Enter the CMYK color.

Figures © Cengage Learning 2013

FIGURE | 5–25 |

Select the mask.

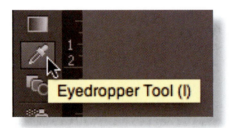

FIGURE | 5–26 |

Choose the Eyedropper tool.

6. Let's use the same color for the mask. Using the Selection tool, click on the mask to select it. See Figure 5–25.

7. Choose the Eyedropper tool in the Tools panel. See Figure 5–26.

8. Place the Eyedropper tool over the purple medallion and click to take a sample of the color. See Figure 5–27. The selected mask will update with the sampled color.

> Note: *You must first select the object you want to change, otherwise, using the Eyedropper tool will change the fill color, not apply it.*

9. Expand the Swatches panel. See Figure 5–28.

FIGURE | 5–27 |

Take a sample of color with the Eyedropper tool.

FIGURE | 5–28 |

Expand the Swatches panel.

10. With the Selection tool, select the face and neck+shoulders. Hold down the Shift key to select more than one object. See Figure 5–29.

11. Click on the peach colored swatch in the Swatches panel to apply the color. See Figure 5–30.

12. Save your file.

Applying Patterns

1. In the Layers panel, select the sublayer **strokes** in the **headdress layer**. To do this, click the circle in the selection column of the sublayer located along the right side of the Layers panel. See Figure 5–31. In the Tools panel, make sure the Stroke box is activated (in front of the Fill box) by clicking on it, and make sure the Fill box is set to "None." Now you're ready to add a new color to the stroke. See Figure 5–32.

FIGURE | 5–29 |

Select the face and neck+shoulders on the lady.

FIGURE | 5–30 |

Select the peach swatch.

FIGURE | 5–31 |

Select an object using the Layers panel.

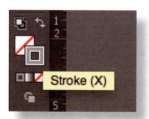

FIGURE | 5–32 |

Stroke box is active: fill box indicates "None."

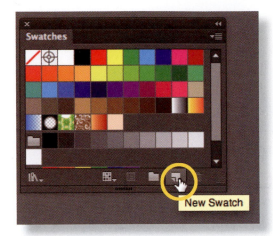

Add a new swatch.

Name the swatch in the Swatch options window.

2. In the Swatches panel, choose the Foliage swatch for the stroke.

3. Select the outer circle object in the headdress layer. Set the stroke to none, and click on the fill color in the Tools panel to activate it. Choose the Pompadour swatch in the Swatches panel.

4. Practice applying colors and patterns to other strokes and fills in the document. Apply color to all the gray areas.

5. Save your file.

Saving Colors

1. Once you have picked colors for the image, you can save them to use over and over using the Swatches panel. Refer to Figure 5–33.

2. In the Layers panel under **face+hair**, select the two hair objects—hold down the Shift key to select both. Notice that the color of the hair is indicated in the Fill box in the Tools panel. Click once on the Fill box (to place it in front of the Stroke box) to activate it.

3. In the Swatches panel, click on the New Swatch icon in the lower-right of the panel window (next to the trashcan) to add the current color. See Figure 5–33.

4. In the dialog box that pops up, enter a descriptive name for your new swatch. See Figure 5–34. Notice you can also change the color mode and color of the saved swatch. Click OK. If you need to get back to the Swatch Options for your new swatch, double-click on it in the Swatches panel.

5. You can also create a new swatch from the Swatches panel options menu. Select both shoulder objects. Click the Swatches panel options icon and select New Swatch. See Figure 5–35. Enter a name for the swatch and click OK.

Create a new swatch using the Swatches options menu.

6. Select each colored area in your image and save the colors in the Swatches panel.

7. Save your collected swatches into a library to use in another document. Click the Swatches options menu icon and, choose Save Swatch Library as AI…. Name your library **lady_colors.ai** and save it in your lessons folder.

8. To open your swatches library, click on the Swatches options menu icon. Choose Open Swatch Library > Other Library (at the bottom of the list).

9. Find your saved swatches library—**lady_colors.ai**—in your lessons folder. Click Open, and the library will appear as a panel in the program.

10. Save your file; you are done for now.

LESSON 2: VEGAS LADY, PART 2

Using a copy of the pre-drawn image from Lesson 1, you will create gradients of color for the fill areas of the image.

Setting Up the File

1. In Illustrator, open the file **chap5L2.ai** in the folder **chap05_lessons**.

2. Verify that your workspace is set to Essentials in the Application bar to ensure you are starting with the default panel layout.

4. Choose View > Fit All in Window.

5. Click on the Gradient icon in the panel dock at the right to expand the Gradient panel. See Figure 5–36.

FIGURE | 5–36 |

Expand the Gradient panel.

FIGURE | 5–37 |

Open the Gradient panel options.

FIGURE | 5–38 |

Click on the gradient fill box to add a default gradient to a selected object.

FIGURE | 5–39 |

Select a color stop.

6. Save this file in your lessons folder. Name it **chap5L2_ yourname.ai**.

Applying a Linear Gradient

1. Select the brown hair pieces of the Vegas lady.

2. In the Tools panel, verify that the fill box is active. In the Gradient panel, click the gradient fill box. See Figure 5–38.

3. In the Gradient panel, select Type: Linear.

4. Notice the color ramp at the bottom of the Gradient panel. It has two colors, one on each side, that blend. The markers under the ramp are called color stops. Point to the leftmost color stop. See Figure 5–39.

> Note: *The little triangle directly above the color stop will turn black when activated.*

5. Now double-click the leftmost color stop to open the Color palette. Notice that the Color panel reflects the white color of the color stop. Click the Color icon if it is not already selected. From the Color panel options menu, choose CMYK. See Figure 5–40. Note, if you want to use a previously saved swatch, click on the Swatches panel icon below the Color panel instead.

FIGURE | 5–40 |

Choose CMYK from the options menu.

Figures © Cengage Learning 2013

6. Click with the Eyedropper on the CMYK spectrum ramp at the bottom of the Color panel to select a new color for the gradient color stop. Pick any color. See Figure 5–41.

Note: *As you click the Eyedropper tool along the Spectrum ramp, notice the gamut warning signs popping up. As discussed previously, you can click on either the Web or the print gamut warnings to snap to an equivalent color within the gamut.*

7. In the Gradient panel, double-click on the rightmost color stop.

8. In the Color panel, choose the CMYK color model again, and assign this color stop a new color.

9. Click on the arrow next to the angle box and select 90 to rotate the angle of the gradient. See Figure 5–42. Or, double-click the number in the angle field and type the number you want, then hit Enter.

10. Move the gradient slider (the diamond shape above the gradient ramp) to the right or left to adjust the midpoint of the gradient.

11. For fun, let's add another color to the ramp. Click under the ramp to create another color stop. See Figure 5–43.

FIGURE | 5–41 |

Select a color in the Color panel. Notice how the color updates on the color stop of the color ramp in the Gradient panel.

FIGURE | 5–42 |

Adjust the angle of the gradient.

FIGURE | 5–43 |

Click under the color ramp to add another color stop.

FIGURE | 5–44 |

Open the Swatches panel Expand it, if necessary, to see all the options.

12. Double-click on the new color stop and select a new color from the Color panel.

> Note: *To delete a color stop, select it and drag it down and away from the Gradient ramp.*

13. Save your gradient by first expanding the Swatches panel. See Figure 5–44. From the Swatches panel options menu, select New Swatch. Enter a name for your new swatch and click OK. See Figure 5–45.

14. The new gradient swatch appears in the Swatches panel.

> Note: *If you don't see it, make sure Show All Swatches is selected from the Show Swatch Kinds menu in the lower part of the Swatches panel. See Figure 5–46.*

15. Deselect everything by using the Selection tool and clicking away from the artboard.

16. Save your file.

FIGURE | 5–45 |

Create a new swatch.

Applying a Radial Gradient

1. Select the Zoom tool and magnify the Vegas lady's lips.

2. Let's apply a radial gradient to the upper and lower lips. Shift-click with the Selection tool to select both parts.

3. Expand the Gradient panel (refer back to Figure 5–36).

4. Click on the gradient fill box in the Gradient panel to apply the last created gradient to the lips.

5. In the gradient box, set the Type to Radial and drag the middle stop away from the bar to delete it.

FIGURE | 5–46 |

Drag a color from the Swatches panel to a gradient stop.

6. Double-click the rightmost color stop. Use the Color panel to select a red color.

> Note: *As an alternative to selecting colors in the Color panel, you can drag a color swatch from the Swatches panel over the selected color stop. To do this, you need to have an undocked version of the Swatches panel open—choose Window > Swatches. See Figure 5–46.*

7. Apply a lighter red color, or white, to the leftmost color stop.

8. Edit the gradient on the bottom and top lips. To do this, click on the Gradient tool in the Tools panel. See Figure 5–47.

9. An interactive gradient editor will appear over each selected lip. See Figure 5–48. Play with the various editing options. See Figure 5–49 for a diagram of the interactive gradient editor options.

10. Save this gradient in the Swatches panel.

11. Using the methods you just learned, create other gradient combinations for the various shapes of the image. For example, use a linear gradient on the lady's hair to add depth.

12. Save your final file.

FIGURE | 5–47 |

Select the Gradient tool.

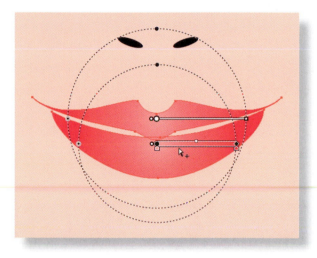

FIGURE | 5–48 |

Use the Gradient tool to adjust the radial gradient.

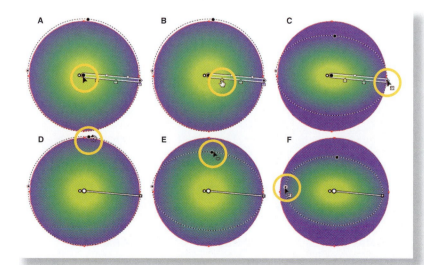

FIGURE | 5–49 |

Gradient tool options: A. position center point; B. adjust blend between color stops, or double-click to access the Color or Swatches panel; C. rotate or extend/collapse the length of gradient; D. rotate; E. non-proportional scale; F. proportional scale. You can also click under the gradient ramp to add more color stops, or remove them by clicking and dragging them away from the bar.

FIGURE | 5–50 |

Example of color wheel.

COLOR IN DESIGN

So many colors, so little time. This becomes apparent when you find yourself hours later still trying to decide what colors to use for your favorite masterpiece. There are several ways to select colors, and different color models to use, in Illustrator. To speed things up, you need to know how colors work together. There is actually a whole art and science to creating a visually appealing palette of hues and, of course, numerous theories to back up the information. In general, these theories are based on an understanding of the color spectrum and usually represented in the form of a color wheel. See Figure 5–50.

As a starting point for picking colors, think in terms of color chords—combinations of colors that work well together. Six basic color chords are described as follows (there are others). For some examples of these color chords, see Figure 5–51.

FIGURE | 5–51 |

Examples of color combinations using color chords.

- ▶ *Dyad (complement or opposite)*: Uses hues that are opposite each other on the color wheel or color spectrum (i.e., orange and blue), plus the addition of black, white, and/or grays.
- ▶ *Monochromatic*: Uses one hue (color) plus the addition of black, white, and/or grays.
- ▶ *Achromatic*: Uses a combination of black, white, and/or grays. No hues.

> Note: *There is a quick way to find dyad colors in Illustrator. In an open file, create an object and fill it with color. Select the object. Open the Color panel. From the Color panel options menu, choose Complement.*

- ▶ *Analogous*: Uses two to three hues, which are adjacent to each other on a standard color wheel (i.e., red, red orange, orange), plus the addition of black, white, and/or grays.
- ▶ *Warm Hues*: Color hues that give the viewer a sense of warmth, such as reds, yellows, and oranges.
- ▶ *Cool Hues*: Color hues that give the viewer a sense of coolness, such as blues and greens.

Another great tool to use in the context of color harmonies is the Color Guide. Located under Window > Color Guide or with the docked Color panel in the Essentials workspace, this is a quick and easy way to find a list of different color harmony rules for a currently selected color. By clicking on the Harmony Rules arrow, the guide takes the selected color (fill or stroke) and provides you with a number of harmony rules, including analogous and complementary. See Figure 5–52. This is a great tool to keep in mind during your color journey. For more on using the Color Guide feature, see Adventures in Design: Harmonizing with Color at the end of this chapter. To practice making your own color chord combinations, see Exploring on Your Own at the end of this chapter.

FIGURE | 5–52 |

Use the Color Guide to pick colors that look good together.

SUMMARY

This chapter introduced you to important concepts about color, including color models, modes, and gamuts. You applied colors, gradients, and patterns to strokes and fills using Illustrator's Color Picker, Color and Swatches panels, and the Eyedropper tool. Using color effectively in your artwork is more than just applying it to strokes and fills, however. It is also about picking colors that are visually enticing and preparing the colors correctly for the artwork's final, anticipated purpose.

▶ IN REVIEW

1. Define the term color gamut.

2. How do different color gamuts affect what colors look like in Illustrator?

3. What is a color model? How does it differ from a color mode?

4. What color model represents the primary colors of light?

5. What is hexadecimal?

6. Briefly describe hue, saturation, and brightness.

7. Four-color process uses what kind of color model?

8. What is a gamut warning in Illustrator?

9. What tool can take a sample of color in an image?

10. Describe complementary colors.

▶ EXPLORING ON YOUR OWN

1. Access the Help > Illustrator Help menu option and read the section "Color." For more advanced information on working with color in Illustrator, read the section "Color Management."

2. Practice your color chords with the color theory lesson.

Instructions:

- ▶ In Illustrator, open a new file, with 6 artboards, each 6 inches by 6 inches.
- ▶ Use the following tools to create a motif (design) for each chord, one per artboard:
    a. *Dyad*: Ellipse tool
    b. *Monochromatic*: Rectangle tool
    c. *Achromatic*: Star tool
    d. *Analogous*: Polygon tool
    e. *Warm Hues*: Any tool
    f. *Cool Hues*: Any tool
- ▶ Color each motif with the appropriate characteristics for each chord.

3. You can learn a lot about color theory and design by surfing the Internet. Do a search for "color theory" or "color

> **Note:** *Review the characteristics of each chord in the section Color in Design.*

design," and plenty of information is bound to pop up. For more information on color in design, see also the next sections, Adventures in Design: The Moods of Color and Adventures in Design: Harmonizing with Color.

4. Find great color schemes and publish your own using the Adobe Labs dynamic color selector program at *http://kuler.adobe.com/* (see Figure 5–53).

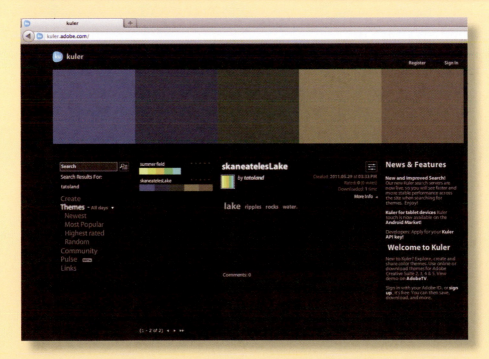

FIGURE | 5–53 |

Adobe's Kuler is a great resource for picking colors that work well together.

adventures
IN DESIGN

THE MOODS OF COLOR

Certain colors and the way they come together can produce a visceral response in a viewer. Colors can be representative of a thought or idea, or they can evoke an emotion. Green brings visions of nature or money. Blue is calming or corporate. Yellow is happy, bright, illuminating. As you have learned, there are several methods for choosing appropriate color combinations: color modes, color chords, and the color wheel. Moreover, colors chosen for a particular piece of artwork or layout directly relate to a design's look and feel. This is a deeper and more subjective aspect to the color selection process; it involves the sense of "mood."

What is the mood that you (or your client) wants to convey in the artwork? Is it to appear classic and professional, warm and inviting, or playful and light? What color combinations will work best to achieve each mood? By identifying a mood for your design, the often-daunting task of picking colors can be easily dispatched.

Professional Project Example

Toni was asked to develop a logo for a small recycling company in upstate New York. Because it was going to be used in print and on the Web, the owner asked her to develop some options for using the logo in color, and the background color would also be used as the color of the recycling bins. To avoid wasting the client's time (and money), Toni asked him to describe the company's mission statement, "personality," and objectives. From that list, Toni was able to determine that it was a small company, serving a rural township, and with a focus on, obviously, recycling. The clients were mostly farmers and very pragmatic, down-to-earth people.

With this in mind, certain color combinations could easily be dismissed: bright or neon colors were out—too urban. So were bold colors like navy blue and red. It was decided that subtle, "earthy" colors were the best place to start—inviting, friendly, and a way to echo the landscape in which the bins would be utilized. After creating several versions of the logo using different color combinations, one with greens and wheat/grain colors became the obvious choice. Various color versions are shown in Figure A–1.

Your Turn

Now it is your turn to play with different color combinations for a logo that Annesa designed. A real estate agent in Vermont commissioned her to create a logo for a brokerage firm. In conversations with the owner, Andrea, Annesa determined that this brokerage was a small, professional, friendly company with personalized service.

Use what you learned about color in this chapter to successfully create combinations of colors. Take some time to explore *http://kuler.adobe.com*. A sample file with four black-and-white duplicates of the brokerage logo is provided in aid_examples/aid2.ai. Select each element in the design and explore different stroke and fill color combinations; create four different versions.

Color Project Guidelines

1. Assume that the logo will eventually go to print, so be sure the aid2.ai document is saved in the CMYK color mode.

2. To adjust different hues and saturation and brightness levels more easily when determining your color combinations, try using the HSB Color panel. See Figure A–2. For example, select one part of the logo and adjust the hue slider of the HSB panel to a color you like. Begin to adjust the S and B sliders to modify the color in saturation and brightness to what might seem appropriate to the description of the company's look and feel. (Here is where some subjective decision making comes in.)

Figures © Cengage Learning 2013

FIGURE | A–1 |

Sample colored versions of the recycling logo.

3. Select another element in the logo and take a sample of the color you just created to fill the selected shape. Leaving the S and B sliders in the HSB Color panel the same, adjust only the H slider to another color of your choice. By adjusting the same component of the HSB color model for each color—in this example, just the H (hue) component—you can quickly create colors that have a similar tone, making for more compatible color combinations.

4. Try this method on another of the logo duplicates, using perhaps a lighter or darker set of colors on each logo shape.

5. For one of the other logo examples, use another technique for quickly choosing colors with the Complement or Invert commands available in Illustrator. See Figure A–3. These options offer variations on a color based on the complement (opposite) or inversion of it on a standard color

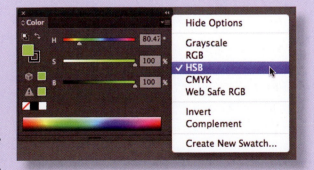

FIGURE | A–2 |

The HSB Color panel.

FIGURE | A–3 |

Select the Complement command in Illustrator.

FIGURE | A–4 |

The CMYK gamut warning icon.

wheel. First, fill a logo shape with a color. Take a sample of that color to fill in another selected shape on the logo. Then, from the Color panel options menu, choose Invert or Complement.

6. Make sure that the colors you have chosen are within the CMYK color gamut. If they are not part of the CMYK color gamut, the print gamut warning—the alert triangle icon in the Color panel—pops up. If the warning comes up, click on the triangle icon to adjust the color to its nearest CMYK equivalent. See Figure A–4.

7. Save your color selections in the Swatches panel.

8. For another version, try using the Color Guide; experiment with using color chords and the vivid/muted, warm/cool, and tints/shades options from the panel's submenu.

9. Do a color test by printing your logos on a color printer. Compare how the color looks printed versus on the screen. As you have learned, color can vary depending on the device displaying it.

Things to Consider

Here are some tips to consider when working with color.

► As a starting point for picking colors, use color chords as described in the section Color in Design.

► If available, pick colors from a swatch book—a book of printable color samples that is usually available for viewing at your local printing bureau. Swatch books will also give you a sense of how colors might look printed on various types of paper.

► Limit the number of colors used in a logo or document if necessary. If you need more than two colors, then plan on working using CMYK values for process color printing.

► Remember the moods of color and how they reflect on your overall design objectives.

HARMONIZING WITH COLOR

Illustrator's Color Guide panel and Recolor Artwork options assist in creating harmonious color combinations for illustrations. This is fantastic if you want to quickly preview various color combinations on a graphic without individually selecting and changing each object in it.

Gianna Foltz, an up-and-coming fashion designer, has a great grasp on using pen and ink with watercolor washes to create what are called *croquis*—quick sketches that designers use to present an idea of what a finished garment will look like. The next step is to create a flat, which is used to create the pattern for construction. These are tighter, more detailed technical drawings that patternmakers use to make a sample garment. Gianna is very adept at using Illustrator for developing these, and she needed a way to create color changes on the fly.

The drawback to her *croquis* technique, which is hand-drawn, was that once she added the color, there was no going back. She also needed a way to experiment with different colors on the flats.

Gianna started to explore several features in Illustrator she thought would be beneficial in her design process. The Recolor Artwork option, in particular, allowed her to try color combinations for her clothing ideas very quickly—a huge bonus when compared to the traditional process of hand-sketching and painting one several times to show multiple color options.

To start, Gianna scanned a black-and-white ink drawing and then placed it in Illustrator. While the illustration was selected, she used Image Trace > Shades of Gray from the Control panel to turn the bitmap scan into vector art. Once it was vectorized, she used Object > Expand to separate the white areas from the sketch. See Figure B–1.

The Image Trace feature takes bitmap art and translates it into vector shapes.

> **Note:** *The amount of detail in the traced image varies depending on the Image Trace option you select.*

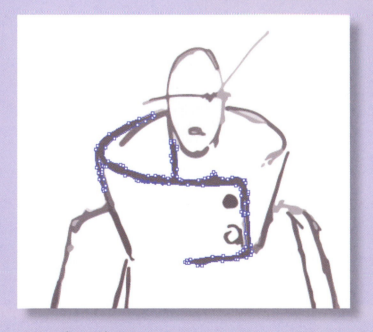

FIGURE | B–1 |

The Image Trace feature takes bitmap art, and translates it into vector shapes.

In order to add color to this image, she added a layer and used the Pen tool to draw shapes that would define the coat. Dragging that layer to the bottom of the Layers panel placed the sketch over the coat shapes. Finally, selecting everything on the sketch layer, she chose Multiply blending mode from the Transparency panel. See Figure B–2.

Gianna used the Color Guide (from the docked panels in the Essentials workspace or Window > Color Guide) to play with harmonious colors based on the current fill color. You can use these colors to color artwork, or you can save them as swatches. The Color Guide options menu in the upper-right corner of the panel provides various color combinations—Tints/Shades, Warm/Cool, and Vivid/Muted. See Figure B–3.

The Color Guide is a great place to explore different color combinations.

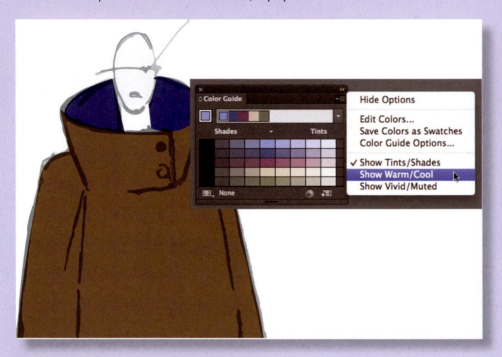

FIGURE | B–2 |

Keeping the painted art on a separate layer, set to Multiply, integrates the traced image with the vector shapes.

FIGURE | B–3 |

The Color Guide is a great place to explore different color combinations.

Figures © Cengage Learning 2013

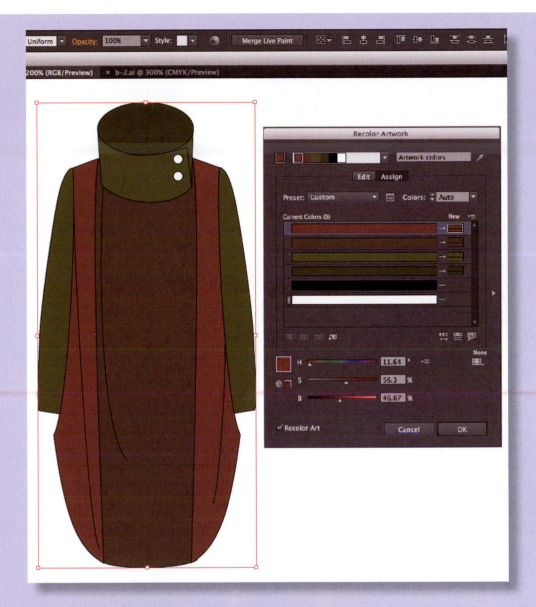

Figure © Cengage Learning 2013

FIGURE | B–4 |

Clicking on a selected object with the Live Paint Bucket tool turns it into something that can be filled with color, even if it wasn't created as a closed shape. Nice!

Gianna then created the flat—a technical drawing—in Illustrator. Each section of the coat was selected and turned into a Live Paint object with the Live Paint Bucket tool (Figure B–4) for adding fill colors. She played with harmonizing the colors using the Recolor Artwork panel. See Figures B–5 and B–6.

FIGURE | B–5 |

The Recolor Artwork panel offers the opportunity to experiment with different color combinations.

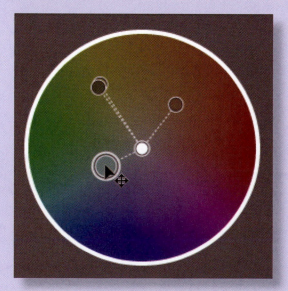

FIGURE | B–6 |

The Edit portion of the Recolor Artwork panel is another area where you can play with color options.

Harmonizing with Color Project Guidelines
Explore the Color Guide

1. Create several objects—a few rectangles or stars would be fine.

2. Select each one and fill it with color.

3. Keep one selected and choose Window > Color Guide. Use the Harmony Rules to see what colors work together. See Figure B–7.

4. From the options menu in the upper-right corner of the Color panel, play with the Warm/Cool and Vivid/Muted options.

5. Select another object and note how the options in the Color Guide update to reflect the new color.

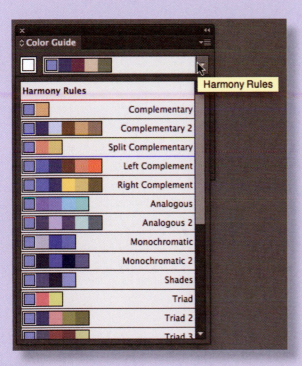

FIGURE | B–7 |

Use the Harmony Rules in the Color Guide panel to experiment with different color chords.

Explore the Recolor Artwork Feature

1. Open colorharmonies.ai from the aid_examples folder. This is an image created using a black marker on newsprint and then scanned and placed in an Illustrator document.

2. Select the placed illustration, and under the Live Trace options in the Control panel, choose the Detailed Illustration, Shades of Gray, or either of the photograph options; they all work nicely. See Figure B–8.

3. While the image is still selected, click the Expand option in the Control panel. See Figure B–9.

FIGURE | B–8 |

Select the scanned image and use Image Trace to turn it into a vector drawing.

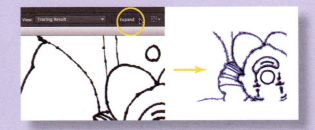

FIGURE | B–9 |

Expand the traced image so that it becomes individual objects that can be selected and colored.

4. Select the Live Paint Bucket tool (Figure B–4) and click somewhere inside the selected image. This will turn every area in the drawing into a separate Live Paint object, which is referred to as a face for the shape, and an edge for the path that defines it. See Figure B–10.

5. Use the Direct selection tool to select a portion of the image and then select a fill color from the Control panel. See Figure B–11.

6. Have some fun selecting and filling all the elements in this illustration.

7. Save your file as clown_yourname.ai in your Lessons folder.

> Note: *When selecting pieces, you sometimes may find weird things highlighting rather than what you wanted. Try deleting those elements (just press the Delete key twice) and reselecting what you really wanted. You can always Edit > Undo [Command Z (Mac) or Ctrl Z (Windows)] if things don't work the first time.*

FIGURE | B–10 |

Clicking on the selected traced image turns each part into a separate Live Paint object.

FIGURE | B–11 |

Use the Direct Selection tool to select and fill the faces in the drawing using the Control Panel.

Orange, Yellow

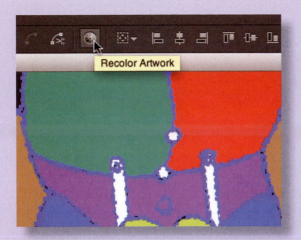

FIGURE | B–12 |

Click on the Recolor Artwork icon to open the panel.

FIGURE | B–13 |

Adjust options in the Recolor Artwork panel. Choose (a) get colors from the selected artwork, (b) link harmony colors, and (c) recolor artwork

8. Next, select all parts of the illustration [Command A (Mac) or Ctrl A (Windows)] and click the Recolor Artwork panel (a color-wheel icon) in the Control panel. See Figure B–12. The panel opens with a list of all the colors used in the selected graphic.

9. Click the Edit button at the top of the panel below the color swatches.

10. Check the following (see Figure B–13):

   a. Get colors from selected artwork
   b. Link harmony colors
   c. Recolor Art

11. Finally, click on a color circle in the color spectrum area and rotate it to adjust all the selected colors in relation to each other. See Figure B–14. Note how the illustration's colors automatically update. Wow!

There are several other things to play with in this Recolor Artwork panel. The rest of the exploration is in your creative hands!

FIGURE | B–14 |

Select the Edit pane, and click and drag the colors around the spectrum to shift the color palette. The selected objects update with the new settings as they change.

| Value and Texture |

charting your course

What brings life to an illustration is the use of value and texture, the last two components in our study of the fundamental building blocks of visual art. (For a review of these elements, see Chapter 3.) This chapter defines value and texture in art and introduces you to value and texture for strokes and fills, including brushes, patterns, filters, effects, and graphic styles. You will learn that the strokes and fills that comprise an Illustrator graphic can be further modified to take what is initially a flat colored illustration and transform it into one that appears to have more tactile characteristics.

goals

In this chapter you will:

► Differentiate between the use of value and texture in illustrative art

► Get a handle on the various attributes of strokes and fills

► Master the use, modification, and creation of Illustrator brush types and the Paintbrush tool

► Explore filters, effects, graphic styles, and the Appearance panel

► Understand the steps for creating and applying patterns

IMPLYING SURFACE

Take a look at the row of Mother Goose images on the first page of this chapter. The goose on the left is the original image—a watercolor Toni did for her daughter. Can you see, maybe even feel, the roughness of the paper on which it was painted? Is the grass smooth or rough? Is the color flat, or does it look more like a gradient in some areas? Now look at the image in the middle. This is a vector drawing of the painting done in Illustrator using only solid, flat colors. The image has a completely different look and feel—very one-dimensional.

Finally, check out the image on the right. This is the same Illustrator image, but with value and texture added. It looks more like the original, with varied strokes and implied surface characteristics, but it is completely digitized and easily altered.

What are value and texture in art? What does it mean to add value and texture to a digitized image? Value is the relationship of light and dark parts within an image, sometimes referred to as tone, shade, or brightness. You experienced the use of value in the previous chapter when you worked with varying fill colors and with gradients, which are blended values of color. There is also value in line; pen strokes in Illustrator have different weights (thicknesses), as do brush strokes. You will learn about value in line in this chapter. Value can also imply a sense of space, which you will encounter in Chapter 9. A good example of this is the illusion that appears when you put a lighter copy of an object below its original, resulting in a shadow effect. See Figure 6–1.

Texture implies surface—how an object might feel if we were to touch it. It informs us of our surroundings, and tells us about the nature of objects—smooth, rough, soft, or hard. Textures in our environment are represented by how light hits a surface, creating highlights and shadows. In Illustrator, the textures you create are simulated, meaning the texture is flat by touch but tricks the eye into thinking it is not. A filter or effect in Illustrator can produce simulated textures, brushes, and patterns—all of which are covered in this chapter.

FIGURE | 6–1 |

The shadow of the word *shadow* is created by changing the value of the text to a lighter gray and adding a slightly blurry texture.

STROKE AND FILL ATTRIBUTES

By now, you should know the difference between a stroke and a fill. A stroke is the defined outline or path of an object, and a fill is the area enclosed by the path. In the previous chapter, you applied the attribute of color to strokes and fills. Luckily for us, strokes and fills have other attributes and appearance effects besides color. See Figure 6–2 and Figure 6–3.

FIGURE |6–2|

Stroke variations.

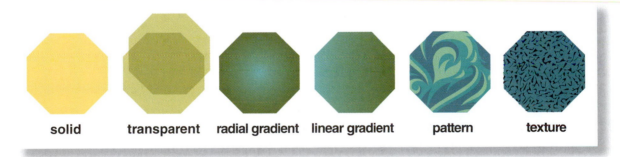

FIGURE |6–3|

Fill variations.

STROKE VARIATIONS

Stroke variations include color, weight (line thickness), solid or dashed lines, line caps and joins, and brush styles. You can change the color of a selected stroke, or fill, in four areas in Illustrator: the Control panel, the Color Picker (accessed by double-clicking on the Stroke or Fill box in the Tools panel), the Color panel, or the Swatches panel (accessed using the Window menu or the docks panel). To change the attributes of a selected stroke, such as the weight, line type, width profile, or line caps and joins, choose Window > Stroke or select the underlined word *stroke* in the Control panel and open the stroke properties. To access brush and pattern types, choose Window > Brushes.

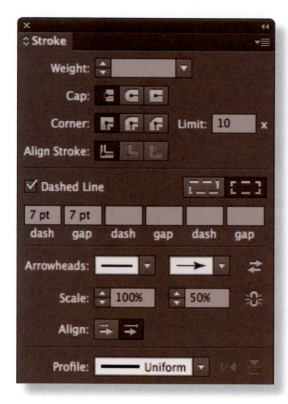

FIGURE | 6–4 |

The Stroke panel.

About Stroke Attributes

Stroke attributes for a selected object are located in the Stroke panel (Window > Stroke). See Figure 6–4. In the Stroke panel, you can alter a stroke's weight, cap, join, and miter limit. You can also create various dashed lines, add arrowheads, or adjust the width profile of a stroke. By default, a stroke's weight is measured in points (pts). If you want a thin line, set the weight to .5 pts; for a thicker line, set it to 20 pts. See examples of stroke weights in Figure 6–5.

> **Note:** *Frequently, panels will collapse to their default state, which hides the additional options in each one. Use the panel's options menu to Show Options when this happens.*

> **Note:** *You can change the unit measurement of a stroke (to picas, inches, millimeters, centimeters, or pixels) by going to Illustrator > Preferences > Units (Mac) or Edit > Preferences > Units (Windows).*

FIGURE | 6–5 |

Example of stroke weights, measured in points.

You can also add different caps to the ends of your strokes. Yes, "cap" might seem like a funny name, but it makes sense; just like you might put a cap on your head for a stylish effect, you can do the same thing with a stroke. To choose different caps, select one of three options in the Stroke panel. See Figure 6–6.

- ► *Butt Cap:* Stroked line with square ends.
- ► *Round Cap:* Stroked line with rounded ends.
- ► *Projecting Cap:* Stroked line with squared ends that takes the weight of the line and extends it equally in all directions around the line including the ends.

Another stylish effect can be added using the line join options. Joins determine the look of a stroke at its corner angles. There are three types of joins. See Figure 6–7.

FIGURE | 6–6 |

Different stroke cap options.

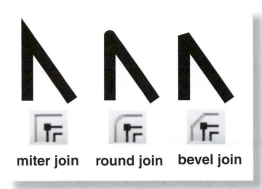

FIGURE | 6–7 |

Options for corners, or miters.

miter join   **round join**   **bevel join**

► *Miter Join:* Creates stroke lines with pointed corners. The miter limit controls when the program switches from a mitered join with a high value (pointed) to a beveled (squared-off) join with a low value. See Figure 6–8.

► *Round Join:* Creates stroked lines with rounded corners.

► *Bevel Join:* Creates stroked lines with squared corners.

Another option is where along the path a stroke will fall—centered, inside, or outside. See Figure 6–9.

From the Stroke panel, you can also create custom dashed lines. To do this, select a stroke and specify a sequence of dashes and the gaps between them.

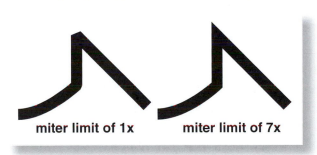

FIGURE | 6–8 |

Miter of a stroke set at 1x and at 7x.

miter limit of 1x   **miter limit of 7x**

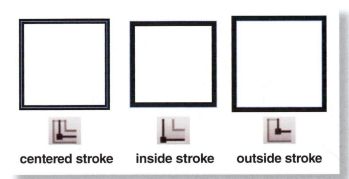

centered stroke   **inside stroke**   **outside stroke**

FIGURE | 6–9 |

Choose where a stroke will be positioned along the path.

See Figure 6–10 for an example. You can also combine cap styles with different dash patterns, resulting in either rounded or squared dash ends.

You can add arrows to the ends of strokes (see Figure 6–11), and select width profile options to adjust the variable width of a stroke, as well as the size of the arrowhead (see Figure 6–12).

FIGURE | 6–10 |

1. Dash pattern: 4 pt. dash, 4 pt. gap.
2. Dash pattern: 4 pt. dash, 4 pt. gap, 2 pt. dash, 1 pt. gap.
3. Dash pattern: 4 pt. dash, 8 pt. gap with round cap.
4. Dash pattern: 4 pt. dash, 8 pt. gap.

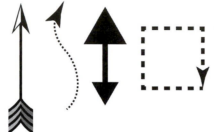

FIGURE | 6–11 |

Arrowheads and tails can easily be added to a stroke from the Stroke panel.

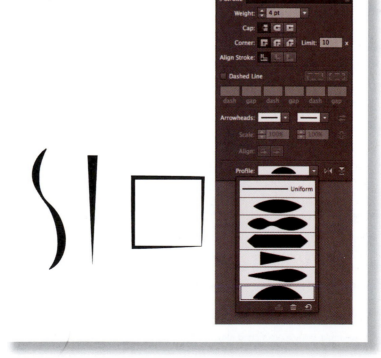

FIGURE | 6–12 |

To vary the width of a stroke select a width profile option in the Stroke panel.

About Brushes

Another very popular stroke variation is the use of brushes. With Illustrator brushes, you can experiment with the texture and value of strokes (paths) without having to wash the brushes when you are done. You can apply Illustrator brush types to selected paths drawn with the Pencil or Pen tool, or paint new paths with the Paintbrush tool. There are five basic brush types (see Figure 6–14):

FIGURE | 6–13 |

Use the Width tool to vary the width of a stroke.

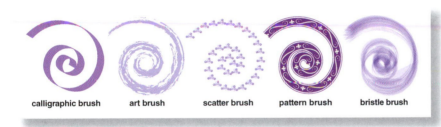

FIGURE | 6–14 |

The five brush types:
1. Calligraphic; 2. Art;
3. Scatter; 4. Pattern;
5. Bristle.

- *Calligraphic*: Calligraphic brush strokes resemble the angled strokes produced by a calligraphic pen.
- *Art*: Art brush strokes resemble sketched or painterly strokes, such as those created with chalk and watercolors. The brushes also include objects, such as arrows, that when drawn stretch evenly along the length of the path.
- *Scatter*: Scatter brushes randomly disperse objects along a path.
- *Pattern*: Pattern brushes produce a repeated pattern—derived from individual tiles— that repeats evenly along a path.
- *Bristle*: Bristle brushes create natural, fluid brush strokes that use opacity variations to simulate real brushes with bristles.

To find these brush types, expand the Brushes panel (see Figure 6–15) or choose Window > Brushes. By

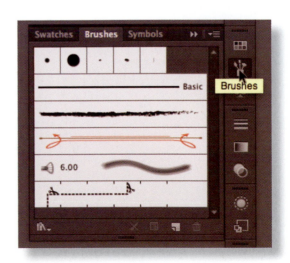

FIGURE | 6–15 |

Expand the Brushes panel.

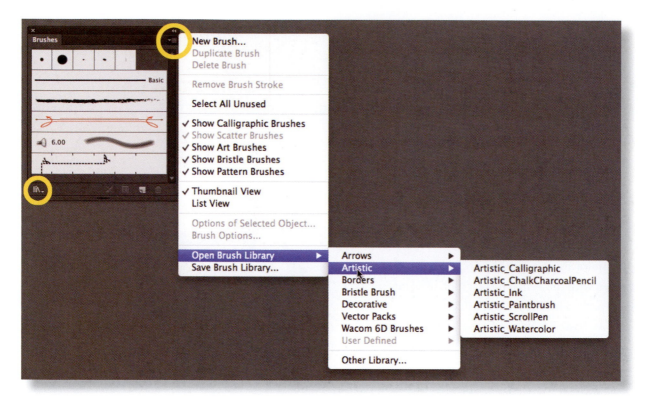

FIGURE | 6–16 |

There are many brushes to choose from!

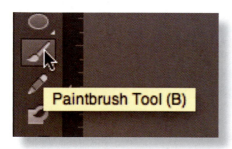

FIGURE | 6–17 |

The Paintbrush tool.

default, some calligraphic and art brushes are provided. To find more, choose Open Brush Library from the Brushes panel options menu, use the Brush Libraries menu on the bottom-left side of the Brushes panel (the icon looks like three books on a shelf), or choose Window > Brush Libraries. See Figure 6–16. You can also create and modify your own brush styles and libraries—and how wonderful is that?

To draw a path and add a brush stroke at the same time, use the Paintbrush tool in the Tools panel (see Figure 6–17). Painting with this tool can sometimes bring unwanted results unless you adjust the tool's settings in its options dialog box.

Note: *Double-clicking on a tool as a way to bring up a tool's options applies to several other tools in the toolbox. You might be surprised by the many options lurking under those tools.*

To open the Paintbrush tool's options, double-click on the tool in the Tools panel. See Figure 6–18.

You will experience painting with brushes and adjusting brush preferences in Lesson 1: The Fish Painting.

FILL VARIATIONS

As demonstrated in Figure 6–3, fills have attributes other than solid colors. Linear and radial gradients were introduced in the previous chapter. You can also apply transparency to fills. Simply select the filled object, expand the Transparency panel as shown in Figure 6–19, by choosing Window > Transparency or by clicking on its icon in the panel dock at the right, and adjust the Opacity setting from 100 (no transparency) to 0 (full transparency). See Figure 6–20.

> Note: *To see the transparency effect on an object, it helps to put another object behind it.*

Patterns are also a great way to have fun with fills. You can apply, create, and transform patterns and save them in the Swatches panel. Use the Show

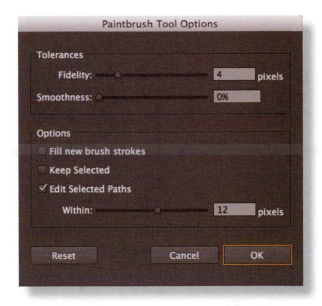

FIGURE | 6–18 |

Double-click on a tool in the toolbox to open its options dialog box.

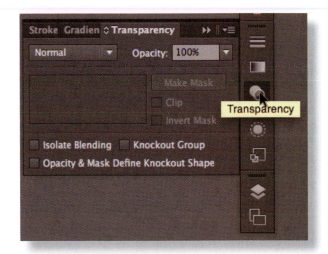

FIGURE | 6–19 |

Expand the Transparency panel.

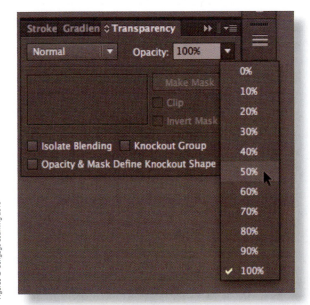

FIGURE | 6–20 |

Adjust the transparency by typing a number in the Opacity field, or selecting a percentage from the drop-down list.

Select to view patterns saved in the Swatches panel.

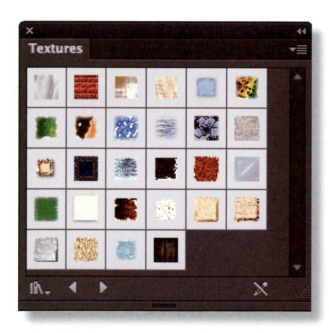

The Textures graphic styles library.

Swatch panel menu to access the Show Pattern Swatches option. See Figure 6–21. Patterns are useful if you want a repeated tile effect or mosaic. Take a look at the fabric patterns at your local textile or clothing store. You will get to play with patterns in Lesson 2: Playing with Custom Brush Styles.

Another way to create fills with varied textures is to use the effects available in Illustrator that are found under the Effects menu.

An effect is considered "live" in that it can be added, altered, or removed at any time. When you apply an effect to an object, it is as if you are laying a cover, or covers, over the object. An effect changes the appearance of the object, but not its original characteristics. An effect and its properties can be changed at any time. When you reshape the original characteristics of the object, the effects applied will adjust accordingly. The Appearance panel (described in the section Using the Appearance Panel) lists the effect(s) applied to an object, and enables you to modify, expand, duplicate, delete, or save them as a graphic style.

A graphic style is a named set of color and stroke attributes, and applied effects that can be stored in a Graphic Styles panel or library. Illustrator comes loaded with many graphics styles (Window > Graphic Styles). You can also create your own styles. You can apply graphic styles to individual fills, strokes, grouped objects, and layers. You can also access graphic styles libraries, such as the Textures library (choose Graphic Styles panel options menu > Open Graphic Style Library > Textures). See Figure 6–22.

In the top half of the Effects menu are vector effects that only can be applied to vector objects, and some of these can be applied to the fill and stroke of a bitmap object using the Appearance panel. The effects in the bottom half of the Effects menu (Photoshop Effects)

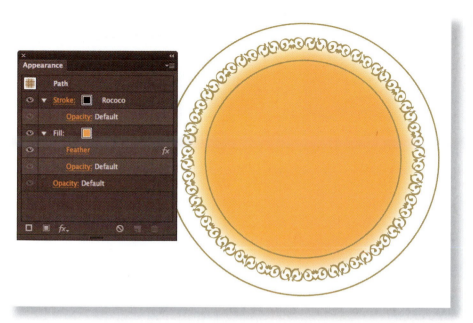

Figures © Cengage Learning 2013

FIGURE | 6–23 |

Filled object with the Rococo art brush outline, a Feather effect, and its stroke and fill attributes in the Appearance panel.

are raster effects and can be applied to either vector or bitmap objects. You can also access the effects using the fx icon at the bottom of the Appearance panel.

> **Note:** *Raster effects are effects that generate pixels, rather than vector data. For more information on Effects, see the Illustrator Help files, Creating special effects.*

You will have the opportunity to work hands-on with effects and graphic styles, and their many quirks, in Lesson 1.

USING THE APPEARANCE PANEL

Once you start applying multiple brushes, patterns, and effects to strokes and fills, you might find it difficult to remember what steps you took to modify all the variations. The Appearance panel comes to the rescue; it is your guide to what fill and stroke variations you have applied to a particular object. Let's say you applied a brush stroke called Rococo, with a Feather effect added to the fill of a selected object. It would look like Figure 6–23. When you expand the Appearance panel from the docked panels it will list the stroke and fill attributes of the selected object.

FIGURE | 6–24 |

Expand the Appearance panel.

If you have a complicated effect or graphic style assigned to an object, such as the Color Halftone graphic style in Figure 6–25, the Appearance panel shows a breakdown of the elements that comprise the object's "look," so you can modify individual parts. For example, refer to Figure 6–25 for the list of elements that produces the Color Halftone graphic style.

Another great thing about the Appearance panel is that in its options menu (see Figure 6–26) you can do some crazy things like add a new fill or stroke, eliminate or modify existing attributes, or, when things get really messy, clear an object's appearance completely.

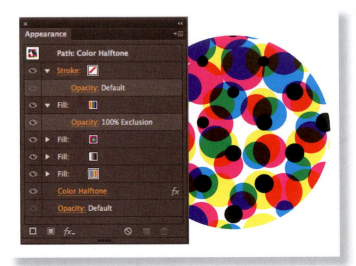

FIGURE | 6–25 |

View the elements of an object's effects in the Appearance panel.

FIGURE | 6–26 |

The Appearance panel's options menu.

Figures © Cengage Learning 2013

FIGURE | 6–27 |

The finished Lesson 1 file.

LESSON 1: THE FISH PAINTING

Once you learn how to apply brush styles to drawn paths, paint directly with the Paintbrush tool, and use graphic styles and effects—all the good things covered in this lesson—there is no turning back your inner artist. See Figure 6–27.

Setting Up the File

1. In Illustrator, open **chap6L1.ai** in the **chap06_lessons** folder.

2. Make sure your Workspace is set to Essentials.

3. Choose View > Fit All in Window.

Applying Brush Styles

For easier reference, all the fish parts are labeled in the Layers panel. The easiest way to select objects is to open the Layers panel, expand the layer called fish, and then select the circle in the selection column to the right of the desired path name. See Figure 6–28.

FIGURE | 6–27 |

The finished Lesson 1 file.

FIGURE | 6–28 |

The elements that comprise the fish layer.

1. Select the fish **body** by clicking on the circle to the right of that sublayer in the Layers panel.

2. Open the Color panel and select a shade of green from the spectrum.

3. Change the stroke color of the body to none. To do this, select the Stroke option in the Color panel, then choose None. If the Stroke option isn't visible, select Show Options on the panel's options menu, or click the up/down arrow next to the panel name to expand it.

4. Select the top fin stripes of the fish. See Figure 6–29.

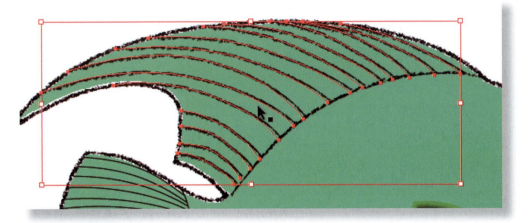

FIGURE | 6–29 |

Select the top fin stripes of the fish.

▶ DON'T GO THERE

When you click once on an object, like the body of the fish, in a document, it will select that object. However, if you double-click on an object, you will be sent to an area of the program called isolation mode. You know you are in isolation mode when the rest of the items on the document become grayed out and the isolated object navigation bar appears in the upper-left of the document window. Isolation mode isolates the selected object from the rest of the items on the document, making it easier to edit.

Feel free to work in isolation mode when editing objects if you find it useful; just be aware that you will need to exit isolation mode to continue working on other areas of the document. To exit isolation mode, click on the left-facing arrow in the upper-left corner of the document window. See more on isolation mode and screen visuals in the Exploring on Your Own section at the end of this chapter.

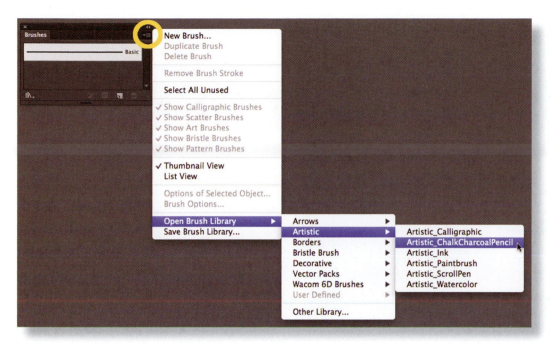

Figures © Cengage Learning 2013

FIGURE | 6–30 |

Open the Artistic_ChalkCharcoalPencil Brush library from the Brushes panel options menu.

5. Apply an art brush to the lines. Use the Brushes panel to open the Artistic_ChalkCharcoalPencil brushes library. See Figure 6–30. Then select the Pencil-Thick option—enlarge the panel, or scroll down to the bottom to find it. The brush stroke is applied to the selected paths. See Figure 6–31.

6. Select the grouped lines of the fish's tail and bottom two fin stripes, and then apply the Pencil_Thick art brush again. Hint: If you are using the Direct Selection tool, hold down Option/Alt and click twice to select the entire group.

7. Save your work in your lessons folder. Name it **chap6L1_yourname.ai**.

8. Select the **eye outline** and choose the Charcoal_Rough art brush (a bit higher in the Artistic_ChalkCharcoalPencil library). Notice that the width of the Charcoal_Rough brush is a bit thick for the eye outline. We need to fix this.

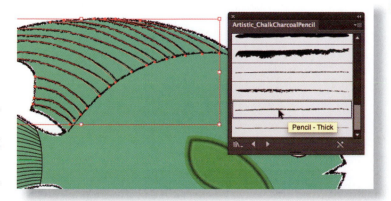

FIGURE | 6–31 |

Selecting a brush type in the Brushes panel applies the style to selected paths.

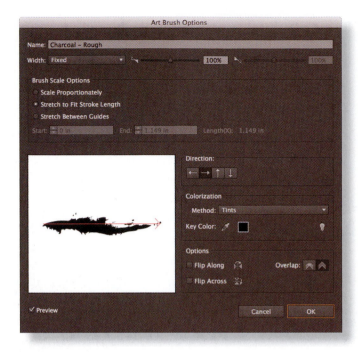

FIGURE | 6–32 |

Change the brush style settings.

FIGURE | 6–33 |

Select Apply to Strokes.

9. Double-click on the Charcoal_Rough brush style icon in the Brushes panel (not the Brushes library). This brings up the Art Brush options for that particular brush. See Figure 6–32.

10. Check the Preview option to see the changes update as you make them. (Move the Options window if it's covering your work.)

11. Change the width setting to 20%, and press Tab to update the change on the eye outline. Much better!

12. Click OK to close the options dialog box. A dialog box will pop up, asking if you would like to apply the new change to the currently selected brush strokes. Select Apply to Strokes. See Figure 6–33.

13. Open the Layers panel and unhide the "**eye swatch**" layer. Select the eyeball and click on the eye swatch on the canvas with the Eyedropper tool to apply it.

14. Save your file again.

Applying Graphic Styles

1. Select the fish's gill.

2. Open the Graphic Styles panel from the docked panels (see Figure 6–34) or choose Window > Graphic Styles.

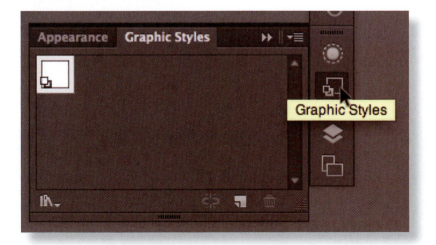

FIGURE | 6–34 |

Expand the Graphic Styles panel.

3. Some graphic styles are provided. To find more, choose Open Graphic Style Library > Image Effects from the options menu in the upper-right corner of the panel.

4. Select the effect called Chiseled in the Image Effects panel to apply it to the gill. See Figure 6–35.

   OK, I know you are itching to try the other graphic styles. Because they are so cool-looking, go for it. Save your file first, and when you are done doodling, come back to the next step.

5. Assign the Chiseled effect to bottom **fin1** and bottom **fin2**.

6. Take a look at what comprises this graphic style in the Appearance panel. Select one of the fins and open the Appearance panel. Notice the many stroke and fill variations that comprise this effect. See Figure 6–36.

7. You can change parts of the effect using the Appearance panel. Make sure the gill or the bottom fins are still selected. Scroll down in the Appearance panel to find the Fill attributes. Click on the Fill color box to bring the Swatches panel forward, or hold the Shift key as you click to bring the Color panel forward. See Figure 6–37. Select a new color for the fill. The color updates right away on the selected objects.

FIGURE | 6–35 |

Select the Chiseled graphic style.

FIGURE | 6–36 |

What a list of attributes for just one graphic style!

FIGURE | 6–37 |

Click on a fill or stroke to change it.

FIGURE | 6–38 |

Click on the Effect name in the Appearance panel to alter its attributes.

FIGURE | 6–39 |

Clear the effect on a selected object.

8. Notice that there is a drop shadow and opacity setting for the fill of the effect. Click on the Drop Shadow text (orange, with a dotted underline) to open its options. Click the Preview option and then type **–0.02 pt** for the X and Y Offsets. Press Tab to see the change on the fin without closing the options box. Add a 0.01 pt Blur. Click OK.

9. Click on the Opacity setting for the green fill in the Appearance panel (toward the bottom). The Transparency panel will come forward. Change the opacity setting in the Transparency panel to 90% to darken the fin effect color. See Figure 6–38.

10. Let's assume you are the indecisive type, and you do not like the effect changes you just made. From the Appearance panel options menu, choose Clear Appearance to remove the appearance effect. See Figure 6–39.

11. The effect has now been removed from the selected objects. Click on the Chiseled style in the Graphic Styles panel to reapply the original, unmodified effect to the gill and bottom fins again.

12. Save your file.

Applying an Effect

1. Choose Effect > Document Raster Effects Settings. Specify the following settings (see Figure 6–40):

▶ *Color Model:* CMYK

FIGURE | 6–40 |

Choose Effect > Document Raster Effects Settings.

▸ *Resolution*: Medium (150 ppi)

▸ *Background*: Transparent

▸ *Options*: Anti-alias

Click OK.

> Note: *If CMYK is not available, use File > Document Color Mode to select that option, and then change the Document Raster Effect Settings in the Effects menu.*

> Note: *When you apply a raster effect to a vector object (as you will be doing in the next steps), it is important to set up the specifications for this conversion in the Document Raster Effects Settings dialog box first. Raster images, otherwise known as bitmap images, are dependent on resolution, which is one of the settings you need to determine in this settings dialog box. Also, you need to determine whether the background of the final object will be filled with white or set as transparent.*

2. Select the fish's body outline (fish outline) within the layer called fish.

3. Choose Effect and under Photoshop Effects, choose Effect Gallery. In the gallery window, choose Sketch, then Torn Edges. Enter the following settings:

▸ *Image Balance*: 25

▸ *Smoothness*: 11

▸ *Contrast*: 17

Click OK to apply the effect.

See Figure 6–41.

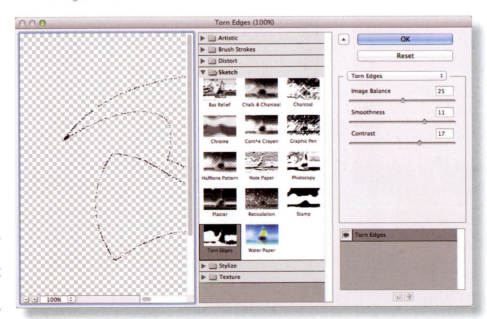

FIGURE | 6–41 |

Choose the Torn Edges option from the Sketch panel.

4. While the fish outline is still selected, use the Stroke panel to set the width to 3 points.

5. Select the bottom **fin1** and bottom **fin2** in the Layers panel and apply another effect to them using the Effect Gallery—you decide which one you like best.

If you want to permanently apply the effect, select the object with the effect and choose Object > Rasterize… (in this case, be sure that Background is set to Transparent). Once you have rasterized an object, it is no longer editable in the Appearance panel, which is why setting the Raster Effects is so important—it establishes the quality of the rasterized art.

Applying a Scatter Brush

1. Choose View > Actual Size to see the whole document.

2. Choose Select > Deselect to deselect all objects in the document.

3. Set the Fill and Stroke colors to their defaults. Hint: a quick shortcut for doing this is to tap the D key.

4. Open the Brushes panel and, from the options menu, choose Open **Brush Library > Decorative > Decorative_Scatter**.

5. Select the Bubbles scatter brush.

6. Double-click on the Paintbrush tool in the toolbar to open the Paintbrush Tool Options dialog box. In the options, be sure that the following are deselected:

    ▶ Fill new brush strokes
    ▶ Keep selected
    ▶ Edit Selected path

    Click OK.

7. In the Layers panel, select the circle in the selection column of the Bubbles layer. With the Paintbrush tool, paint two strokes of bubbles coming from the fish's mouth. See Figure 6–42.

> **Note:** *Some of these options might be selected. Keeping Edit Selected path selected automatically edits the shape of your paths as you draw over them, which can be frustrating. On your own, try drawing with and without these options selected to see the varying results.*

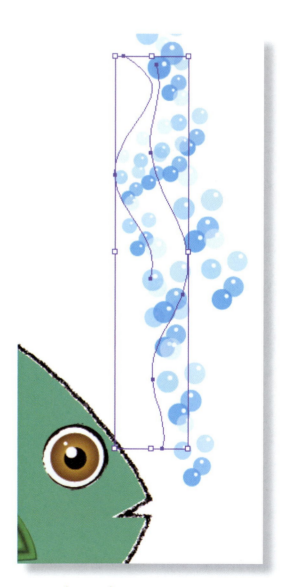

FIGURE | 6–42 |

Paint with the Bubbles scatter brush.

8. With the Selection tool, Shift-click on the bubble paths to select both of them. In the Appearance panel, click on the word Bubbles to open the Brush Definition window, and then double-click the Bubbles icon to open the Bubbles scatter brush options. See Figure 6–43.

9. In the options window, set the following:

   ▸ *Size*: Random, 72% to 125%

   ▸ *Spacing*: Random, 60% to 97%

   ▸ *Scatter*: Random, 6% to −62%

   ▸ *Rotation*: Fixed, −79°

   ▸ *Rotation relative to*: Page

   ▸ *Colorization Method*: None

   Check the Preview option at the lower left to see how you like things, click OK, and then click Apply to Strokes to have the changes take effect.

10. Select the bubble paths and adjust their position, if necessary, so it appears as if the fish is actually breathing. Save your file.

Making Water and Waves

1. Choose View > Actual Size. Use the Layers panel to select the water; click on the circle at the right of the layer name.

2. Open the Gradient panel and make sure that the fill is active. Create a linear gradient with a light blue at the right and a dark blue at the left. Refer back to Chapter 5, Lesson 2, Vegas Lady, Part 2, for a refresher on how to do that.

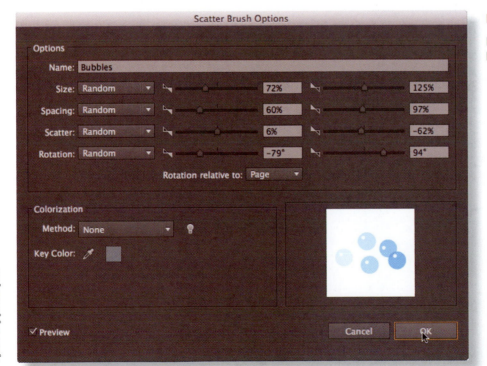

FIGURE | 6–43 |

Modify the scatter brush options.

FIGURE | 6–44 |

Create a gradient and adjust the direction.

FIGURE | 6–45 |

Adjust the opacity and blending mode of the water.

3. In the Gradient panel, enter 90 for angle. The direction of the gradient is altered, with the dark blue color on the bottom and the light blue color on the top. See Figure 6–44.

4. While the water is still selected, use the Transparency panel to set the Opacity to 50%, and the Blending Mode to Multiply. See Figure 6–45.

5. Select None for the stroke color of the gradient-filled rectangle, if necessary.

6. Choose Select > Deselect, or click outside the artboard with either Selection tool.

7. Open the Brushes panel and click on the books icon at the bottom left of the panel. From the drop-down menu, choose Artistic > Artistic_ChalkCharcoalPencil.

8. Choose the Chalk brush (the top one in the list).

9. Set the Brush stroke to 1 pt in the Control panel, click the Brush tool in the Tools panel, and then paint some foamy waves at the top of the water you just created.

10. Select the waves and use the Appearance panel to change the stroke color to blue or white (try both!). See Figure 6–46.

11. Save your file.

> Note: *In the finished example for this lesson, there is some seaweed added. If you'd like to continue experimenting, create a new layer and then try using the brushes from the Artistic_ScrollPen brush library to add the seaweed.*

FIGURE | 6–46 |

Add and adjust the waves.

LESSON 2: PLAYING WITH CUSTOM BRUSH STYLES

Creating custom brush styles in Illustrator requires a special lesson. Just as you can save swatches to a custom library, so can you create your own brush styles and save them as a library to use whenever necessary.

Setting up the File

1. Launch Illustrator, open the New Document dialog box, set the Profile to Print, set the Size to Letter, and then set the Units to Inches. In the Advanced area of the New Document window, ensure that the Color Mode is set to CMYK, and set the Raster Effects to Medium (150 ppi). See Figure 6–47.

2. Make sure that your Workspace is set to Essentials.

3. Choose View > Fit All in Window (try the keystroke shortcut: Command 0 (Mac)/Alt Ctrl 0 (Windows). This will be your working document for creating new brushes and patterns.

Creating a Calligraphic Brush

You will start with a Calligraphic brush, since those are the easiest to create, and then move on to develop Scatter, Art, and Pattern brushes. Finally, you will save these brushes in a custom library so that you can use them whenever you like.

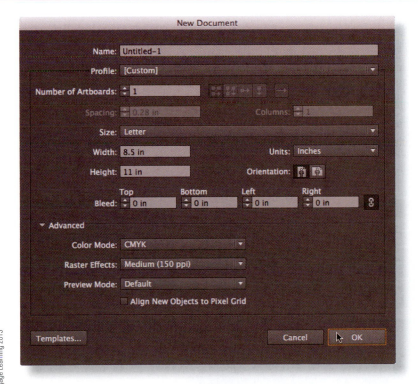

FIGURE | 6–47 |

Create a new Print document, and then set to CMYK color mode.

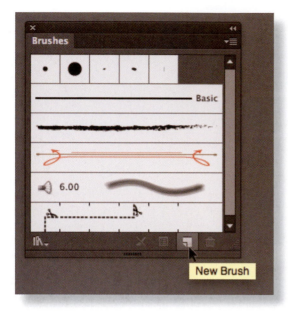

FIGURE | 6–48 |

Create a new brush.

1. Open the Brushes panel and click on the New Brush icon at the bottom—Figure 6–48.

2. You will be presented with the New Brush dialog box, and Calligraphic is automatically selected for you. Click OK.

3. In the Options window, give your brush a name.

4. There are a few ways to create the brush; one is to adjust the circle by squashing and rotating it using the Brush Shape Editor under the Name field. The other is to adjust the Angle, Roundness, and Size using the sliders or text fields. Use these settings (see Figure 6–49):

   ▶ *Angle*: –50°, Fixed

   ▶ *Roundness*: 14%, Fixed

   ▶ *Size*: 15 pt, Fixed

   Then click OK.

5. Select the Paintbrush tool from the Tools panel Make sure that your new brush is highlighted in the Brushes panel and start painting!

> Note: *To adjust the settings for your brush, double-click on the Paintbrush tool to open its options.*

6. Use the Selection tool to select everything on your artboard (or use the keystroke shortcut: (Command A (Mac)/Ctrl A (Windows)) and delete it. Save the file as **brushes_yourname.ai**, and keep it open.

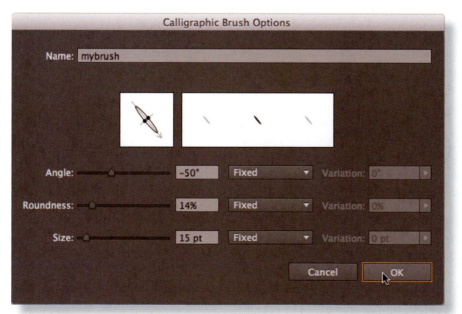

FIGURE | 6–49 |

Calligraphic Brush options.

Editing Brushes

While you can edit existing brushes, it's usually smarter to duplicate existing brushes and edit the copies, or create new ones so all the originals remain in their default state.

1. In the Brushes panel, click and drag your new brush to the New Brush icon at the bottom of the panel to create a copy of it. Then double-click on the copy's icon to make changes to the way the brush paints: set the angle to 121°, the roundness to 12%, and the size from 15 pt to 9 pt. Click OK, and if asked, choose not to update the existing strokes.

2. Use the Paintbrush tool to test your new brush.

3. Save your file.

Creating a Scatter Brush

You may have noticed that the Scatter Brush option isn't available when choosing to create a new brush from scratch. That's because scatter brushes rely on artwork that's attached to a path. So, you need to start with some artwork first.

Let's start with a simple object—a star—for the scatter brush stroke. Once you see how easy it is to create this, you should have a great time experimenting with other options.

1. Select the Star tool (under the Rectangle tool) in the Tools panel and draw a star. You can decide how many points you want as you draw by tapping the up arrow key to add more, and the down arrow key to reduce the number.

2. Set the fill color to anything you want using either the Swatches or the Color panel, and set the stroke to None.

> Note: *You cannot use gradients, blends, other brush strokes, mesh objects, bitmap images, graphs, placed files, or masks in objects you intend to use in a brush.*

3. Draw two more stars of different sizes and with different numbers of points, keeping them close together. See Figure 6–51 for an example.

4. With the Selection tool, select all the stars and then open the Brushes panel.

5. Open the options menu of the Brushes panel and choose New Brush. (Or, click on the New Brush icon at the bottom of the Brushes panel—it looks like a little pad.)

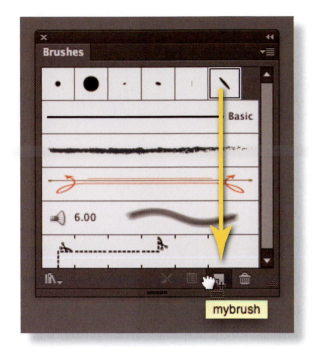

FIGURE | 6–50 |

Drag your brush over the New Brush icon to create a duplicate.

FIGURE | 6–51 |

Star graphics for a Scatter Brush.

Figures © Cengage Learning 2013

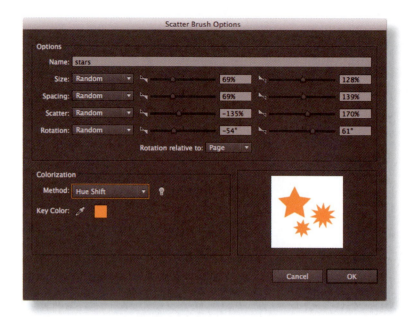

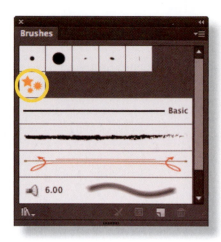

FIGURE | 6–53 |

The new brush is made available
in the Brushes panel.

FIGURE | 6–52 |

Settings for the Scatter brush.

6. For brush type, select Scatter Brush option and click OK. In the Scatter Brush Options dialog box, enter a name for your brush. You can determine the settings for how the scatter brush will work, or try the settings indicated in Figure 6–52. Once you have determined your settings, click OK. Notice that your new brush is available in the Brushes panel, just below the Calligraphic brushes (see Figure 6–53).

5. Select the Paintbrush tool. Create at least three starry paint strokes in the drawing area to the right of your original stars (see Figure 6–54).

Another way to modify a scatter brush stroke without changing the actual brush is to change the color. This is possible only if you choose Hue Shift in the Brush Options dialog box (refer back to Figure 6–52).

6. If you didn't enable this setting, double-click on your star scatter brush in the Brushes panel to edit it. The Scatter Brush Options dialog box opens. Check the Preview option at the bottom left, and then alter any settings for the brush, if you wish. At the bottom right, be sure that Hue Shift is selected for Colorization Method and click OK. If you get a warning asking you if you want to apply the new settings to existing strokes, choose Leave Strokes.

7. Using the Selection tool, select one of the existing strokes on the artboard, and click on the revised star brush in the Brushes panel to update the stroke.

8. Select another stroke and open the Color panel. Show options, establish that the stroke color is active, and then select a new color from the spectrum, or mix one using the color sliders. Change another star stroke to a third color. Obviously, you could turn a starry night into confetti or fireworks fairly easily! See Figure 6–55 for an example of what this can look like.

9. Save your file.

FIGURE | 6–54 |

Starry brush strokes using the new scatter brush.

Original Art Brushes

Art brushes are similar to scatter brushes in that you need to start with some artwork before you can choose this option in the New Brush window.

1. Select the Pencil tool in the Tools panel, set the fill color to a light hue (yellow, blue, or pink, for instance), set the stroke to None, and then draw a wide, biomorphic shape somewhere on the artboard or canvas area (see Figure 6–56).

2. The smoother the shape, the more interesting the brush will be. Using the Direct Selection tool (the white arrow), click a point to adjust its position and handles. Also, you can use the Add Anchor Point and Delete Anchor Point tools (under the Pen tool) to edit the shape.

3. Select the shape with the Selection tool—make sure that all the anchor points are solid—then click on the little pad icon at the bottom of the Brushes panel to open the New Brush dialog box (see Figure 6–57).

FIGURE | 6–55 |

Changing the color of a scatter brush.

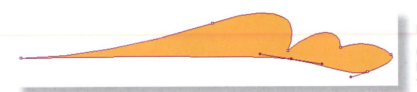

FIGURE | 6–56 |

Create a wide, smooth, biomorphic shape with the Pencil tool.

4. Choose Art Brush and click OK. The Art Brush Options dialog box opens with options for width, scale, direction, and colorization. Leave everything as it is for now and click OK.

5. Select the Paintbrush tool in the Tools panel, verify that the new art brush is selected, and then paint some strokes.

6. Double-click on the new art brush icon to edit the brush's options. In the Brush Options window, and select Hue Shift for the Colorization Method, then click OK. Choose not to apply this brush to existing strokes, if asked.

7. Paint a few more strokes.

8. Select one of the new strokes and choose a new stroke color from the Color or Swatches panel. Fun, right?

> Note: *If the colors don't change, delete all the paths and try again with new strokes.*

9. Save your file.

FIGURE | 6–57 |

Create a new Art Brush using the biomorphic shape.

FIGURE | 6–58 |

Set the Colorization method for any brush to Hue Shift to be able to change its color.

Making Pattern Brushes

Admittedly this is one of the more difficult brushes to create since it involves at least two different pieces of artwork, and up to five depending on how intricate you want it to be. It's good to know how it works, though, just in case. See Figure 6–59.

1. Add a new layer to your custom brush file and, in the Layers panel, drag it below the existing **Layer 1**. Keep the new layer selected.

2. From the File menu, choose Place (File > Place), navigate your way to the **chap06_lessons/assets** folder, and then select the **patternbrush.psd** file. You'll use this as a template to avoid frustration the first time through this process. Click the Place button.

3. Adjust the position of the Photoshop file, if necessary, and then choose Template from the Layers panel options menu. That will dim the Photoshop file a bit so you can see what you're doing (see Figure 6–60).

FIGURE | 6–59 |

Examples of Pattern Brushes.

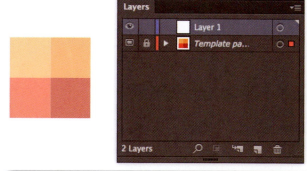

FIGURE | 6–60 |

Add a layer and place a file to use as a template.

Figures © Cengage Learning 2013

4. Highlight the top layer (**Layer 1**, unless you renamed it). You will work on this layer.

5. Select the Rectangle tool and hold down the Shift key as you draw to create a perfect square; match the size of the whole square on the template: click and drag from the top-left corner of the square to the bottom right, then be sure to deselect it [press Command Shift A (Mac) or Ctrl Shift A (Windows)].

6. Set the stroke color to black and, with the Line tool, draw a vertical line through the square. Hold down the Shift key to ensure that it's perfectly straight. Use the Selection tool to center it. Or, to be even more precise, open the Align panel from the Window menu. Select both the square and the line and click the Horizontally Align Center icon in the Align panel (see Figure 6–61).

7. Make sure only the line is selected, and use the Object menu to select Path > Divide Objects Below. This will split the square in half.

8. Repeat this process with a horizontal line, centered in the square, so you end up with 4 quadrants of equal size. Deselect all.

9. Select each quadrant and use the Control panel or the Color panel to select a different fill color for each of them. Set the strokes to None, if necessary. See Figure 6–62.

Pattern brushes are so named because they use patterns placed along a path. You need to make this square graphic into a pattern swatch before you can make it into a brush.

10. Select all four quadrants of the pattern square, and open the Swatches panel. With the Selection tool, drag the pattern square over to the Swatches panel and drop it. See Figure 6–63.

11. Keep the pattern square selected on the artboard, open the Brushes panel, and click on the New Brush icon in the Brushes panel. Select Pattern Brush to pick the type you want. Click OK.

Figures © Cengage Learning 2013

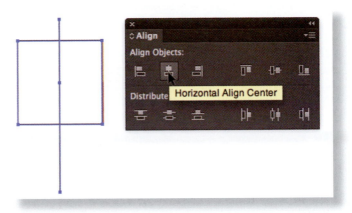

FIGURE | 6–61 |

Use the Align panel to organize several objects in relation to each other.

FIGURE | 6–62 |

The finished graphic for a Pattern Brush.

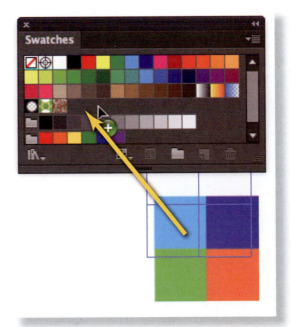

FIGURE | 6–63 |

Drag the pattern graphic onto the Swatches panel to make it into a swatch.

FIGURE | 6–64 |

The pattern brush settings.

FIGURE | 6–65 |

A custom pattern brush stroke.

12. In the Pattern Brush Options window, your pattern square will be positioned automatically in the first rectangle, which establishes the look of a basic stroke. Click the second rectangle, which will determine the outer corners, and choose your pattern swatch from the list—it should be named something like New Pattern Swatch 1, since it wasn't named when you dragged it into the Swatches panel. (You'll be experimenting a lot more with patterns in Chapter 10.)

13. Click the third box and select the same pattern swatch for inner corners.

14. Set the Colorization method to Hue Shift. See Figure 6–64. Click OK.

15. Draw a large rectangle or a circle with the Rectangle or Ellipse tool, and while it's still selected, make sure the stroke attribute is active in the Tools panel. Then click on your new pattern brush in the Brushes panel (see Figure 6–65).

16. Save your file. Well done!

Saving a Custom Brush Library

1. To save these brushes, first use the Brushes panel options menu and choose Select All Unused. Once they are selected, click the trash can icon at the bottom right of the Brushes panel to eliminate them from your set. Click Yes when asked if you're sure you want to do this. See Figure 6–66.

Note: *It's important that you have used each of your new brushes in this file, or Selecting All Unused will select your brushes as well.*

FIGURE |6–66 |

Delete any unused brushes from the Brushes panel.

FIGURE | 6–67 |

Save this brush library with the other Illustrator brush presets for easy access.

2. Select Save Brush Library from the Brushes panel options menu.

3. Give your brush library a name in the Save Brushes as Library dialog box.

4. If you are working on your own computer, save the file in the Brushes folder inside the Illustrator application folder [Adobe Illustrator CS6 > Presets > en_US > Brushes (Mac)/C:\Users\user_name\AppData\Roaming\Adobe\Adobe Illustrator CS6 Settings\en_US\x64\Brushes (Windows)] See Figure 6–67. If not, save it in the **chap06_lessons** folder.

5. Now that you have saved these brushes in a library, you can close this file and delete it from your lessons folder, if you want.

LESSON 3: CREATING GRAPHIC STYLES

As with brushes and colors, Illustrator comes with several dozen graphic style libraries you can choose from. Let's take a look at how to use the Appearance panel to create a new graphic style. You will create one fill style and one stroke style. The key part of this process is that you are limited to using stroke and fill variations and effect options only.

Setting up the File

1. Open a new Illustrator document, and set the profile to Print and the size to Letter. Set the color mode to CMYK and the raster effects to Medium (150 ppi).

2. Organize your workspace to make accessing the panels you'll use easier. Drag the Color panel away from the dock, then the Swatches panel, the Appearance panel, and finally, the Graphic Styles panel. See Figure 6–68.

3. Use the Rectangle tool to draw a small square—hold down the Shift key to constrain the shape. Or, to be more precise, click once with the Rectangle tool and set the size to 1 in x 1 in.

FIGURE | 6–68 |

Drag panels from the dock so they are always accessible.

The First Fill

1. Select an orangish fill color, and set the stroke to None.

2. Keep the square selected and then, at the bottom of the Appearance panel, click on the FX icon to reveal the options. Select Stylize > Feather. See Figure 6–69.

3. In the Feather options window, set the Radius to .1 in. Click the Preview box to see how that looks, then click OK.

The Second Fill

1. Let's add another fill to this style; click on the Add New Fill icon at the bottom of the Appearance panel. See Figure 6–70.

2. Click on the fill color in the Appearance panel and change it to pink.

3. Right now, this new fill is covering the first one, so we need to make it a bit smaller. Click the FX icon at the bottom of the Appearance panel again, go to Path, and select Offset Path. Alternatively, you can use Effect > Path > Offset Path from the menu. Set the offset to −0.08 in. Click OK.

> **NOTE:** *If things don't seem to be changing in your square as you make these alterations, be sure that it's still selected; otherwise, nothing will happen.*

4. Use the FX icon one more time to select Distort & Transform, and then choose Roughen. In the Roughen dialog box, set Size to 1%, Detail to 20, and Points to Smooth. Click the Preview box to see how that looks (see Figure 6–71), and then click OK.

FIGURE | 6–69 |

Use the FX icon at the bottom of the Appearance panel to add effects to the fill.

FIGURE | 6–70 |

Add a new fill using the Appearance panel.

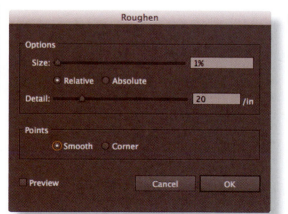

FIGURE | 6–71 |

Add some texture using the Roughen effect.

5. Click on the triangle to the left of this fill in the Appearance panel to reveal the effects you've added to it. Note that it has an automatic opacity assigned to it. Click on the word Opacity to open that panel. Set the Opacity to 50% and the Blending Mode to Hard Light. See Figure 6–72.

The Final Fill

1. We'll add one last fill to this style; click the Add New Fill icon again (or use the Appearance panel's options menu at the top right to choose Add New Fill) and set the fill color to bright yellow. Remember to keep the square selected in order to apply this new fill to it.

2. Again, it's covering the first two squares, so use the FX option to select Path, then Offset Path. Change the Offset to –0.125. Click OK.

3. Since the Photoshop filters are part of the Effect options, let's apply one of those to this fill. Select Effect Gallery from the FX menu and then open the Artistic options.

FIGURE | 6–72 |

Adjust the opacity and blending mode.

4. Click the Palette Knife effect, and specify a Stroke Size of 12, a Stroke Detail of 3, and a Softness of 6 (see Figure 6–73), then click OK.

5. Click on the triangle next to this fill in the Appearance panel to access the Opacity settings. Click on the word Opacity to set the Opacity to 50% and the Blend Mode to Overlay.

This is looking pretty good! Let's make it into a Graphic Style so we can apply it to something.

6. Save your file as **myStyles_yourname.ai** in your Lessons folder.

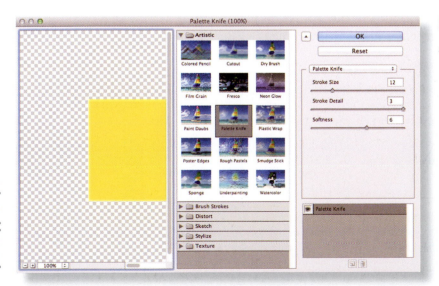

FIGURE | 6–73 |

Add a Photoshop effect.

FIGURE | 6–74 |

Add your style to the Graphic Styles panel.

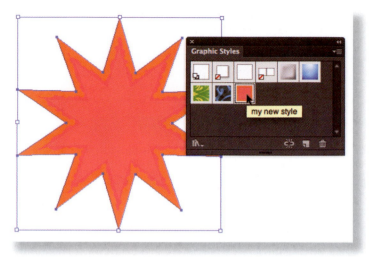

FIGURE | 6–75 |

Apply your new style to a shape.

Making & Using a Graphic Style

1. Make sure the Graphic Styles panel is visible, and that the square you created is selected. Then use the panel's options menu to select New Graphic Style. Give your style a name and click OK. A new style icon will appear in the panel (see Figure 6–74).

2. Use the Star tool to draw a star in your document and keep it selected.

3. Make sure the fill color is active in the Color panel or the Tools panel, and then click on your new graphic style in the Graphic Styles panel. Figure 6–75.

How cool is that?

This style is just about fills. You can add a stroke color to any object filled with this Graphic Style if you want. Let's create a Graphic Style for strokes.

Creating Stroke Styles

1. In the same Illustrator document in which you've been working, select the Line tool and draw a horizontal line about 6 inches long—hold down the Shift key to keep it straight.

2. Use the Stroke panel (Window > Stroke, or pop it open from the dock) and set the weight to 20 points.

3. Set the stroke color to lime green using the Color panel.

4. Use the Appearance panel options menu to add a new stroke, and set the width to 10 points and the color to magenta. You can use the Appearance panel to do this, rather than the Stroke panel; click the Stroke Weight box arrow and select the value (10). Or,

double-click the Stroke Weight box and type the value. Then, Shift click on the color box to open the Color panel. See Figure 6–76.

5. Make sure the magenta stroke is highlighted in the Appearance panel and select Stylize > Scribble from the FX menu. Use the Snarl setting from the Settings pop-up menu and click OK. See Figure 6–77.

6. Add one last stroke to this, with a weight of 5 points and a turquoise stroke color. See if you can make all these alterations using the Appearance panel, rather than the Stroke and Color panels.

7. Click the word Stroke to open the Stroke panel and make this a dashed line with 3-point dashes and gaps. See Figure 6–78.

8. Save your file.

Creating, Applying, & Saving the Style

1. If it's not still selected, use the Selection tool to highlight the stroke and click on the New Graphic Style icon at the bottom of the Graphic Styles panel.

> **Note:** *When you create a style this way, you don't have the option to name it. If you do want to give it a name, double-click on it in the Graphic Styles panel to open the Options window.*

2. Use the Star tool again to draw another star. This time, set the fill to None, and for the stroke, select your new style from the Graphic Styles panel. See Figure 6–79.

3. Select Save Graphic Style Library from the Graphic Styles panel options menu. Illustrator should automatically direct you to the Graphic Styles folder in the Illustrator application folder. Click Save, and you're done!

4. Save your file.

If you have time, use the Appearance panel to make additions or other changes to these two new styles, and add the variations to the Graphic Styles panel. Or, make a new style that uses both fills and strokes; the process is the same.

FIGURE | 6–76 |

Use the Appearance panel to set the stroke attributes.

FIGURE | 6–77 |

Add a Snarl effect to the stroke.

FIGURE | 6–78 |

Make the stroke a dashed line.

FIGURE | 6–79 |

Name the stroke style and apply it to an object.

SUMMARY

Let me guess. After this chapter, you are hooked on painting with Illustrator—so many brushes and effects to fool around with, so little time and digital screen space. As you learned with every stroke and fill, your drawing can suddenly come to life with variations on value and texture. These variations can be modified again and again with the Appearance panel, and used over and over in custom libraries.

▶ IN REVIEW

1. Define value in drawing and painting.

2. Define texture in drawing and painting.

3. What are caps and joins?

4. What are the five brush types and their characteristics?

5. Define a Graphic Style in Illustrator.

6. How can the Appearance panel enhance your workflow?

7. What are the steps to edit brush styles applied to a particular stroke?

8. What is opacity?

9. What does the Document Raster Effects Settings do under Effects in the menu bar?

10. How do you save custom brushes and graphic styles to use again?

► EXPLORING ON YOUR OWN

1.   Access the Help > Illustrator Help menu option. Read the section called "Painting."

2.   Explore the Blob Brush tool in the Tools panel. This tool creates outlines and filled shapes from brush strokes (as opposed to stroked paths). To get the Blob Brush tools options, double-click on the Tool in the Tools panel. See Figure 6–80.

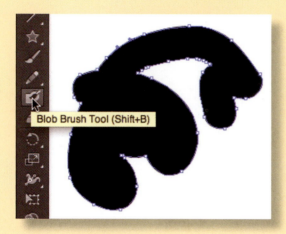

FIGURE | 6–80 |

The Blob Brush on a stroke with a variable width option applied.

3.   What is isolation mode?

You might have already ended up in isolation mode unintentionally – it could happen if you accidentally double-click on an object rather than a single-click to select it. A double-click on an object sends you into isolation mode, which could be a good thing if that's where you want to be. Here's the word from the Illustrator help files on isolation mode: Isolation mode isolates objects so that you can easily select and edit particular objects or parts of objects. You can isolate any of the following: layers, sublayers, groups, symbols, clipping masks, compound paths, gradient meshes, and paths.

In Isolation mode, you can delete, replace, and add new art relative to the isolated art. As soon as you exit isolation mode, replaced or new art is added at the same location as the original isolated art. Isolation mode automatically locks all other objects so that only the objects in isolation mode are affected by the edits you make—you don't need to worry about what layer an object is on, nor do you need to manually lock or hide the objects you don't want affected by your edits.

When isolation mode is active, the isolated object appears in full color, while the rest of the artwork appears dimmed. The isolated object's name and location (sometimes referred to as "bread crumbs") appears in the isolation mode border, and the Layers panel displays only the artwork in the isolated sublayer or group. When you exit isolation mode, the other layers and groups reappear in the Layers panel. See Figure 6–81 and Figure 6–82.

Take a moment to explore isolation mode. Open **chap6LIfinished.ai** in the **chap06_lessons** folder and double-click on an object in the fish scene to enter isolation mode. Exit isolation mode by clicking the arrow in upper left of the document window (refer to Figure 6–81).

4.   As you explore the world of brushes, you may wish to add brushes to your toolset. One great location for downloading brushes is the Adobe Exchange (http://www.adobe.com/cfusion/exchange/index.cfm). In the Adobe Exchange, navigate to the Illustrator Exchange and choose Brushes from the categories

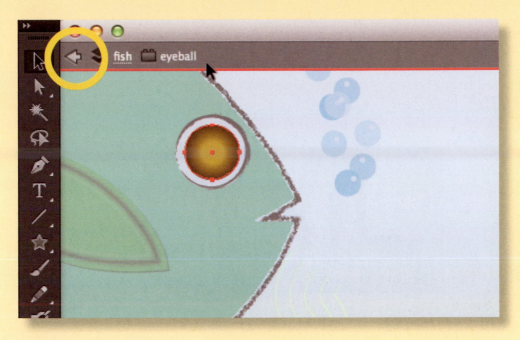

FIGURE | 6—81 |

Isolation mode of selected object.

FIGURE | 6—82 |

Exit isolation mode.

menu. Here you will find a variety of brushes to choose from. You may be required to create an account and/or login to the Adobe site to download the brushes. Once the files have been downloaded from the Illustrator Exchange, access your new brushes by opening the Brushes panel's options menu, and then choosing Open Brush Library > Other Library… to locate your downloaded brush files.

Explorer PAGES

Reggie Gilbert

Illustration by Reggie Gilbert, showing close-up line and full-color versions.

About Reggie Gilbert

Reggie Gilbert spent most of his teen years in Los Angeles skateboarding and wrecking shop (Reggie's words!) on trains and dark alleyways, so art was always something he was thinking about—paint on his shoes and screen print on the fat laces— at the time some people thought he was a kook. Now people are getting rich from it. While he was laid up after breaking his leg in a snowboarding accident, he learned Illustrator. Since he could not move around much, every day he sat and scanned in doodles and cleaned them up in Illustrator. After a few months of not taking his new Illustrator skills too seriously, a local audio cable manufacturer caught wind that he was drawing exclusively vector images and asked if he could draw some technical illustrations for the company. "Sure," he said, and his professional illustration career started.

Illustration representing Reggie's signature, freestyle drawing method. Compliments of Reggie Gilbert.

What are Reggie's predictions for the future? Cars are going to be belching out water instead of carbon; he is going to be killing it (illustrating) for several more years. Then his computer is going to melt down and—due to the fact he never backs up— he will lose everything he has ever done. He will then move to Costa Rica or Ecuador to surf and chill in a hammock, never to be heard from or use the Pen tool again.

Enjoy Reggie's freestyle illustration and design work and his other exciting projects at TechVector: *http://www.techvector.com*

Illustration of a spray can from sketch to 3D rendering using Illustrator. Compliments of Reggie Gilbert.

Botanical vector set for purchase, among others, at YouWorkForThem (*http://www.youworkforthem.com*).

"As an artist, don't ever lose sight of how lucky you are to be able to do art and make money from it. I've done it all—dug ditches, flipped burgers—so I recognize how fortunate I am to be doing what I'm doing."

Technical illustration by Reggie Gilbert.

ITALIAN MARINATED MUSHROOMS

PREPARATION

Mix together oil, water, freshly squeezed lemon juice, bay leaf, garlic, peppercorns, and salt in a large stainless steel saucepan. Bring to a boil over medium-high heat. Reduce heat, cover and simmer for 15 minutes.

Strain using a sieve (or remove garlic and peppercorns using a slotted spoon) and return to a simmer over low heat.

Drop the mushrooms and roasted pepper into the simmering marinade, stirring gently from time to time, for about 2–4 minutes. If the mushrooms are very small, remove from heat after just 1 minute.

Remove pan from heat and allow to stand, uncovered, while the mushrooms cool.

Serve at room temperature or refrigerate in a plastic container. Refrigerate for up to 2 to 3 days. After mushrooms have marinated, taste and adjust seasonings; after a day or two, you may want to add fresh herbs for an extra layer of flavor, since the marinated herbs will have mellowed, imparting their flavor to the oil. Remove bay leaf before serving.

INGREDIENTS

2/3 cup extra virgin olive oil
1/2 cup water
1 bay leaf
juice of 2 lemons
3 garlic cloves, crushed
1 large shallot, minced
6 whole peppercorns
1/2 teaspoon sea salt
1/4 tsp. each basil and oregano
pinch of finely minced rosemary
1/4 tsp. red hot pepper flakes
1 pound small mushrooms
1 roasted red pepper, chopped

| Working with Type |

charting your course

For the novice graphic designer, selecting typefaces and designing with type are often neglected—an afterthought to the overall image or layout. Type, however, plays a vital role in visual communications, from business cards to logos and signage to party invitations. Designing with type, or working with the appearance of printed characters, is called typography. This chapter will introduce you to the methods for creating, formatting, exporting, and importing type in Illustrator. Basic design techniques for making appealing and readable layouts are also provided. Of all the design skills you're developing, working successfully with type is one of the most important.

goals

In this chapter you will:

▶ *Practice the three methods of creating type in Illustrator: type at a point, type in an area, and type along a path*

▶ *Discover the quirks of typefaces, font families, and font formats*

▶ *Format type with ease*

▶ *Get an overview of importing, exporting, installing, and embedding fonts*

▶ *Learn basic design techniques when choosing and working type*

▶ *Become familiar with typographic terms*

CREATING TYPE IN ILLUSTRATOR

There are three methods for creating type in Illustrator:

► Type at a point
► Type in an area
► Type on a path

FIGURE | 7–1 |

The Type tool and its expanded options.

TYPE AT A POINT

Not unlike typing in any basic word processing program, to type at a point, you click in a document with the Type tool and start typing. The Type tool, located on the Tools panel, has a big T on it (no chance of missing that!). When you click and hold the tool, several more type tools are revealed, which we will investigate soon enough. The first three tools listed create horizontal type, while the last three create vertical type. See Figure 7–1 and Figure 7–2.

To type at a point, follow these steps:

1. Create a new document in Illustrator.

2. Select the Type tool in the Tools panel. The cursor changes to what is called an I-beam; this is your starting mark. The small arrow at the top left determines where the type will first appear. See Figure 7–3.

3. Click anywhere on the document and start typing.

4. Hit Return or Enter to start a new line. To insert a letter, word, or line within the existing text block, click between any two letters and start typing.

Horizontal text is easy to read, and the most common format for that reason.

Vertical text is very difficult to read and looks unbalanced.

For that reason, if you must fit type into a vertical space, turn it sideways instead.

FIGURE | 7–2 |

An example of horizontal and vertical text.

Figures © Cengage Learning 2013

▶ DON'T GO THERE

Do not click on an existing object with the Type tool. Otherwise that object converts to an area-type shape or assumes you want to type along its path. To be on the safe side, hide or lock any objects that might get in your way.

Type at a point involves clicking with the Type tool and then typing. You must use the Enter or Return key to start a new line.

FIGURE | 7–3 |

Some text typed at a point. The circled I-beam is the active text cursor.

5. To select the block of text, use the Selection tool, or Command click (Mac) or Ctrl click (Windows) on the text.

Note: *When you choose View > Show Bounding Box and select the text block using the Selection tool, transform handles appear around it. This makes it easy to move, scale, and rotate text. See Figure 7–4.*

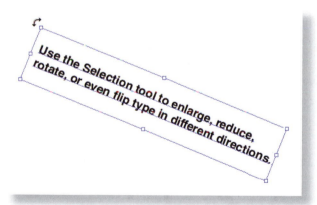

FIGURE | 7–4 |

Transform a text block using the bounding box.

6. There are several methods to select and edit individual characters, words, sentences, or paragraphs. Experiment with each to determine which works best for you.

> ▶ If the text block or path is already selected, just double-click on the text with the Selection tool to switch to the Type tool and get the I-beam cursor. With the I-beam, click in front of and then drag over the text you want to change.

> ▶ Select the Type tool in the Tools panel. With the I-beam, click in front of and then drag over the text you want to modify.

> ▶ If you want to select a single word, place the I-beam anywhere within the word and then double-click. Clicking three times will select a whole line of type.

> ▶ To select an entire block of text at once, click at the beginning once, then shift-click at the end, or use the Command A/Ctrl A keystroke shortcut.

TYPE IN AN AREA

There are two ways to type in a defined area. To define a rectangular area, click and drag with the Type tool (see Figure 7–5) and then start typing within the area. Illustrator will put line returns in automatically when it reaches the right edge of the text field. To type inside another kind of shape, create the shape first, then click with the Type tool or Area Type tool on the object's path, which converts it to a container for the text. See Figure 7–6.

If you type more than can fit in the defined area, a little red box with a plus sign shows up at the bottom of the text block, indicating that part of the text is hidden or "overset." See Figure 7–7. To fix this problem, you can either use a smaller point size for the font (see the section Formatting Type) or scale the text area larger. To scale, choose View > Show Bounding Box, then select the area and adjust the transform handles. When you scale a defined shape, the object's size changes but the point size of the text does not. This is different than scaling text at a point, which will enlarge or reduce the text itself, unless you hold down the Shift key. See Figure 7–8 and Figure 7–9.

> Note: *Be aware . . . if you use the Scale tool on a text block, you will be enlarging the type as well as the shape.*

There is also an Area Type Options dialog box (see Figure 7–10), which includes options to numerically change the width and height of a text area, create rows and columns, and adjust offset and text flow. To access box, select some area type on the document, and either choose Type > Area Type Options from the menu bar or double-click the Type tool in the Tools panel.

FIGURE | 7–5 |

Drag with the Type tool to define an area.

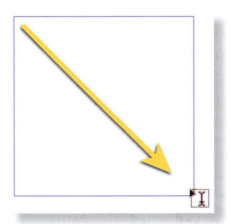

FIGURE | 7–6 |

Create a text container out of any shape.

Just click on the stroke of a shape to convert it into a container for text, then just start typing. Note how the i-beam cursor changes to have a dotted circle around it, rather than a dotted square.

Figures © Cengage Learning 2013

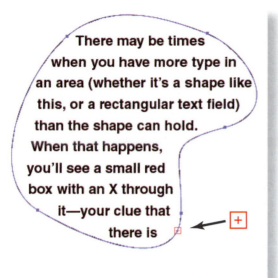

There may be times when you have more type in an area (whether it's a shape like this, or a rectangular text field) than the shape can hold. When that happens, you'll see a small red box with an X through it—your clue that there is

FIGURE | 7–7 |

The little box with the plus sign in the corner of the text block indicates hidden text called "overset" type.

There may be times when you have more type in an area (whether it's a shape like this, or a rectangular text field) than the shape can hold. When that happens, you'll see a small red box with an X through it—your clue that there is "overset" type.

FIGURE | 7–8 |

Scale or edit the shape of a text block to include overflow text.

FIGURE | 7–9 |

Always hold down the Shift key when scaling text so as not to distort it.

While type size should be determined using points, beginning typographers have a tendency to want to scale it larger or smaller rather than using specific point sizes. To ensure that it doesn't distort, **always** hold the Shift key when scaling text.

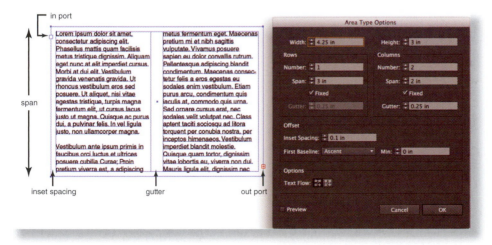

FIGURE | 7–10 |

Select the type with the Selection tool first, then double-click the Area Type tool in the Tools panel to access these options.

You can specify columns for area type using the Area Type Options (Figure 7–10) and, you can also thread (or flow) type from one text field to another. Selected type fields have two little boxes, called ports, one on each side. To connect a text block with overflow text with an empty text block, use the Selection tool and click on the out port of one text block (the box with the red plus sign in it at the bottom right). If you have already created a shape for the next text field, click directly on the path of the next block to initiate the thread. If you haven't, then just click and drag to create one. See Figure 7–11 and Figure 7–12. If you want to release threaded text, select one of the linked boxes and choose Type > Threaded Text > Release Selection or Remove Threading.

Lorem ipsum dolor sit amet, consectetur adipiscing elit. Phasellus mattis quam facilisis metus tristique dignissim. Aliquam eget nunc at elit imperdiet cursus. Morbi at dui elit. Vestibulum gravida venenatis gravida. Ut rhoncus vestibulum eros sed posuere. Ut aliquet, nisi vitae egestas tristique, turpis magna fermentum elit, ut cursus lacus justo ut magna. Quisque ac purus dui, a pulvinar felis. In vel ligula justo, non ullamcorper magna.

Vestibulum ante ipsum primis in

faucibus orci luctus et ultrices posuere cubilia Curae; Proin pretium viverra est, a adipiscing metus fermentum eget. Maecenas pretium mi et nibh sagittis vulputate. Vivamus posuere sapien eu dolor convallis rutrum. Pellentesque adipiscing blandit condimentum. Maecenas consectetur felis a eros egestas eu sodales enim vestibulum. Etiam purus arcu, condimentum quis iaculis at, commodo quis urna. Sed ornare cursus erat, nec sodales velit volutpat nec. Class aptent taciti sociosqu ad litora torquent per

FIGURE | 7–11 |

Click on the out port of a text field to initiate the threaded text option. Then click on the in port of the next text field.

FIGURE | 7–12 |

If there is no second text field, click on the out port of the first field, and click and drag to create a second one.

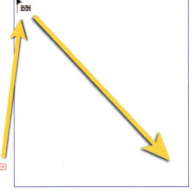

Lorem ipsum dolor sit amet, consectetur adipiscing elit. Phasellus mattis quam facilisis metus tristique dignissim. Aliquam eget nunc at elit imperdiet cursus. Morbi at dui elit. Vestibulum gravida venenatis gravida. Ut rhoncus vestibulum eros sed posuere. Ut aliquet, nisi vitae egestas tristique, turpis magna fermentum elit, ut cursus lacus justo ut magna. Quisque ac purus dui, a pulvinar felis. In vel ligula justo, non ullamcorper magna.

Vestibulum ante ipsum primis in

TYPE ON A PATH

In Illustrator you can also create text that flows along an open or closed path. To do this, use the Type tool, Type on a Path tool, Vertical Type tool, or Vertical Type on a Path tool, depending on your preference. Click on any defined path and start typing. See Figure 7–13.

At some point, you might need to move text along its path and adjust its orientation (i.e., bend text around an ellipse). To move text along a path, first create the path, and then select it with the Selection tool. A bracket appears at the beginning, middle, and end of the path. Place your cursor over the middle bracket until a little icon that looks like an upside-down T appears. Click and drag on the middle bracket to move the path. See Figure 7–14 and Figure 7–15. The brackets on each end of the type line adjust the distance between the beginning and end of the typed line. See Figure 7–16. Be aware that moving the brackets at the start and end points toward the type will make it disappear. If this occurs, pull the brackets back out.

> Note: *As you adjust the path using the brackets, avoid clicking on the little boxes, or ports, at each end of the line. This initiates the threaded area type option discussed in the previous section.*

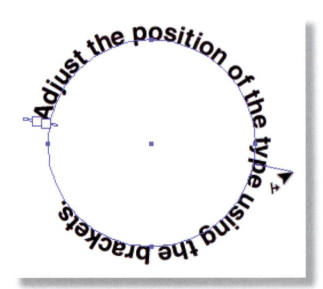

FIGURE | 7–14 | and FIGURE | 7–15 |

Select, then move, the middle bracket to adjust the text on a path.

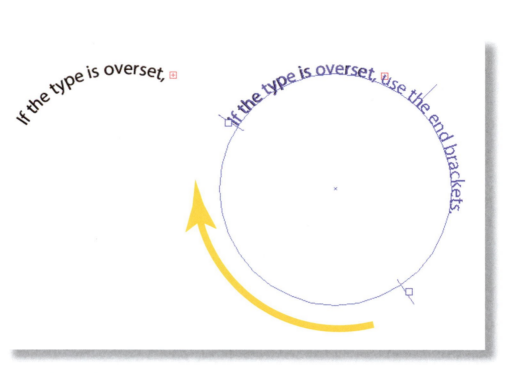

FIGURE | 7–16 |

If all the text isn't showing (overset), use the Selection tool and move the end
bracket to adjust the distance between the beginning and the end of the text line.

Of course, there are more goodies to tinker with in the Type on a Path Options box.
Select some type on a path and choose Type > Type on a Path > Type on a Path
Options, or double-click the Type tool in the Tools panel. See Figure 7–17. I highly
recommend selecting Preview in this box and exploring the different options available.

FIGURE | 7–17 |

The Type on a Path Options window.

TYPE TIPS

There are a couple of miscellaneous things you should know about creating type. You can use either the Type tool or the Area Type tool to create type within a text field or shape—clicking on the edge of any shape will automatically toggle the Type tool to the Area Type tool. By the same token, you can click on a path with the Type tool—it automatically shifts into Path Type mode.

You can also create area type within an open path rather than a closed shape by using the Area Type tool. See Figure 7–18.

Another somewhat odd thing about creating type is that, usually inadvertently, empty type paths represented by an anchor point are created when you click the Type tool in the artwork area and then choose another tool. To clean up these stray type markings and containers, choose Object > Path > Clean Up and select the Empty Text Paths option. See Figure 7–19. To delete all unnecessary anchor points in a file, choose Select > Object > Stray Points.

The Type tool is "sticky" and will continue to type on the same line or in the same field until you either click on the Type tool in the Tools panel, or Command click (Mac) or Ctrl click (Windows) away from the text. Once you've done that, you can click with the tool to start typing somewhere else.

FIGURE | 7–18 |

You can use the Area Type tool along an open path to create an unusual margin along one side.

FIGURE | 7–19 |

Use Object > Path > Clean Up to delete any inadvertently placed text points.

FORMATTING TYPE

You have probably formatted plenty of text in word processing programs—selected typefaces and sizes, used the bold and underline options, copied, pasted, and justified paragraphs, and worked with letter and line spacing. These familiar formatting options are also available in Illustrator.

FIGURE | 7–20 |

The Character panel used to format type.

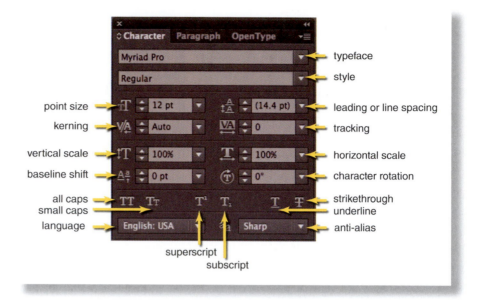

To format specific characters, such as style and size, leading, tracking, and kerning, choose Window > Type > Character to bring up the Character panel. To modify familiar paragraph options, such as paragraph justification and indentation, use the Paragraph panel, which is usually grouped with the Character panel. See Figure 7–20 and Figure 7–21. To access more options for both panels (by default they are hidden), open the options submenu (in the upper-right corner of the panel) and select Show Options. In addition, most commonly used character and paragraph features can be found in the Control panel for any selected text object. Definitions for some of the formatting options, such as tracking, leading, and kerning, are provided in the section Designing with Type.

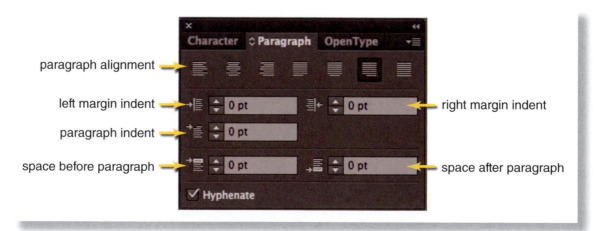

FIGURE | 7–21 |

The Paragraph panel used to format type.

Another kind of formatting that is somewhat specific to Illustrator is changing the appearance of type. You can change the basic fill color or stroke of type by selecting the text and changing the color, as you would any object, from the Control panel, Color panel, or by double-clicking on the Fill or Stroke box in the Tools panel. Using this same method, you can also change transparency, effects, and graphic styles. See Figure 7–22.

If you want to apply a gradient to text, you must convert the text to outlines (the underlying path structure and shape of each letter) before assigning a gradient color to it. To do this, select the text path, choose Type > Create Outlines, and then apply the gradient. See Figure 7–23. Creating outlines is also a necessary step if you want to manipulate the individual anchor points of a letterform, or need to use text in a custom art or pattern brush. Be aware that once you have converted type to outlines, character and paragraph options for the type are no longer available. You will not be able to fix typos either, so make sure you proofread the text carefully first!

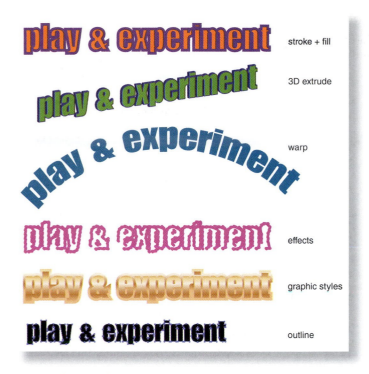

FIGURE | 7–22 |

There are an infinite number of ways to play with text. Just be careful not to compromise the message by using inappropriate options!

FIGURE | 7–23 |

The top line indicates text when normally selected. Below is the text selected after converting it to outlines. The bottom image is what it looks like with a gradient fill.

THE STORY OF FONTS AND TYPEFACES

Before we start discussing the ins and outs of working with type, it's important to clarify the difference between fonts and typefaces. It's true that the terms "font" and "typeface" are used more interchangeably than in the past, due to the way software programs render textual content. And, in this book, you will find these terms used interchangeably at times. Nevertheless, it's important to understand the distinction. A typeface is the design of the letters—what the type looks like. Serif, sans serif, stroke weight, the size relationships between lowercase letters and capitals, and many more features are considered and developed to create each letter form or character in a single typeface. A font is the actual "thing" that creates the type digitally. It is the software that enables the application to display the typeface onscreen.

Fonts are funky. If you have worked with type on a computer, you have experienced the quirks (or, rather, the frustration) of fonts—that is, the digital code that creates the letters themselves. Suppose, for example, you find the perfect typeface—the design of the letters—"Groovalicious Tweak," and use it extensively in a document. You send the document to a friend who tries to open it on his or her computer. However, a warning comes up indicating "Groovalicious Tweak" font is nowhere to be found. Furthermore, unless otherwise specified, the missing font will be substituted with Times New Roman (or something like that), and . . . so much for your typographic vision. This predicament occurs when one computer has a font installed and the other does not. To avoid this, designers often send font files along with their documents or embed (save) the fonts within the document.

Typefaces often come in families—a group of similarly designed typesets. For a particular typeface within a family, you can choose a style, such as bold, italic, or medium. In Illustrator, you can select typefaces in digital font formats like TrueType and OpenType (see the next section below Font Formats) using the Character panel (Window > Type > Character) or the Type menu (Type > Font). Each typeface family has a name, sometimes derived from the artist who first created the design. For example, Figure 7–24 shows some of the typeface designs in the Photina family.

Photina Regular
Photina Italic
Photina Semibold
Photina Semibold Italic
Photina Bold
Photina Bold Italic
Photina Ultra Bold
Photina Ultra Bold Italic

The Photina typeface family, designed by José Mendoza y Almeida.

TrueType and OpenType (see next section below Font Formats) using the Character panel (Window > Type > Character) or the Type menu (Type > Font). Each typeface family has a name, usually derived from the artist who first created the design. For example, Figure 7–26 shows some of the typeface designs in the Helvetica family.

FONT COPYRIGHT

Unless you use license-free fonts (freeware), fonts are protected by copyright law. Using someone else's font requires permission, just as when you use someone else's image or photograph. Even though you have the ability in Illustrator to embed (save a font's outlines for viewing in other applications), select, and format any font installed on your computer, that doesn't necessarily mean you have the right to showcase it in your Illustrator creations. This is especially true if your work is designed for commercial purposes. You are reminded of this fact when you save a document and a font embedding notification pops up. See Figure 7–25. Play it safe, and contact the creator of the font to determine whether a given font can legally be embedded and used in your document. You can often find the font creator's information in the Read Me files or in documentation that accompanies the font before installation. You can also select the font's filename, and Ctrl-click > Get Info (Mac), or right-click > Properties (Windows) for information on that particular font.

Note: *From AIGA, the professional association of design: "When necessary, it is acceptable for font data to be embedded in file formats such as EPS and PDF for printing and previewing purposes." For more information see http://scripts.sil.org/cms/scripts/page .php?site_id=nrsi&id=UNESCO_Font_Lic*

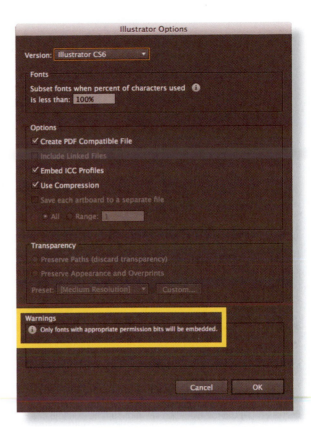

FIGURE | 7–25 |

Depending on their license agreements, fonts used in your artwork might prompt the font embedding notification when you go to save the document.

FONT FORMATS

Just as there are different ways in which a device, such as a computer or printer, renders a digital image (i.e., as bitmapped pixels or vectored outlines), so it is for fonts. A font's format, generally speaking, provides the instructions for how a digitized font is either printed on paper, presented on screen, or both. As is the nature of technology, font formats have evolved quickly over time, and it behooves us to have some understanding of the current font technologies.

Interestingly, in the 1980s it was Adobe Systems that made the most significant advancements in how computers handle text. It started with PostScript, a page description language that stores objects or glyphs (character shapes on a page or screen) not as fixed resolution bitmaps but as programmatically defined outlines or shapes. The nice thing about PostScript-derived glyphs is that they can be reliably recreated at any size. In other words, it does not matter if you choose 12-point type or 72-point type; the document will always look crisp and clean when you print it.

To some extent, each of the three most common font formats uses PostScript. These are Type 1, TrueType, and OpenType.

- ▶ *Type 1*: A resolution-independent digital font type that can translate a font from the screen to a high-quality font in print. Adobe is the original designer and manufacturer of Type 1 and maintains its standards. However, other companies have designed and released their fonts using the Type 1 format. Type 1 fonts are commonly used by graphic designers whose work specifically goes to print.

- ▶ *TrueType*: The standard for digital fonts. It was first developed by Apple Computer Corporation and subsequently licensed to Microsoft Corporation. Each company has made independent extensions to this format, some of which can be used on either or both Windows and Macintosh operating systems. Within a single font format, TrueType has the ability to translate fonts for print and screen, avoiding the bitmapped look when size and resolution are changed. TrueType fonts are great for graphic designers who create work for both print and screen (i.e., CD-ROM and Web).

- ▶ *OpenType*: This type was developed jointly by Adobe and Microsoft. It is currently the most sophisticated form of font technology. It is an extension of the TrueType font.

OpenType fonts have several advantages over previous font types. One, they are cross-platform compatible, meaning you can use a single font file for both Macintosh and Windows computers—no more font substitution issues. Also, they can support expanded character sets and languages, because they contain more variations of glyphs in a single font set, including nonstandard ones like old-style figures, fractions, ligatures, and alternate characters (letters with swashes, for instance).

OpenType has opened new doors for typographers, providing better control over type layout and design. Illustrator CS6 supports OpenType layout features with OpenType-formatted fonts. A single character in the OpenType format can have several glyph (shape and symbol) variations to broaden its linguistic and typographic options. For example, variations on the number "2013" in the font Warnock Pro (an OpenType font) could be alternated as you see in Figure 7–26, using the OpenType panel (Window > Type > OpenType).

To view and choose glyphs for any currently selected font format, choose Type > Glyphs. For the glyphs available for the font Myriad Bold (a Type 1 formatted font) and Warnock Pro (an OpenType formatted font), see Figure 7–27. The OpenType version has many more glyph variations.

It is easy to identify a font's format, whether Type 1, TrueType or OpenType. When you select a font, choose Type > Font or Window > Type > Character. To the left of each font name you have installed on your computer is a small icon indicating the font type. See Figure 7–28.

2013 small capitals
2013 "typical"
2013 numerators
2013 denominators
2013 superscript
2013 subscript

FIGURE | 7–26 |

Example of glyphs for numbers in Warnock Pro, which is an Open Type font.

Figure © Cengage Learning 2013

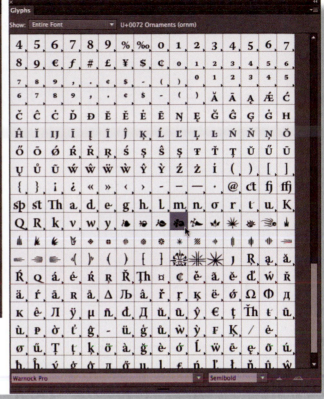

FIGURE | 7–27 |

Part of the glyphs list for Myriad Bold (Type 1) and Warnock Pro. Many typefaces designated as "Pro" are Open Type fonts.

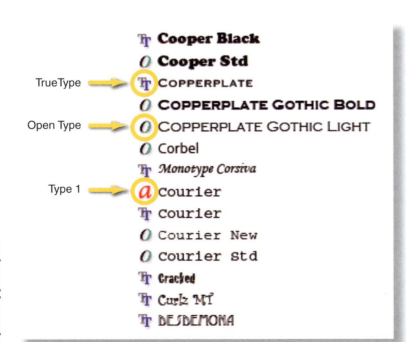

FIGURE | 7–28 |

An example of part of the font list installed on Toni's computer. Notice the icons next to the font names indicating the font's format: "TT" indicates a TrueType font, "O" indicates an OpenType font, and "a" indicates a Type 1 font.

FONT COMPATIBILITY

As you encountered in the "Groovalicious Tweak" situation, fonts go missing when they are used in a document but are unavailable on a computer system. For easy identification, Illustrator highlights missing fonts. See Figure 7–29. You can then use the Find Font command (Type > Find Font) to replace the missing fonts with

FIGURE | 7–29 |

If a font is not installed, Illustrator warns you, and if you choose the Highlight Substituted Fonts option in Document Setup, then Illustrator will highlight any type that is affected.

installed ones or identify the missing fonts so you can install them. Choose whether to highlight the substituted fonts or glyphs, as well as choose other global Type options with the Document Setup dialog box under File > Document Setup. See Figure 7–30.

Another thing that merits mention is the issue of legacy text. The term legacy in Illustrator refers to earlier versions of an Illustrator file format. Thus, legacy text refers to text used in earlier versions of the program. Because Illustrator (since version CS2) has a more efficient way of dealing with text composition, called the Adobe Text Engine, legacy text must be updated before you can edit it. When you open an Illustrator file created in an older version, a dialog box asks if you would like to update

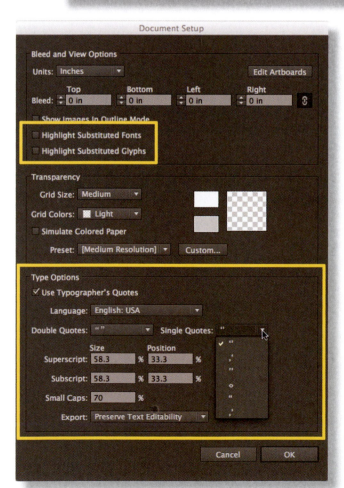

FIGURE |7–30|

Select File > Document Setup to open the Document Setup diallog box and access the Type options.

any legacy text in the document. If you choose to update, slight variations in the text layout might occur; however, you can then edit the text. If you choose not to update, the legacy text will be preserved (indicated by an "X" in its bounding box when selected) and can be viewed, moved, and printed, but not edited. See Figure 7–31.

LESSON 1: RECIPE CARD

Note: *When an original font is not available, it is possible to outline the text, thus changing the letters into vector objects. Be wary of copyright infringements, however.*

In this lesson, you experience creating type and applying formatting options while constructing a graphically pleasing recipe card. Figure 7–32 is a visual reference of the completed file.

FIGURE | 7–31 |

Type created in older versions of Illustrator is considered Legacy text. Choose Update it if you need to edit it in any way.

FIGURE | 7–32 |

The completed Recipe Card lesson.

FIGURE | 7–33 |

The Tulip Cafe logo is an example of type on a path.

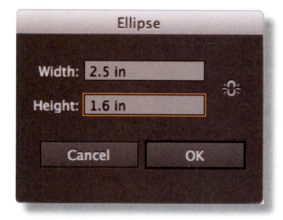

FIGURE | 7–34 |

Specify an exact size for the ellipse.

FIGURE | 7–35 |

Fit the ellipse shape over the logo.

Setting Up the File

1. In Illustrator, open **chap7L1.ai** file in the folder **chap07_lessons**.

2. Make sure your workspace is set to Essentials.

3. Choose View > Fit All in Window.

4. Open the Layers panel. Be sure the **text on a path** layer is highlighted. Notice the other layers are locked (indicated by the lock icon to the left of the layer name), so you cannot accidentally select or place items in those layers.

Creating Type on a Path

1. Let's create some type on a path that looks like that shown in Figure 7–33. Use the Zoom tool to zoom in on the tulip logo in the upper-left corner of the document (look familiar?).

2. Select the Ellipse tool in the Tools panel. Click once over the logo to open the Ellipse tool options Type **2.5 in** for Width and **1.6 in** for Height. See Figure 7–34. Click OK. The ellipse shape will be created on the document.

3. Choose None for the fill color of the ellipse, then position it so it fits over the tulip logo. See Figure 7–35. Remember that the ellipse object can be moved either by clicking and dragging directly on the outline or by using the up/down and left/right arrow keys.

> **Note:** *To move a selected object in larger increments, press the Shift key while using the up/down and left/right arrow keys.*

4. Cut the ellipse shape into two sections: a top section to create one line of curved text and a bottom section for the other line of curved text. First select the ellipse, then select the Scissors tool in the Tools panel. See Figure 7–36.

5. Place the cursor over the anchor point on the left side of the ellipse shape and click the anchor point to cut the path. Do the same on the anchor point on the right, breaking the shape into two halves. See Figure 7–37.

> **Note:** *When you attempt to click over an anchor point to cut it with the Scissors tool, a warning box might come up as follows: "Please use the Scissors tool on a segment or an anchor point (but not an endpoint) of a path." This warning comes up when you have not directly clicked on a segment or anchor point on the selected path. Exit the warning box and try again.*

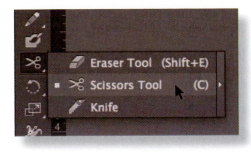

Figures © Cengage Learning 2013

FIGURE | 7–36 |

The Scissors tool is used to cut paths.

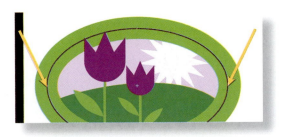

FIGURE | 7–37 |

Cut the ellipse in half using the Scissors tool.

6. Choose Window > Type > Character to open the Character panel. For Font type and style, choose **Arial Black.** If that's not available, use Arial and set the style to Bold. For font size, enter **19 pt**. See Figure 7–38.

> Note: *If Arial Black is unavailable, choose another font to play with, such as Helvetica or Verdana.*

FIGURE | 7–38 |

Format the type in the Character panel.

7. Now you are ready to type some text on the defined paths. Select the Type on a Path tool in the Tools panel. See Figure 7–39. Then click on the top line segment of the ellipse you just cut in half to convert the path into a text path. A blinking cursor will appear on the path line.

8. Type **TULIP HILL CAFE.**

9. In the Control panel, click on the Align Center icon next to the word *Paragraph* to center the text on the path. See Figure 7–40.

10. Adjust the alignment of the text. Choose the Selection tool in the toolbox and select the text path. Click and drag the middle bracket to the right or left until it is centered along the path. See Figure 7–41.

11. Use the Control panel to set the fill to white and the stroke to none.

12. Choose Type > Type on a Path > Type on a Path Options. In the options box, choose Preview to view changes directly on the document. Take a moment to explore the Type on a Path Options. What does the 3D Ribbon Effect do? How about the Align to Path and Spacing options? Once you have explored all the options, set the type to the following specifications then click OK to exit the options window.

> ► *Effect*: Rainbow
>
> ► *Align to Path*: Center
>
> ► *Spacing*: 0 pt

FIGURE | 7–39 |

Select the Type on a Path tool.

FIGURE | 7–40 |

Choose the Align Center option to center the text.

FIGURE | 7–41 |

Center the text line on the path.

13. With the Type on a Path tool, click on the lower segment of the ellipse you cut in half.

14. Type **SYRACUSE** along the path. Adjust the text alignment, position, and color of this lower segment the same way you did with the top segment of text. Refer back to Figure 7–33 for an example of the final result.

> Note: *If your type appears upside down, you might need to use the Flip option in the Type on a Path Options window to fit the text upright on this lower path.*

15. Save the document; name it **chap7L1_yourname.ai**.

Creating Type in an Area

1. Choose View > Actual Size to see the whole document.

2. Open the Layers panel.

3. Lock the **text on path** layer. To do this, click on the blank box to the left of the layer's name and a lock icon will appear.

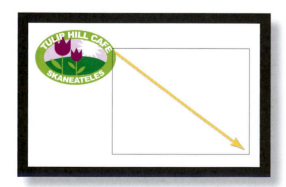

FIGURE | 7–42 |

Use the guides to click and drag a text field.

4. Unlock the **logo** layer. To do this, click on the lock icon to the left of the layer's name.

5. Select the **logo** layer. You are going to build a text block in this layer. The reason for doing this, rather than creating a new layer, is to prepare for a later step. Eventually you will wrap the text block around the logo image, and to do this, both objects need to be on the same layer.

6. Select the Type tool in the Tools panel.

7. Click and drag a text field that spans two columns; use View > Guides > Show Guides to help you position the top-left corner, as well as determine the width. See Figure 7–42 for the approximate height.

Figures © Cengage Learning 2013

FIGURE | 7–43 |

Imported text filling
a defined area.

PREPARATION
Mix together oil, water, freshly squeezed lemon juice, bay leaf, garlic,
peppercorns and salt in a large stainless steel saucepan. Bring to a boil
over medium-high heat. Reduce heat, cover and simmer for 15 minutes.
Strain using a sieve (or remove garlic and peppercorns using a slotted
spoon) and return to a simmer over low heat.
Drop the mushrooms and roasted pepper into the simmering marinade, stirring gently from time to time, for about 2-4 minutes. If the
mushrooms are very small, remove from heat after just 1 minute.
Remove pan from heat and allow to stand, uncovered, while the
mushrooms cool.
Serve at room temperature or refrigerate in a plastic container. Refrig-
erator for up to 2 to 3 days.
After mushrooms have marinated, taste and adjust seasonings; after a
day or two, you may want to add fresh herbs for an extra layer of
flavor, since the marinated herbs will have mellowed, imparting their
flavor to the oil. Remove bay leaf before serving.

8. Let's put some text in the text block. Make sure a blinking cursor is at the top-left part of
the text block. If not, choose the Type tool and click in the upper-left corner of the text
block to initiate the blinking cursor.

9. Choose File > Place from the menu bar. Look for **chap7_lessons/assets** and select the
recipe.docx text file. Click Place, and leave the Microsoft Word options at their default.
Click OK. The text should fill the defined area. See Figure 7–43.

10. Select the text box with the Selection tool, then choose Type > Area Type Options. Enter
2 for Columns Number (see Figure 7–44), and then click OK.

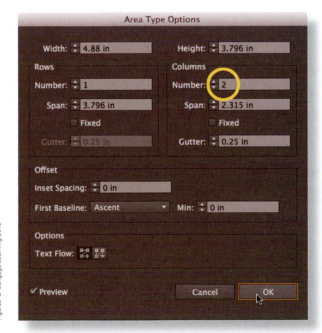

FIGURE | 7–44 |

Create two columns in
the Area Type Options.

FIGURE | 7–45 |

The text will overlap the logo a bit. Not to worry.

11. The text will overlap the logo image. You will fix this in the next exercise. See Figure 7–45.

12. Save your file.

Wrapping Text Around an Object

When wrapping text around an object, the text and object must be on the same layer. In addition, the text block needs to be positioned below the objects you want it to wrap around. Let's fix this.

1. Open the Layers panel. Expand the **logo** layer. Select the sublayer with either no label or the word "PREPARATION" (this is the type you just placed), then click and drag it underneath the logo group sublayer. See Figure 7–46.

2. Select the logo image in the document or select the sublayer **logo group** in the **logo** layer.

3. Choose Object > Text Wrap > Make from the menu bar and click OK when Illustrator tells you what's going to happen. Notice that the text now wraps around the logo. Choose Object > Text Wrap > Text Wrap Options and set the Offset to **6 pt**. Click OK.

FIGURE | 7–46 |

Move the text layer below the layers that make up the logo graphic.

Note: *If the text does not wrap around the image, select the logo again, choose Object > Text Wrap > Release, then repeat steps 1 through 3. See Figure 7–47.*

4. Save your file.

Formatting the Text

1. Select the two-column text block with the Selection tool. Then, with the Type tool, click on some text in the text block and choose Select > All from the menu bar to select all of the recipe text.

2. In the Control panel or Character panel (Window > Type > Character), enter **Arial Regular** for Font Type and Style and **10 pt** for Size.

3. We need to do a bit more formatting to make this easier to read. With the Type tool, locate the beginning of each paragraph and add a return. Look at Figure 7–48 to see where those line breaks should occur.

4. Add a few extra returns before the text "Remove pan…" so it lines up with the first line of the instructions. See Figure 7–48.

FIGURE | 7–47 |

The text block wraps around the edge of the logo graphic.

Mix together oil, water, freshly squeezed lemon juice, bay leaf, garlic, peppercorns, and salt in a large stainless steel saucepan. Bring to a boil over medium-high heat. Reduce heat, cover and simmer for 15 minutes.

Strain using a sieve (or remove garlic and peppercorns using a slotted spoon) and return to a simmer over low heat.

Drop the mushrooms and roasted pepper into the simmering marinade, stirring gently from time to time, for about 2–4 minutes. If the mushrooms are very small, remove from heat after just 1 minute.

Remove pan from heat and allow to stand, uncovered, while the mushrooms cool.

Serve at room temperature or refrigerate in a plastic container. Refrigerate for up to 2 to 3 days.

After mushrooms have marinated, taste and adjust seasonings; after a day or two, you may want to add fresh herbs for an extra layer of flavor, since the marinated herbs will have mellowed, imparting their flavor to the oil. Remove bay leaf before serving.

FIGURE | 7–48 |

Use the Type tool to insert paragraph breaks.

Note: *You might be wondering why we are using such an unexciting (yet versatile and easily readable) font family such as Arial. It is mainly for compatibility purposes when working through this lesson. Whether you are working on a Mac or Windows, you will most likely have the ever-so-common Arial font installed. If, by chance, you do not, or you prefer to use a different typeface for this lesson, that is perfectly acceptable. Just be aware that different type styles will vary in size and shape and might affect the text layout of this particular lesson. And that's OK. For now, it is all about exploring the tools.*

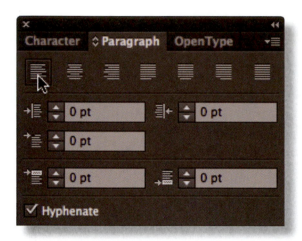

FIGURE | 7–49 |

Align the text using the Paragraph panel.

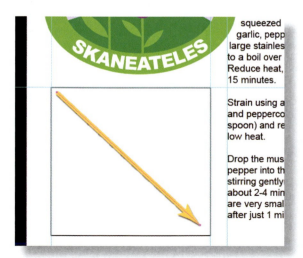

FIGURE | 7–50 |

Create a text area for the ingredients.

5. Click and drag through the word "PREPARATION" with the Type tool. In the Character panel (Window > Type > Character), enter **Arial, Bold and set the size to 11 pt.**

6. Change the color of the word "PREPARATION." Select the Eyedropper tool and click on one of the tulips in the logo to make the selected text purple.

7. Click on the Paragraph panel tab (docked with the Character panel). Make sure the selected text is set to Align left. See Figure 7–49.

8. We can't really make these mushrooms without knowing the ingredients! With the Type tool, click and drag a text area between the first column's guides. See Figure 7–50.

9. Use File > Place and place the ingredients.docx file, found in chap07_lessons > assets > ingredients.docx. Leave the Microsoft Word default options as they are and click OK.

10. Click anywhere inside the text area with the Type tool, and from the Menu bar, choose Select > All, or use the Command A (Mac), Ctrl A (Windows) shortcut. Delete any extra line spaces at the top of the text field.

11. Use the Control panel to set the Character to Arial, the Style to Regular, and the size to 8 pt. Then click on the Align Center option.

12. With the Type tool, add a line space between the word "INGREDIENTS" and the olive oil.

13. Highlight the word "INGREDIENTS" with the Type tool, and then select the Eyedropper tool in the Tools panel.

14. Click on the word "PREPARATION" with the eyedropper. The Eyedropper will sample the color, as well as the typeface, point size, and style. Nice!

15. Oops. With "INGREDIENTS" still highlighted, choose the Align Center option in the Control panel again.

16. One small detail remains; click the Selection tool, and then use the right arrow key to move the text area to the right a bit so it's centered under the logo. See Figure 7–51.

17. Save your file.

Adding a Headline

1. Choose Select > Deselect to deselect any items on the document.

2. Select the Type tool and click the I-beam to the right of the logo just above the two-column text block. Check the Control panel and reset the paragraph format to flush left, if necessary. Type in the recipe name: **Italian Marinated Mushrooms**. Refer back to Figure 7–32.

3. Highlight the recipe name. In the Character panel, enter **Arial Black** (or **Arial Bold**, if you don't have **Arial Black**), and **19 pt** for size. Leave Kerning and Leading set to **Auto**. Set Tracking to **−31**. At the bottom of the Character panel, click on the TT icon to make the title all capital letters.

4. Select the recipe name with the Selection tool and position it so that the top of the letters is aligned with the top guide, and the left is aligned with the PREPARATION column. See Figure 7–51.

5. Let's add some color to the title. While it's still selected, open the Gradient panel, make sure the fill option is forward, and click on the down arrow next to the black-and-white gradient. See Figure 7–52.

6. Remember, gradients can't be applied to type. To solve this problem, select the text with the Selection tool so the baseline is visible, then choose Type > Create Outlines to convert the text to compound paths and shapes.

7. Select the gradient swatch called greens in the Swatches panel. The text should be filled with the gradient color.

> **Note:** *Once you convert type to outlines, it loses its instructions for character and paragraph adjustments. Therefore, it is advisable to set the formatting options for your type and spell check before converting to outlines.*

8. While all the letters are still highlighted, select the Gradient tool and click and drag from the top of the letters to the bottom. Zoom in if necessary to see what you're doing.

9. Save your file.

FIGURE | 7–51 |

The centered and formatted ingredients text.

FIGURE | 7–52 |

The type won't fill with a gradient until it's converted into outlines.

FIGURE | 7–53 |

Use the greens gradient swatch to fill the letters and the Gradient tool to adjust it.

FIGURE |7–54 |

Apply a Graphic Style to the border.

Adding the Final Look

1. Open the Layers panel, collapse the **logo** layer and lock it, then unlock the **border** layer.

2. Select the white outline.

3. Open the Graphic Styles panel, and then click on the panel's options icon at the top right. Choose Open Graphic Style Library > Other Library, and navigate your way to the assets folder in the **chap07_lessons** folder. Open the graphicstyles.ai file.

4. Select the third border style to apply it to the white stroke. See Figure 7–54.

5. Choose Select > Deselect.

6. Open the Symbols panel (via Window > Symbols, or in the Dock, click the icon that looks like a club). Click on the tulip symbol to select it.

7. Select the Symbol Sprayer tool in the Tools panel, then click and drag to create several tulips at the lower right.

8. Take some time to play with the Symbol Sprayer Modifier tools under the Symbol Sprayer.

9. When you're pleased with the results, save your file. The recipe card is complete.

DESIGNING WITH TYPE

Like color, type evokes a look and feel. And like designing with color, designing with type is an endless adventure in exploring options for the "tone of voice" of the message it communicates, either in print or on the Web. With that in mind, there are several fundamental "rules" regarding typography that should never be broken until you have mastered them.

When given a visual comparison of what works "well enough" and what works "really well" in typography, it is easy to see the difference between an amateur- and professional-looking document. See Figure 7–55 and Figure 7–56 to get an idea of what we mean. A few simple type style and formatting changes make all the difference.

When working with type, take into account the text's readability and visual impact, specifically the formatting and flow of the type for readability, and the use of contrast and appropriate font selections for visual impact. Following is a list of typography tips to ensure that your typography is readable and to create the appropriate "voice" for your message. Compare and contrast these suggestions with the two visuals of the Tulip Cafe business cards (Figure 7–55 and Figure 7–56).

Tulip Hill Cafe

Elizabeth Alexanders, Master Chef

315 555 1234 (800 555 1234)
www.tulipcafe.com
liz@tulipcafe.com
15 Ocean View Way, Santa Monica, CA 12345

FIGURE | 7–55 |

A business card design that could seriously use some layout and typographic improvement.

SPACING AND ALIGNMENT

Line Length

Have you ever started to nod off reading a book? Chances are, it wasn't just a bad plot or boring subject that put you to sleep. It could be due to long lines of type that are difficult to read and cause fatigue and eyestrain. Your eyes get so tired that they can't find the beginning of the next line, and you start reading the same one over and over again. And too-short lines of text can break up the text flow, so you need to find the right balance. The accepted rule of thumb is that a line of type should have 55 to 60 characters, or approximately 9 to 10 words, for optimal readability. The actual width of the line would vary, depending on the size of the type.

Leading or Line Spacing

Leading refers to the space between lines of type. It is measured in points from baseline to baseline. Depending on the typeface used, leading can vary for optimal readability. See Figure 7–57.

Word and Letter Spacing

▶ **Tracking:** The process of adjusting the space between characters in a block of text. See Figure 7–58. The spacing between words and letters is a subtle thing that can really improve text legibility. Most typefaces available today are designed with correct spacing between characters. However, you might find yourself wanting to adjust these defaults if, for example, you want to work with ALL CAPS or type that is larger than 18 points.

▶ **Kerning:** An even subtler variation of character spacing, kerning refers to the space between two letters. For most letters, kerning is relatively uniform; however, in some cases, such as with A and V, kerning must be adjusted to appear consistent and more readable. See Figure 7–59. Kerning is also very useful when working with decorative type in large headlines.

TULIP HILL CAFE

Elizabeth Alexanders
Master Chef

315 555 1234 (800 555 1234)

www.tuliphillcafe.com
liz@tuliphillcafe.com
15 LakeView Way
Skaneateles, NY 12345

FIGURE | 7–56 |

A business card design that works better—is more visually appealing and readable—when simple typographic design principles are applied.

Sed eu dui non lorem vestibulum ultrices sed non orci. Maecenas sed lectus urna. Integer tempus elit urna. Nullam molestie elit eu ligula ultrices venenatis. Phasellus et congue nisl. Integer erat orci, congue a semper pellentesque, vulputate non augue. Aenean semper tellus vitae urna bibendum viverra. In ac urna tortor.

Sed eu dui non lorem vestibulum ultrices sed non orci. Maecenas sed lectus urna.

Integer tempus elit urna. Nullam molestie elit eu ligula ultrices venenatis. Phasellus

et congue nisl. Integer erat orci, congue a semper pellentesque, vulputate non

augue. Aenean semper tellus vitae urna bibendum viverra. In ac urna tortor.

Sed eu dui non lorem vestibulum ultrices sed non orci. Maecenas sed lectus urna. Integer tempus elit urna. Nullam molestie elit eu ligula ultrices venenatis. Phasellus et congue nisl. Integer erat orci, congue a semper pellentesque, vulputate non augue. Aenean semper tellus vitae urna bibendum viverra. In ac urna tortor.

FIGURE | 7–57 |

Type that has too little or too much line spacing is difficult to read. Use the Character panel or the Control panel to adjust it.

Sed eu dui non lorem vestibulum ultrices sed non orci. Maecenas sed lectus urna. Integer tempus elit urna. Nullam molestie elit eu ligula ultrices venenatis. Phasellus et congue nisl. Integer erat orci, congue a semper pellentesque, vulputate non augue. Aenean semper tellus vitae urna bibendum viverra. In ac urna tortor.

Sed eu dui non lorem vestibulum ultrices sed non orci. Maecenas sed lectus urna. Integer tempus elit urna. Nullam molestie elit eu ligula ultrices venenatis. Phasellus et congue nisl. Integer erat orci, congu.

Sed eu dui non lorem vestibulum ultrices sed non orci. Maecenas sed lectus urna. Integer tempus elit urna. Nullam molestie elit eu ligula ultrices venenatis. Phasellus et congue nisl. Integer erat orci, congue a semper pellentesque, vulputate non augue. Aenean semper tellus vitae urna bibendum viverra. In ac urna tortor.

FIGURE | 7–58 |

Tracking is the process of adjusting the space between all the characters in a block of text.

Note: *Setting the kerning in the Character panel to Auto often will work just fine. However, you should check what your text selection looks like using the Optical option. Optical kerning automatically adjusts the spacing between two selected characters based on their shapes. Kerning and tracking manually are absolutely essential for point sizes larger than 18.*

a curved letter and a straight one require typical spacing

balloon

two curved letters should be very close

two straight letters need more space between them

FIGURE | 7–59 |

Kerning is the process of adjusting the space between two letters.

▶ DON'T GO THERE

The differences between tracking and kerning are so subtle that novice designers often get the two terms confused. Tracking provides global spacing of words and letters, whereas kerning works between two specific characters.

Justification

Justification is the alignment of lines of text or text blocks. Documentation with lots of text is usually formatted with a left justification—aligned to the left margin (flush left) and ragged on the right. You can also choose to align text to the right margin (flush right) with the left side ragged; however, the resulting text is not as easy to read. For a more formal look, all lines might be justified on both the right and the left sides (no ragged edges). Often, newspaper or magazine articles have this type of look. Centered justification works well with small amounts of copy. See Figure 7–60.

FLUSH LEFT Sed eu dui non lorem vestibulum ultrices sed non orci. Maecenas sed lectus urna. Integer tempus elit urna. Nullam molestie elit eu ligula ultrices venenatis. Phasellus et congue nisl. Integer erat orci, congue a semper pellentesque, vulputate non.

FLUSH RIGHT Sed eu dui non lorem vestibulum ultrices sed non orci. Maecenas sed lectus urna. Integer tempus elit urna. Nullam molestie elit eu ligula ultrices venenatis. Phasellus et congue nisl. Integer erat orci, congue a semper pellentesque, vulputate non.

CENTERED Sed eu dui non lorem vestibulum ultrices sed non orci. Maecenas sed lectus urna. Integer tempus elit urna. Nullam molestie elit eu ligula ultrices venenatis. Phasellus et congue nisl. Integer erat orci, congue a semper pellentesque, vulputate non.

JUSTIFIED Sed eu dui non lorem vestibulum ultrices sed non orci. Maecenas sed lectus urna. Integer tempus elit urna. Nullam molestie elit eu ligula ultrices venenatis. Phasellus et congue nisl. Integer erat orci, congue a semper pelle tesque, vulputate non.

FIGURE | 7–60 |

Examples of justification.

FONT SELECTION AND SIZE

Proportional vs. Fixed Pitch

Fonts are distinguishable by their style and the way in which their individual letters and characters are spaced. Spacing of characters can be either fixed pitch (also called fixed-width or mono-spaced) or proportional. A fixed-pitch font is usually what is defined as a typewriter font, where each character takes up the same amount of space and is representative of how old-style typewriters used to reproduce letterforms. Modern digital type and printable text are generally designed using proportional spacing, where each letter is given just the amount of space it needs to look visually appealing and legible. Proportional fonts can be formatted better on a page and actually improve readability over fixed-pitch fonts. See Figure 7–61.

FIXED WIDTH Sed eu dui non lorem vestibulum non orci. Maecenas sed lectus urna. Integer Nullam molestie elit.

FIXED WIDTH Sed eu dui non lorem vestibulum non orci. Maecenas sed lectus urna. Integer Nullam molestie elit.

PROPORTIONAL Sed eu dui non lorem vestibulum ultrices sed non orci. Maecenas sed lectus urna. Integer tempus elit urna. Nullam molestie elit.

PROPORTIONAL Sed eu dui non lorem vestibulum ultrices non orci. Maecenas sed lectus urna. Integer tempus elit urna. Nullam molestie elit.

FIGURE | 7–61 |

Examples of fixed-pitch (mono-spaced) and proportionally spaced fonts.

SERIF Sed eu dui non lorem vestibulum non orci. Maecenas sed lectus urna. Integer Nullam molestie elit.

SERIF Sed eu dui non lorem vestibulum non orci. Maecenas sed lectus urna. Integer Nullam molestie elit.

SANS SERIF Sed eu dui non lorem vestibulum ultrices sed non orci. Maecenas sed lectus urna. Integer tempus elit urna. Nullam molestie elit.

SANS SERIF Sed eu dui non lorem vestibulum ultrices non orci. Maecenas sed lectus urna. Integer tempus elit urna. Nullam molestie elit.

Serif vs. Sans Serif

It is important to know the difference between serif and sans-serif type styles because both types play a vital role in the readability of either print or Web-based documents. Serif typefaces are letterforms with "feet" or cross lines at the ends of each letter stroke. Sans-serif fonts do not have these "feet." Serif typefaces usually have a more formal look, whereas sans-serif typefaces often look bolder and more modern. See Figure 7–62.

For printed documents containing lots of text, serif typefaces such as Times New Roman, are easier to read. This is why

FIGURE | 7–62 |

Examples of serif and sans-serif font faces.

newspapers traditionally use serif type styles for their copy. For screen-based text, like that on a Web site, sans-serif typefaces are recommended, such as Arial, Helvetica, or Verdana. This is especially true when working with type sizes that are less than 12 points (the little "feet" of certain serif fonts get lost when the text is viewed on a lighted screen). Using a combination of serif and sans-serif type styles in a layout provides contrast and a design hierarchy. It's important to stick with just two or three font families or typefaces to avoid confusing the viewer and hampering readability. For Web page designs, for example, you might use a serif family for the topic headings and a sans-serif family for the body copy (main text areas). On the other hand, in the business card example (refer to Figure 7–56), which will be printed, notice that a sans-serif font (Arial Black) is used for the business title while a serif font (Goudy Old Style) is used for the address and contact information.

Contrast

To really put some "oomph" in your type design, the principle of contrast is critical. Contrast is when something is different from something else, and it is commonly used in design to heighten visual impact. Here are six characteristics of type that can be manipulated to create contrast; notice how these characteristics are used or not used to produce contrast in the two business card examples.

- ▶ **Size:** Font size variation offers contrast, such as a 20-point headline above 10-point body text.
- ▶ **Weight:** Most font families and font formatting options come in varying weights for the purpose of providing contrast, such as medium, light italic, bold, or condensed versions. See Figure 7–63.
- ▶ **Structure:** Within a layout, a combination of serif and sans-serif fonts offers contrast.
- ▶ **Form:** Form implies a font's shape. For example, a good contrast of form would be uppercase type set against lowercase type.
- ▶ **Color:** Type color can make a huge impact on a design, especially how it might contrast with a colored background or other colored objects. Be sure there is sufficient contrast when working with colored copy, such as white text on a black background or dark blue text on a white background. Avoid combinations like yellow text on a white background, or dark blue text on a black background. Whenever using light type on a dark background (for print, especially), consider using a bold version, which will prevent thin strokes and serifs from disappearing.
- ▶ **Direction:** You can change the direction of text to provide contrast. For example, put text on a curved path, slant it, or place it sideways (not stacked!) along a page.

Gill Sans Light
Gill Sans Regular
Gill Sans Bold
Gill Sans Ultra Bold

FIGURE | 7–63 |

Provide contrast with variations of font weight rather than using several different typefaces.

Figure © Cengage Learning 2013

SUMMARY

One of Illustrator's great strengths is its ability to work with type, offering you ample flexibility and versatility for creating, formatting, and managing type. With such control over typography you can focus on the often-overlooked subtleties of type design, and watch your design work transcend from amateur to professional.

▶ IN REVIEW

1. What tool do you use to type at a point? To type in an area? To type on a path?

2. What does the command Type > Create Outlines do? When would you use it?

3. Name three font formats and describe their characteristics.

4. What has happened when your document is missing a font?

5. What is legacy text?

6. When wrapping text around an object, the object and text must be on the same layer. Does the text need to be below or above the object in the layer stack?

7. Describe the difference between serif and sans serif type.

8. Define leading, kerning, and tracking.

9. Name at least four general design tips for working with type.

10. What should you do when you use someone else's font in your commercial artwork?

▶ EXPLORING ON YOUR OWN

1. Choose Help > Illustrator Help and read the topic Type.

2. Illustrator CS6 comes loaded with an array of templates you can use for basic layouts, such as cards and postcards, business sets, and stationery. In Illustrator, choose File > New From Template… and explore the various templates provided. Some of them are already designed; others are blank templates with common layout sizes you can use as a starting point. The Illustrator template format is .ait, and you can find templates under Templates > Blank Templates. Using your newfound typography skills, create your own logo design (or other layouts) using one of these templates.

Note: *To save your own layouts for repeated use, choose File > Save As Template… You will work more with layout in Chapter 8.*

3. Adobe is a leader in digital type technologies, and it provides a wealth of information on type, such as type design, terminology, and typeface licensing and copyright FAQs, on its Web site *http://www.adobe.com/type.*

4. There are plenty of places online where you can buy fonts and font symbols (image glyphs such as Dingbats) in just about any style you can imagine. However, there are also many places that offer fonts for free use, usually with only a minimum requirement of crediting the font creator. Do a search for "free fonts" on the Web.

5. Explore the topics of "typography" and "typographic design" online. Good places to start are *http://ilovetypography.com* and *http://www.alistapart.com/*

6. Open a magazine or a Web browser and put on your typographer's hat. Critique the text you see —analyze its design, visual impact, and legibility. What simple things would you do to improve text that is difficult or perhaps even "boring" to read? Adjust the leading (line spacing)? Change the font? Change the color? Make it bigger or smaller? Become a type critic.

7. Visit some fun online sites that use typographic design with Flash animation; for example, *http://evan-roth.com/typo_illus.php.* Select the sites with the word "typo" in the title.

Explorer PAGES

Michael Fleishman

"Drawing and painting! I can't help myself; I gotta do it. It has been this way since I can remember. As a kid, drawing— and by extension, painting— was a sheer joy. As a student, drawing and painting (said in one breath) was MY thing. Teaching (and writing about these creative endeavors is the shared, continued joy of that rich, multilayered, and incredibly satisfying experience. I tell my students and readers that drawing/painting is THE thing."

About Michael Fleishman

A Day in the Life

"Good morning, good morning," says Michael Fleishman. "I feel fine." And from me to you, Fleishman also feels that he's a lucky guy (eight days a week)—he's always had a direction.

Born and raised in Pittsburgh, PA, he wasn't a particularly motivated student, and certainly no football hero. But he *was* a distinctly dedicated rock-and-roller. These days, it's a little hard for him to carry that weight, but he still plays. "My wife tells me I have too many guitars," he smiles, "But, oh! darling, we can work it out."

Yeah yeah yeah. Growing up, Mike's dream was to do exactly what he's doing right now, his art was his ticket to ride. Ultimately, he let it be in the Steel City, and his little piggies eventually led him to Yellow Springs, OH. "From this little matchbox of a town I've scribbled with folks here, there, and everywhere. And my writing career was established here, as well. The book gig is the direct offspring of my illustration career. I wouldn't have predicted that I'd be a paperback writer ... but get back, here I am—maybe I'm amazed just a bit, ya know?"

He was a contributing editor at *The Artist's Magazine*, and has written for a variety of publications, including *How Magazine, Step Inside Design, Computer Arts Projects* (UK), and the *Artist's and Graphic Designer's Market*. Mike is the author of two earlier books for North Light (now out of print), followed by *Starting Your Career as a Freelance Illustrator*

or *Graphic Designer* (Allworth Press, 2001), *Exploring Illustration* (Thomson/Delmar, 2004), and *How to Grow as an Illustrator* (Allworth Press, 2007).

However, that was yesterday. "My book, *Drawing Inspiration: Visual Artists at Work* (Cengage), is just out," he tells us. "This full-color, 400-page text was done with a little help from my friends: 188 international contributors and 465 illustrations. It was a long and winding road; I'm so tired ... this was indeed the most monumental—but most gratifying—project of my career."

Mike has always enjoyed dual passions—the doing and teaching of art. For the last eight years, he's taught both Graphic Design and Fine Arts at Edison Community College in Piqua, OH (where he's also Program and Staff Coordinator). At ECC, he's been honored to receive a regional SOCHE Excellence in Teaching award (2006), as well as a national teaching excellence award from NISOD (2004).

He was a featured presenter at DesignWorld, How's annual conference in 2002, the NISOD annual conference in 2004, and ICON 4 (the National Illustration Conference) in 2005. "I've been a visiting artist at Kendall College of Art and Design plus a guest lecturer at Savannah College of Art and Design, and Minneapolis College of Art and Design. I'm currently serving on the board of directors for ICON6."

Hey bulldog, if you can tell him how many Beatles song titles are in this bio, this boy might give you a prize. It may only be a badge or something, but tomorrow never knows. The end.

 Learn more about Mike at www.michaelfleishman.com

About the Work of Michael Fleishman

In his words, Michael shares with us the inspirations for this work. Also, see Michael's Adventures in Design at the end of Chapter 9. "What encourages ... encourages an artist to make a drawing? As a kid, a box of crayons and a blank sheet of paper was probably all you needed. You didn't have to work at it. But today, drawing may be your work. Artists are not really born with a silver pencil in their mitts. You *want* to draw. You *have* to draw. You *go for it* and draw every day. You *improve* over time.

I can speak to what makes the *vocation* of Illustration a perfect job for me—it's the joy of it. If this job isn't enjoyable—first and foremost—why do it? There are other ways to break a sweat, save the world, or just make money (and, yes, more money than an illustration gig). Drawing is just plain *fun*. And do understand that the world of Illustration is a business of people. Realize that you don't live in a vacuum.

Now, 'fun' is certainly a great motivator, but even the most enjoyable gig can beg for inspiration. Don't discount the inspiration of sheer *energy* and *work*—blood, sweat, and tears—plus *passion* (another critical muse). If one is working on an interesting project that inspires great passion, you may not need much motivation. Adrenaline and excitement are prime movers and shakers. But if you can't connect in some way, it might be a totally different story.

The chapter spots (see Figure 1) from my book, *How to Grow as an Illustrator* (Allworth Press), are ganged together to discuss *linear character*: process, concept, and product. The theme of the book is, well, *growing*—developing—as a viable professional (and maybe we should make that, a *whole* professional, which actually means you're growing as a whole *person*). This idea is advanced by the very organic nature of these drawings—in style, execution, and concept.

While these are digital drawings done in Adobe Illustrator, I push a softer, natural line quality. The 'lines' are actually tweaked, brushed

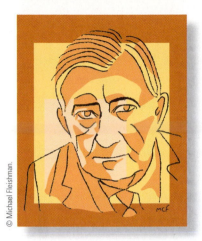

Figure 2: Portrait of Josef Albers, from Mike's book *Drawing Inspiration: Visual Artists at Work*.

strokes, of course. Leaves grow in number to reflect chapter position (1 leaf for Chapter 1 to the 15 leaves of Chapter 15). Stems sway or contort to become actual chapter numbers. Sprouts and grounded seedlings accumulate to the number of the next chapter. This is purposely subtle—I like the idea that an illustration can prompt a viewer to work a little for a bigger pay off.

This direct thread of concept to style and composition also factors into my portrait of Josef Albers, Mrs. Albers' Boy, Joe (see Figure 2) from my book, *Drawing Inspiration: Visual Artists at Work* (Cengage). Here I gently nod to Albers color theory, lightly touching on his *Homage to the Square*.

Finally, as a point of contrast and comparison, I include a much older digital illustration: *Topp Dawg* (see Figure 3). It's more a hybrid, actually: drawn by hand with a hairline pen nib on a napkin (at a decidedly tiny scale, I must add); scanned in at somewhere between 200 to 600 percent (my standard ballpark to achieve instant and marvelous, wonderfully craggy line quality); line finessed in Photoshop; then placed in Illustrator for the color plate.

Figure 1: Chapter spots from Mike's *How to Grow as an Illustrator* book.

Figure 3: Topp Dawg.

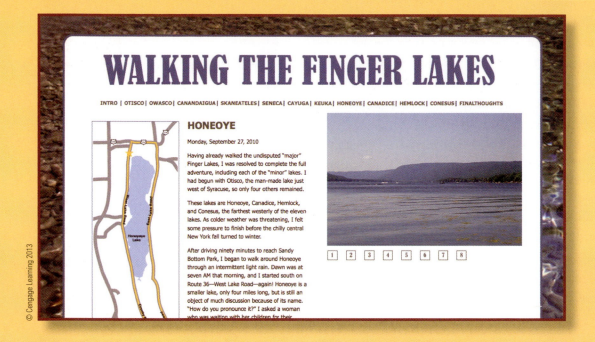

WALKING THE FINGER LAKES

HONEOYE

Monday, September 27, 2010

Having already walked the undisputed "major" Finger Lakes, I was resolved to complete the full adventure, including each of the "minor" lakes. I had begun with Otisco, the man-made lake just west of Syracuse, so only four others remained.

These lakes are Honeoye, Canadice, Hemlock, and Conesus, the farthest westerly of the eleven lakes. As colder weather was threatening, I felt some pressure to finish before the chilly central New York fall turned to winter.

After driving ninety minutes to reach Sandy Bottom Park, I began to walk around Honeoye through an intermittent light rain. Dawn was at seven AM that morning, and I started south on Route 36—West Lake Road—again! Honeoye is a smaller lake, only four miles long, but is still an object of much discussion because of its name. "How do you pronounce it?" I asked a woman who was waiting with her children for their

| 1 | 2 | 3 | 4 | 5 | 6 | 7 | 8 |

| Object Composition |

8

charting your course

You have learned the basic components of drawing in Illustrator: creating lines and shapes with the Pen tool, and then enhancing objects using value, texture, color, and type. The next step is to combine, group, and organize objects to produce more complex and complete illustrations or graphic layouts. This process is called composition. In this chapter, you will explore features for combining paths and shapes, such as grouping, the Pathfinder panel, and clipping masks. You also will explore the process for creating a layout, which introduces you to the organization and elements of composition in design. In addition, you will work with layers and layout tools, such as rulers, guides, and grids, as well as extensive information on importing content. Finally, you will venture further and build a layout for a Web page.

goals

In this chapter you will:

- ▶ *Get a handle on grouping objects*
- ▶ *Create compound paths and shapes using the Pathfinder panel*
- ▶ *Reveal artwork using clipping masks*
- ▶ *Develop an understanding of design composition*
- ▶ *Learn workflow and organizational techniques for developing compositions and layouts*
- ▶ *Learn what works when importing content*
- ▶ *Gain practical experience working with layers*
- ▶ *Practice working with rulers and guides*

COMBINING PATHS AND SHAPES

So far, you have been drawing simple paths and shapes. Now you will learn how to get more complex with your object construction through the process of combining (or compounding) paths and shapes. This is something Illustrator does very well through the use of grouping, the Pathfinder panel, and clipping masks.

GROUPING

Grouping objects is easy, and you might be familiar with it from other programs. It is a common way to consolidate objects so they can be manipulated as a single unit. To create a group, select the objects you want to include and choose Object > Group. See Figure 8–1. To release a group, select the grouped object with the Selection tool and choose Object > Ungroup.

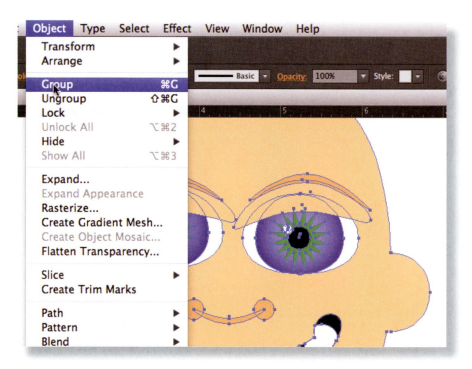

FIGURE | 8–1 |

Create a group.

If you create a group from a series of objects on several layers, when you choose Object > Group, the objects are combined into a single layer and named <Group> on a sublayer. When you open the grouped layer, each individual item is stacked in sublayers. See Figure 8–2. The Layers panel then allows you to select either the whole group or the individual sublayers. You can also select and modify individual objects within a group by using the Group Selection or Direct Selection tool in the Tools panel. To modify the stacking order of a group—how objects are arranged in front of or behind each other—select an individual object using the Group Selection tool, and choose Object > Arrange. See Figure 8–3 and Figure 8–4. You can also arrange the stacking order of objects that are not grouped, so long as they are on the same layer.

> Note: *The feature named "Drawing Modes," located at the bottom of the Tools panel, allows you to Draw Behind or Draw Inside selected art objects. For more information on Drawing Modes, see Exploring on Your Own section, #2, at the end of this chapter.*

If you like to keep things organized, especially when you have many objects overlapping, you can group grouped objects (called nesting). For example, let's say you draw a face. First, you group the two eyes together so you can move them around easily. Then you choose the head, nose, mouth, and the grouped eyes and make them into a larger group that can then be selected as a whole. To practice this idea, complete Lesson 1: Creating Groups.

FIGURE | 8–2 |

The individual parts of a grouped object are available in sublayers.

FIGURE | 8–3 |

The Group Selection tool selects individual parts of a group.

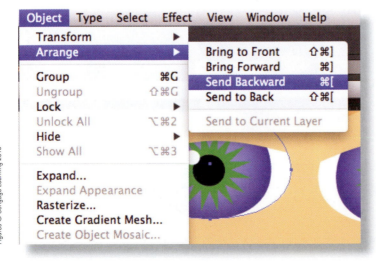

FIGURE | 8–4 |

You can select elements within a group and rearrange their stacking order using Object > Arrange.

Figures © Cengage Learning 2013

COMPOUND PATHS, SHAPES, AND THE PATHFINDER PANEL

Using the geometric shape tools and creating simple paths with the Pen tool will not cut it when constructing more complex objects. You need to be able to combine these simple paths and shapes into new and different objects. There are various ways to do this in Illustrator. When constructing more complex shapes, you may not get the result you want on the first try. It usually takes some experimentation with the available tools in Illustrator to get things right.

As a point of reference, it is important to understand the difference between a simple path or shape in Illustrator versus compound paths and shapes. See Figure 8–5. You have been working with simple paths and shapes. A compound path is comprised of objects that overlap and create a "window" or negative space at that point. Think of it like punching a hole in a shape. A compound shape is a combination of two or more objects—they appear to be a single element, yet each part is still editable in some ways. See Figure 8–5.

To create a compound path, select two or more objects and choose Object > Compound Path > Make. To release the paths, select them and choose Object > Compound Path > Release.

A compound shape is composed of two or more paths, compound paths, groups, blends, text, or other compound shapes that intersect one another to create new and editable shapes. To create a compound shape, select the desired paths, choose

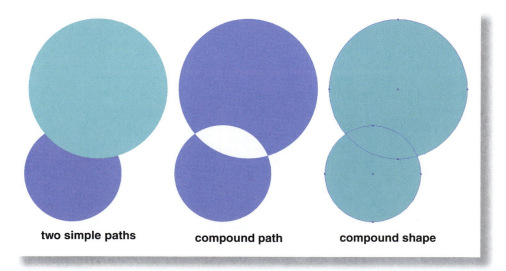

two simple paths   **compound path**   **compound shape**

FIGURE | 8–5 |

Identify simple paths and shapes versus compound paths and shapes.

Window > Pathfinder, and, in the submenu of the Pathfinder options, choose Make Compound Shape. See Figure 8–6. To release, choose Release Compound Shape.

Understanding the difference between a compound path and a compound shape can be confusing. The bottom line is that the individual elements in a compound shape can be manipulated separately. This difference makes sense when looking in the Layers panel. Objects merged into a compound path create a single layer or sublayer. However, objects within a compound shape are contained in a single layer or sublayer, but each part is editable in sublayers or sub-sublayers. See Figure 8–7.

Commands to combine compound paths and shapes are available in the Pathfinder panel (Window > Pathfinder) or from Effect > Pathfinder. The Pathfinder panel contains two sections of commands: Shape Modes and Pathfinders. Shape Modes allow you to add, subtract, intersect, and exclude objects. Pathfinders allow you to divide,

FIGURE | 8–6 |

Make a compound shape.

FIGURE | 8–7 |

View a compound path and compound shape in the Layers panel.

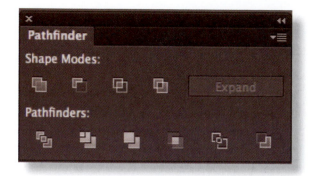

FIGURE | 8–8 |

The Pathfinder panel.

trim, merge, crop, outline, and subtract objects. See Figure 8–8 and Figure 8–9, and the Pathfinder examples in Figure 8–24. The Expand option in the Pathfinder panel maintains the shape of the compound object, but you can no longer select the individual components.

Generally, expanding an object is useful when you want to modify the appearance attributes and other properties of specific elements within it, when you have created an object that is native to Illustrator and need to import it to a different program, or if you are finding that the attributes assigned to the object (i.e., transparency, gradients, or blends) are presenting printing difficulties. For more details on each Pathfinder combination, choose Help > Illustrator Help, go to Index, and look for information on Pathfinder effects. You also get to explore the Pathfinder exclusively in Lesson 2: Hands-on with the Pathfinder Options.

The Pathfinders in the Pathfinder panel are filters, which are not editable, unlike effects, in the Appearance panel. However, Pathfinder effects in the Effects menu are editable. To use the Pathfinder effects, first group selected paths or shapes. Choose Object > Group, then choose Effect > Pathfinder and the Pathfinder option of your choice.

Note: *Illustrator also provides a Shape Builder tool. With this tool, you can select overlapping shapes and quickly merge or subtract shape areas. See more about the Shape Builder tool and how to use it in Exploring on Your Own at the end of this chapter.*

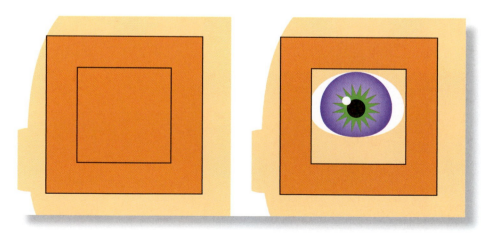

FIGURE | 8–9 |

Create a compound shape using the Subtract option in the Pathfinder panel.

CLIPPING MASKS

Masking is a universal concept in graphic design. A mask is an object that hides or reveals other objects. A mask in Illustrator is referred to as a clipping mask, which can be a vector object or group whose shape becomes like a window that reveals other objects or artwork behind it. See Figure 8–10 and Figure 8–11. You will make masks in Lesson 3: Clipping Masks.

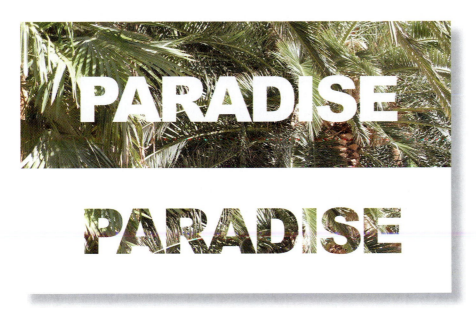

FIGURE | 8–10 |

Before and after Object > Clipping Mask > Make is applied.

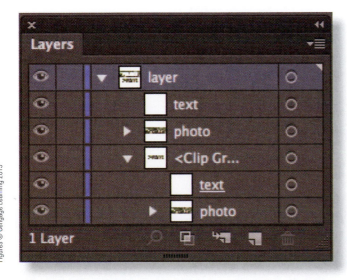

FIGURE | 8–11 |

A clipping mask's object resides on the same layer or sublayer.

What you should know about clipping masks:

► Only vector objects can be masking objects, such as a path, a compound shape, a text object, or a group of these. However, they can mask any type of artwork, such as bitmapped photographs or other vector objects.

► The masking object must reside above or in front of the object being masked.

► Masked objects are moved into the clipping mask's group in the Layers panel if they do not already reside there.

► When an object is converted to a clipping mask, it loses all its previous attributes and is assigned no fill or stroke.

► When using more than one vector object as a mask, the objects must first be converted into a single compound path or shape.

LESSON 1: CREATING GROUPS

This lesson will familiarize you with grouping and how grouped objects are indicated in the Layers panel. Your completed file will look like Figure 8–12.

FIGURE | 8–12 |

The completed file.

Setting Up the File

1. Open the file **chap8L1.ai** in the folder **chap08_lessons**.

2. Make sure your workspace is set to Essentials.

3. Select the Zoom tool and magnify the funny face.

Grouping Face Parts

1. With the Selection tool, Shift-click the teeth and the mouth shape. Do not select the head. See Figure 8–13.

2. Choose Object > Group to group the two pieces.

3. Deselect all by clicking on a blank area of the artboard or choosing Select > Deselect.

> Note: *To test if the objects are grouped, use the Selection tool to move the mouth section around and see if both pieces move as one.*

4. Use the Selection tool and Shift click to select all the eye pieces—the pupils, eyeballs, and eye color. See Figure 8–14.

5. Choose Object > Group to group the parts.

> Note: *If you made a mistake in your grouping, choose Object > Ungroup to release the grouped state.*

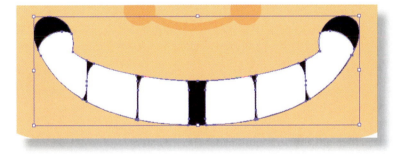

FIGURE | 8–13 |

Select the teeth and the mouth shape.

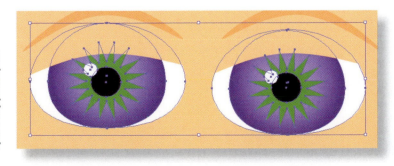

FIGURE | 8–14 |

Select all parts of the eyes.

FIGURE | 8–15 |

Select all the face pieces using the Layers panel.

FIGURE | 8–16 |

The Group Selection tool.

FIGURE | 8–17 |

Name the layers.

6. Select each piece of the face, including the mouth group, eye group, eyelids, and head. The easiest way to do this is to Shift click on the circles next to each sublayer in the Layers panel. See Figure 8–15.

7. Choose Object > Group to consolidate the objects and groups into one larger group. This becomes a "nested group" or "groups within a group"—an even more detailed way to organize a file.

> Note: *The shortcut key command to group is Command G (Mac) or Ctrl G (Windows).*

8. Deselect everything by clicking on a blank area of the artboard.

9. To maintain the "groupness" of the objects and yet select individual parts of the whole for modification or adjustment, use the Group Selection tool (hidden under the Direct Selection tool). See Figure 8–16.

10. With the Group Selection tool, practice selecting individual parts of the face.

11. Save the file. Name it **chap8L1_yourname.ai**.

Examining Groups in the Layers Panel

1. Choose Window > Layers.

2. Expand the layer named **face**. Then expand the sublayer named <**Group**>. Notice the groups within groups.

3. Double-click on the topmost group title within the **face** layer (<**Group**>), and rename the whole group **face**.

4. Within the **face** group, name any unnamed groups or sublayers. See Figure 8–17. Naming layers and sublayers is the only way to keep track of what's where. You can probably imagine the complexity of the Layers panel in a more detailed illustration!

Figures © Cengage Learning 2013

5. Collapse the subcategories of the **face** layer to save room in the Layers panel. See Figure 8–18.

Creating a Jester Hat

1. Choose View > Fit All in Window.

2. Unhide the layer named **jester hat**.

3. Zoom in on the half-completed jester hat drawing.

4. Select the colored sections of the jester hat. See Figure 8–19.

5. Choose Object > Group.

6. Make a duplicate for the other side of the hat, and flip it into place in one step. First, select the Reflect tool (hidden under the Rotate tool) in the Tools panel. See Figure 8–20.

FIGURE |8–18|

Collapse the subcategories of a layer.

FIGURE | 8–19 |

Select the colored sections of the jester hat.

FIGURE |8–20 |

The Reflect tool.

7.   Next, hold down the Alt/Option key and click in the center of the hat (on the left edge of the orange area) to open the Reflect options box.

> **Note:** *The yellow arrow in Figure 8–19 indicates where to click.*

8.   In the Reflect options box, choose Vertical and click the Copy button (do not click OK). See Figure 8–21. A flipped copy of the half-jester-hat is created. See Figure 8–22.

FIGURE |8–21|

Create a flipped copy of an object using the Reflect tool.

FIGURE |8–22|

A new copy is created to the left of the first half.

> **Note:** *If necessary, you can move the new copy into place incrementally by selecting it with the Selection tool and then clicking the right/left or up/down arrow keys (hold Shift to move in larger increments). To adjust the increment distance, choose Illustrator > Preferences > General (Mac) or Edit > Preferences > General (Windows) and enter an amount in the Keyboard Increment option.*

9. Select both halves, and choose Object > Group, or Command G (Mac) or Ctrl G (Windows).

10. Select the grouped halves, the middle star, and the blue rim, and choose Object > Group to create one larger group. See Figure 8–23.

Finishing the Character

1. Choose View > Fit All in Window and position the jester hat above the funny face.

2. To complete the character, unhide the layer named **glasses** in the Layers panel.

3. Let's group all the parts of the glasses. Expand the **glasses** layer to see the parts.

4. In the Layers panel, click on the target icon of the **glasses** layer (right side). Notice that the parts of the glasses are also selected in the layer's sublayers and in the document.

5. Choose Object > Group to consolidate the pieces.

6. Save and close your file.

FIGURE | 8–23 |

Click the target icons in the Layers panel to select all the parts of the jester hat.

LESSON 2: HANDS-ON WITH THE PATHFINDER OPTIONS

The best way to learn the options for constructing compound paths and shapes is to play with each shape mode and pathfinder variation in the Pathfinder panel. For an example of this lesson, see the Pathfinder panel variations in Figure 8–24.

Setting Up the File

1. Open the file **chap8L2.ai** in the folder **chap08_lessons**.

2. Make sure your workspace is set to Essentials.

3. Zoom in on the first set of fish under the Shape Modes heading. See Figure 8–25.

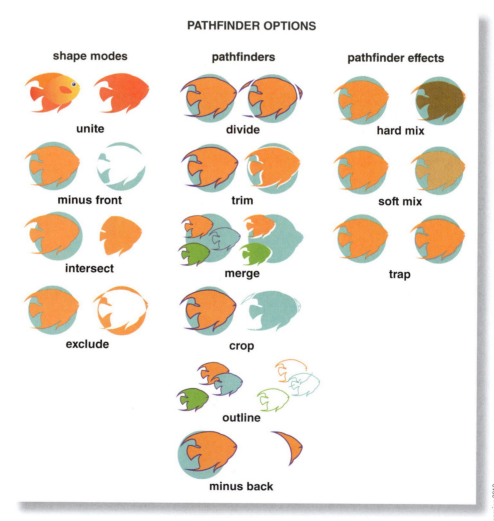

PATHFINDER OPTIONS

shape modes · pathfinders · pathfinder effects

unite · divide · hard mix

minus front · trim · soft mix

intersect · merge · trap

exclude · crop

outline

minus back

FIGURE | 8–24 |

Variations of shapes that have been modified using the Pathfinder. Note that there are three additional options under Effects Pathfinder.

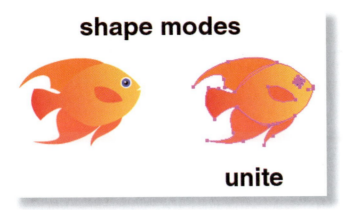

FIGURE | 8–25 |

Zoom in on the first set of fish.

Exploring the Shape Modes

1. Select all the parts of the fish above the Unite label.

2. Choose Window > Pathfinder. In the Pathfinder panel, choose the Unite option. See Figure 8–26.

3. The fish parts merge. The Unite option merges the selected objects into a single element. The paint attributes (stroke and fill) from the frontmost object (the fish's gill) are applied to the new object.

4. Select the fish and circle above the Minus Front label.

5. Choose the Minus Front option in the Pathfinder panel. This option subtracts the frontmost objects from the backmost object. Use this command to delete areas of an object, much like a cookie cutter.

6. Select the fish and circle above the Intersect label.

7. Choose the Intersect option in the Pathfinder panel. This option deletes portions of the top object that are not overlapping the base object and leaves only the

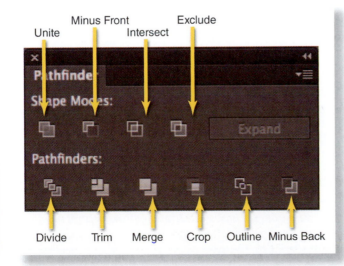

FIGURE | 8–26 |

The Pathfinder panel options.

overlapping parts. The paint attributes of front-most objects are applied to the new object.

8. Select the fish and circle above the Exclude label.

9. Choose the Exclude option in the Pathfinder panel. With Exclude, any portions of the selected elements that overlap become transparent—a compound path in a way, except that each shape becomes a separate element rather than overlapping objects.

Exploring the Pathfinders

1. Choose View > Fit All in Window.

2. Zoom in on the upper-right side of the document to see the first fish under the Pathfinders heading.

3. Select the fish and circle above the Divide label.

4. Choose the Divide option in the Pathfinder panel. This option divides overlapping areas of selected paths into separate, nonoverlapping closed paths or lines. The new objects maintain their original fill and stroke attributes. To get a better idea of how the division works, select and pull apart the divided sections with the Group Selection tool.

5. Select the fish and circle above the Trim label.

6. Choose the Trim option in the Pathfinder panel. With Trim, the frontmost object is preserved, whereas parts of the object(s) behind it and overlapping it are deleted. Objects retain their original fill attributes, and stroke colors are deleted. Once again, pull the trimmed areas apart to see the effect.

7. Select the fish and circle above the Merge label.

8. Choose the Merge option in the Pathfinder panel. Using Merge causes all the objects to divide into separate pieces, except for any that have the same fill color as the backmost object. Other fill attributes are not changed, and strokes are deleted. Pull the merged areas apart to see the effect.

9. Select the fish and circle above the Crop label.

10. Choose the Crop option in the Pathfinder panel. With Crop, the back object acts like a cookie cutter, eliminating any portion(s) of the front object that extend outside the edges. The cropped object's fill color changes to match the backmost object.

11. Select the fish above the Outline label.

12. Choose the Outline option in the Pathfinder panel. Nothing tricky here— filled objects turn into stroked objects. The fill colors of the original objects become the stroke colors, and the fills are removed. If the shapes are overlapping, this option will divide them where they intersect.

Note: *If you cannot see the stroke lines, it is possible that the stroke weight needs to be readjusted in the Stroke panel (Window > Stroke) or in the Control panel.*

13. Select the fish and circle above the Minus Back label.

14. Choose the Minus Back option in the Pathfinder panel. This option subtracts the backmost selected object from the frontmost objects. Anything that overlaps the frontmost objects is deleted. The paint attributes of the frontmost objects are applied to the new object. The objects must partially overlap for this command to create an effect.

15. Save and close your file.

LESSON 3: CLIPPING MASKS

Clipping masks are commonly used and easy to create, as you will learn in this lesson.

Setting Up the File

1. Open the file **chap8L3a.ai** in the folder **chap08_lessons**.

2. Choose View > Actual Size.

3. Open the Layers panel.

Creating the Mask Effect

1. Expand the **mask 1** layer in the Layers panel. Notice there are two sublayers: the **text group** and a **photo group**.

2. Expand the **text** sublayer. Each letterform is in its own layer and labeled as a compound path rather than type. To turn type into compound paths, as in this example, select the type and choose Type > Create Outlines.

> Note: *Creating compound paths from type can be useful when you want to work with the type as an image, need it to be compatible with certain printers, or when you do not want to worry about whether the proper font is installed to render the type correctly. It is not necessary to convert type to outlines when working with clipping masks; it was set up like this in this lesson in case you did not have the correct font on your computer.*

3. Select the text in the document with the Selection tool.

4. Choose Object > Compound Path > Make to convert the letterforms into one compound path. This is necessary when you are using more than one object in a mask in this case, multiple letterforms.

5. Select the text (now invisible) and the photo. To do this, either drag a marquee with the Selection tool around everything, or Shift click each target icon of each sublayer in the **mask 1** layer panel.

6. Choose Object > Clipping Mask > Make. The photo is revealed through the letters.

7. Notice in the Layers panel that both pieces are in a clip group layer. See Figure 8–27.

8. Select the photo by clicking on its target icon in the Layers panel.

9. With the Selection tool, move the photo around in the document. Notice that it stays behind the text mask.

10. Save this file in your lessons folder and then close it.

Creating Another Clipping Mask

1. Open the file **chap8L3b.ai** in the folder **chap08_lessons**.

2. Choose View > Actual Size.

3. Select the Star tool (hidden under the Rectangle tool) in the Tools panel. See Figure 8–28.

4. Press the D key to set the default fill and stroke options (white for fill, black for stroke) if they are not already selected in the Tools panel.

5. Click and drag over the water to create a star shape. Remember that you can add more points to the star by tapping the up arrow key as you draw.

6. Create two more stars over the photo. See Figure 8–29.

7. Choose the Selection tool. Shift click the stars and choose Object > Compound Path > Make to combine the three shapes into a compound group.

FIGURE | 8–27 |

Both parts of the clipping mask are grouped under one layer.

FIGURE | 8–28 |

Create several stars with the Star tool.

FIGURE | 8–29 |

Create stars.

8. Select the compound group (the stars) and the photograph, and choose Object > Clipping Mask > Make.

Note: *To release the mask, choose Object > Clipping Mask > Release.*

9. Choose Select > Deselect. Select the Group Selection tool (hidden under the Direct Selection tool) and practice adjusting individual parts of the mask or the photo underneath.

Note: *Selecting the spirals stars can be tricky, since there is no fill or stroke associated with them. You must click directly on a path edge to select it. See Figure 8–30. You can also choose View > Outlines as a way to select the paths more easily.*

10. Save the file in your lessons folder.

Figure © Cengage Learning 2013

FIGURE | 8–30 |

You can move the star and the photo as a group by selecting it with the Selection tool, or move only the star using the Group Selection tool.

ABOUT COMPOSITION

Author Otto G. Ocvirk and contributors define composition best in their book *Art Fundamentals: Theory and Practice*—"An arrangement and/or structure of all the elements, as organized by principles, that achieves a unified whole. Often used interchangeably with the term 'design.'" Reflect for a moment on things in your life that seem compositionally complete—your car, your house, the flower in the vase sitting on your table, your favorite TV commercial, or a song. These things came to being through the combination of predefined elements of design. See Figure 8–31.

For graphic or multimedia designers, the elements derived are from those in visual art. We have studied these explicitly through the use of Illustrator—line, shape, value, texture, and color. How these elements are organized brings about the sense of completeness in a drawing or layout. In traditional art study, the principles of organization include concepts such as harmony, variety, proportion, dominance, movement, and economy. The study of these concepts and their effective interaction with one another is more than we can get into in a book about Illustrator, but is not to be overlooked in your own study of visual art and graphic design. In this section, you will be introduced to a general process by which to organize and produce a compositionally sound design. You'll also learn about some of the tools available in Illustrator for organization and workflow.

FIGURE | 8–31 |

Composition is everywhere—in the design of clothing, buildings, signage, or a mosaic of ceramic tiles.

THE LAYOUT PROCESS

The creative process comes to fruition in many ways. Typically, it starts with the identification of an objective, whether it's to design a pair of slippers or a logotype. The second step, sometimes referred to as incubation, is the often unconscious process of letting ideas drift through your mind. Illumination follows—you have an idea (or several) and start to shape those ideas as rough sketches. Refinement, in the shape of tight, or comprehensive, sketches, comes next. The final piece requires creating and/ or assembling materials or content and digitally preparing them for production.

Start with an Idea

No matter what process you follow, a design always starts with a vision or idea. Sometimes the idea is perfectly realized in your mind, and it is simply a matter of getting it into a tangible form. Other times, the idea is enhanced or modified as you go through the design process. Either way, you have to start with an idea—and something that drives you to make it "real."

Make a Comprehensive Layout (Comp)

The next step is to put your idea into tangible form or comprehensive layout or comp. Comps help to visualize what an overall design will look like before you begin the development stages. Often a comp starts as a series of cursory sketches (called thumbnails), then it is refined into a more detailed drawing. A professional

FIGURE | 8–32 |

Thumbnail sketches and tight roughs of logo ideas for library book bags, and the finished digital artwork.

designer will sketch ideas on paper first, scan them, then use the most successful sketch as a template for constructing a final, digital version. See Figure 8–32.

When it comes to page layout, setting up content areas within a grid structure works effectively. Content areas are designated, blocked-out spaces where information will be placed, such as images, copy, and logos. Using the grid-mapping idea, a starting grid for a Web page might look something like Figure 8–33, with each area labeled for easy reference.

If you are creating multiple pages requiring a similar look, keep the positioning of content consistent from page to page. For example, in the creation of a Web page design—something you will practice in Lesson 4: Practicing the Process—Building a

Rough sketches for different Web page layout ideas.

FIGURE | 8–33 |

Web Page Design—it is important that the position of text, images, and navigational (button) elements is visually appealing and consistently easy to use as you click from page to page. After all, a Web page is not a static design—it is an interactive experience.

After identifying content areas comes the most creative and interesting part of the process: applying design elements and principles to get the "look and feel" appropriate to the topic. Usually this is done in a very fluid fashion, knowing that the final version will be completed once there is client approval of the design idea (if that is the case), and the final content pieces are gathered. Figure 8–34 shows the layout for a site about walking around the Finger Lakes in New York.

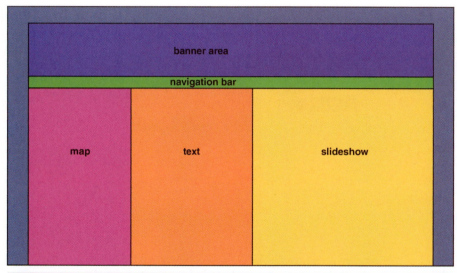

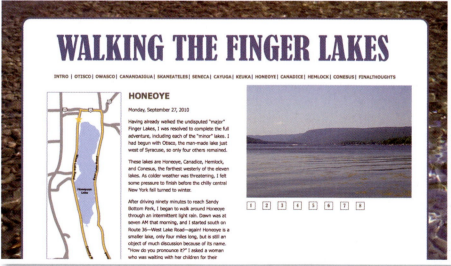

FIGURE | 8–34 |

The blocked content areas and the final layout for the Web site content pages.

> ▶ DON'T GO THERE
>
> Many novice designers fall short on their designs because they do not take the time to sketch multiple ideas on paper first. Experience shows that starting with thumbnails and roughs can alleviate headaches and missed deadlines later on.

Gather Content

When you have your initial sketch, you have a better idea of what kind of content you need to fill each content zone area. Gathering content for your layout can be the most time-consuming and challenging part of the whole process. In some instances you might have to create all the content—images and copy—yourself, or procure the content from other sources (i.e., your client or an outside resource, such as another artist or writer, image source, or font repository). This is where issues of copyright come into play. If you create your own content or use copyright-free material, there is no need to worry about the permission process. However, if you use others' materials, such as another company's logo or a photo taken by someone else you need the correct permissions for using them in your work.

Another aspect of content gathering is getting the content into the right format for your use. For example, if Illustrator is to be used as the medium for integrating your content (see the next section), make sure the content can be successfully imported into the program. Are the images and photos you want to use in the correct file format for Illustrator to read? Is the written copy translatable in the Illustrator environment? I will not go into detail about each importable file format supported by Illustrator (you can review that information in the Illustrator Help files), but here is a quick list: EPS, Adobe PDF or PSD, SVG/SVGZ, PICT, WMF/EMF, DXF/DWG, Freehand, CorelDraw, CGM, raster formats (i.e., GIF 89a, JPEG/JPEG2000, PNG, TIFF, BMP), and text formats, such as plain text/ASCII (.txt), Microsoft RTF (.rtf), Microsoft Word (.doc), and Microsoft Word DOCX (.docx).

Assemble Content

After content is gathered, you assemble it in a design program (i.e., Illustrator or InDesign). There are two steps to integrating content into your final layout: properly importing content from outside the program, creating content in Illustrator when necessary, and accurately formatting, sizing, and positioning content.

Importing When you have the content in an appropriate format (see the previous section, Gathering Content), it is placed imported into Illustrator in one of several ways—using the Open, Place, or Paste commands, or, if available, dragging and dropping.

► *Open (choose File > Open)*: Opens artwork in a new Illustrator document. Vector artwork is converted to Illustrator paths, which you can modify with any Illustrator tool. Bitmap artwork can be modified with only some tools, such as transformation tools (scale, rotate, etc.) and image filters.

► *Place (choose File > Place)*: Places artwork into an existing Illustrator document. You can place the artwork in one of two ways—linked or embedded. Linked artwork remains independent of the Illustrator document, which is good if you need to keep the document's file size down. However, if you move your Illustrator document to another spot on your computer, the linked files must be moved, too, and possibly be relinked to the Illustrator document. This is very similar to how fonts are read by Illustrator—the fonts must be available on your computer for Illustrator to find and display them. The other option is to embed the artwork, which is when Illustrator copies the artwork into the document, increasing the file size and keeping everything in a single file. The option to link or embed a file is available when you choose File > Place. Select the link option if you want to link the artwork, or unselect the option to embed it. See Figure 8–35. To identify and monitor linked and embedded files, choose Window > Links. In the Links panel, you can also change a linked file into an

> Note: *The Clipboard is a temporary holding place for the most recent thing that was copied or cut. The next time you copy or paste something, it "forgets" what that was and replaces it with the new data.*

FIGURE | 8–35 |

If the placed file will be part of the final artwork, it may be smarter to embed it. If you need it only for reference and will be deleting it later, use the link option.

The Align panel.

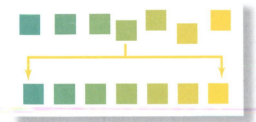

FIGURE | 8–44 |

Before-and-after example of using the Align tool. The boxes on the bottom have been aligned horizontally and spaced evenly.

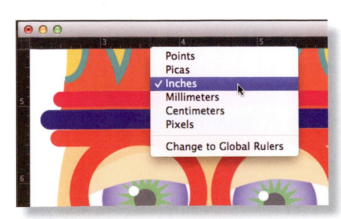

FIGURE | 8–45 |

Set the measurement unit of the rulers.

For more details about layers, choose Help > Illustrator Help and do a search on "layers."

Other features that keep your work organized while integrating content in a document include the Align panel, Rulers, Grids, Guides, Smart Guides, and Snap to Grid or Point. The Align panel is located under Window > Align. The other features are found under the View menu.

- ▶ The **Align panel** aligns selected objects horizontally right, left, or center or vertically top, bottom, or center, in relation to either themselves or the artboard. It also horizontally or vertically distributes selected objects evenly, using either the objects' edges or the anchor points as the spatial reference. See Figure 8–43 and Figure 8–44.

- ▶ **Rulers** are designed to measure and place objects on the artboard accurately. To turn the rulers on, choose View > Rulers > Show Rulers. To turn them off, choose View > Rulers > Hide Rulers.

- ▶ When turned on, both a horizontal and a vertical ruler appear along the top and left edges of the document. To change the measurement unit of the rulers, Ctrl click (Mac) or right-click (Windows) on a ruler and select a new measurement unit from the drop-down menu. See Figure 8–45. Or, use Illustrator > Preferences > Units & Rulers (Mac) or Edit > Preferences > Units & Rulers (Windows). The upper-left corner of the document, where the vertical and horizontal rulers meet, is called the Ruler Origin. Setting the ruler origin is useful when, for example, you are working on an object that is 2 by 3 inches on an $8\frac{1}{2}$ -by-11-inch document. You can set the ruler origin at 0, 0 in the upper-left corner of the 2-by-3 area, rather than the $8\frac{1}{2}$-by-11 area, for more precise positioning. To set the ruler origin, place the cursor where the rulers intersect, then click and drag the crosshair to the new origin. See Figure 8–46. To restore default settings, double-click the Ruler Origin.

- ▶ The **Grid** in Illustrator is located under View > Show Grid. A grid of lines or dots appears on the artboard, and it can be used to position objects with precision. Grids do not print. To adjust Grid settings, such as color, style, subdivisions, and whether the grid appears over or below the artwork, choose Illustrator > Preferences > Guides & Grid (Mac) or Edit > Preferences > Guides & Grid (Windows).

embedded file (see Figure 8–36), or choose the Embed option in the Control panel of the selected image.

- ▶ *Paste (choose Edit > Paste)*: Pastes copied artwork into the document. This method is useful when transferring content from one Illustrator document to another (and from other programs as well, like Photoshop, Word, or Flash). Before pasting artwork into Illustrator, the copied artwork is saved in the Clipboard. You can think of a clipboard as a virtual holding place for copied information. It sits in this temporary space (your computer's memory) until you are ready to paste it or until you copy or cut something else. To specify copy and paste preferences, choose Illustrator > Preferences > File Handling & Clipboard (Mac), or Edit > Preferences > File Handling & Clipboard (Windows).

- ▶ *Dragging and dropping*: This option can also transfer artwork from one document to another, most commonly between different Illustrator files, or between Illustrator and Photoshop or InDesign. If you are a Mac user, you can also drag a copy of Illustrator artwork to the desktop, which converts the artwork into a pictClipping file that you can drag into another open Illustrator document. Be aware that for this to work, you need to be able to see both files—the open Illustrator document, and the pictClipping file on the desktop.

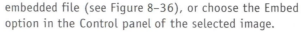

FIGURE | 8–36 |

The Links panel lets you easily identify and modify your placed files.

Problems can arise when importing content into Illustrator, or other programs for that matter. For example, you cannot place a CorelDraw file that is saved in a newer version than the version that Illustrator supports. If the file is in a vector format (which, if it is CorelDraw, it will be), it often helps to save the file in the Encapsulated PostScript (EPS) format, rather than its native file format, then place it into Illustrator. EPS is a standard, cross-platform file format that recognizes both vector and bitmap information. The Adobe Creative Suite has been designed so that most of the programs integrate fairly seamlessly with each other in terms of importing different file formats, as well as copying and pasting between different programs. For instance, Photoshop can save paths as vector paths to edit in Illustrator, and Illustrator can export movie clip symbols to use in Flash. You can paste a Photoshop image or Illustrator element directly into InDesign.

One issue that might arise is trying to open a newer version of an Illustrator file while you're in an older version of the software (i.e., opening a CS6 file using CS5). In this case, you usually get a dialog box that says something like Figure 8–37. The conversion will probably work, but you might lose some information. One other thing: When you attempt to place artwork and can't access the file you want to import, it's your clue that the file has been saved in a format that Illustrator cannot read.

Organizing After content has been imported into Illustrator or created it directly in the program, it should be organized. While this is certainly optional, it is

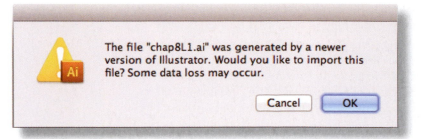

FIGURE | 8–37 |

This is the dialog box you will see if you attempt to open a file created in Illustrator CS6 using Illustrator CS5 software.

highly recommended, especially to those of you who would rather close the door of a dirty bedroom than clean it up. You cannot leave all your content in one unnamed layer and expect to find what you need quickly or without frustration.

Use the Layers panel to name, select, move, categorize, hide, and link elements on your document. You have already worked a lot with layers in previous lessons, such as the Elizabeth's Eye lesson in Chapter 3. You will also get to work with layers in Lesson 4 of this chapter. To see what the Layers panel can do for you, see Figure 8–38 through Figure 8–42.

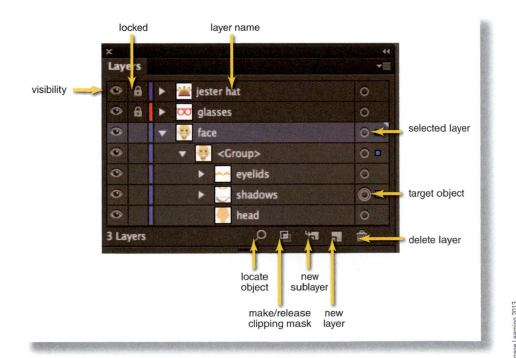

FIGURE | 8–38 |

Basic layer options.

FIGURE | 8–39 |

Click and drag a layer to a new location in the layer stack.

FIGURE | 8–40 |

More layer options are available in the Layers panel options menu.

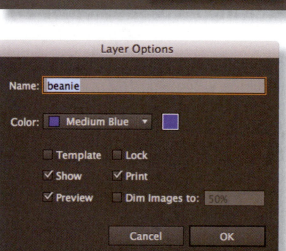

FIGURE | 8–41 |

From the Layers panel options menu, choose Options for "layername". . . to open the specific options of a selected layer.

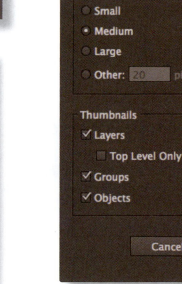

FIGURE | 8–42 |

From the Layers panel options menu, choose Panel Options . . . to adjust how you view layers in the panel.

Figures © Cengage Learning 2013

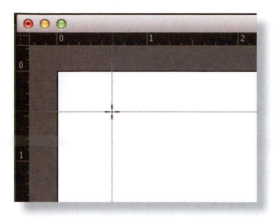

FIGURE | 8–46 |

Click and drag the crosshair to the new origin.

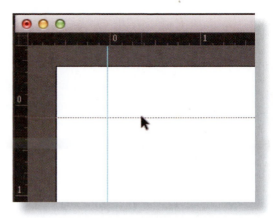

FIGURE | 8–47 |

Drag ruler guides from the horizontal and vertical rulers.

▶ **Ruler Guides** and **Guide Objects** are useful for aligning your work. To create ruler guides, choose View > Rulers > Show Rulers and drag guidelines from the horizontal and vertical rulers on the edges of the document (see Figure 8–47). Guide Objects can be any vector object(s) you decide to turn into a guide. To create a Guide Object, select the object and choose View > Guides > Make Guides. To hide, lock, release, and clear guides, choose View > Guides. Guides do not print. To adjust guide colors and style, choose Illustrator > Preferences > Guides & Grid (Mac) or Edit > Preferences > Guides & Grid (Windows).

▶ **Smart Guides** (see Figure 8–48 and Figure 8–49) have a "snap-to" ability, which helps you create, align, edit, and transform objects relative to other objects. With Smart Guides turned on (View > Smart Guides), your cursor acts like a magnet; within a certain distance, it will snap to edges, anchor points, or intersections for precise sizing and positioning. If you prefer to use Smart Guides without the color lines and XY information, choose Illustrator > Preferences > Smart Guides (Mac) or Edit > Preferences > Smart Guides (Windows) and uncheck the display options.

▶ **Snapping** allows for even more precise positioning by snapping objects to the Grid (when visible) or anchor points. Choose View > Snap to Grid or Snap to Point.

FIGURE | 8–48 |

Use Smart Guides to snap to anchor points.

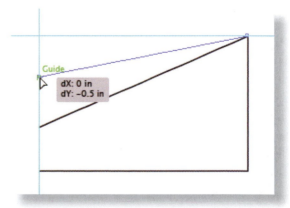

FIGURE | 8–49 |

Use Smart Guides to align paths and shapes.

Fine-Tune and Output

Fine-tuning involves fixing the details of a layout: adjusting colors, aligning items, and playing with subtle text formatting, like line and character spacing. In this phase, you also prepare your final work for its intended output: selecting the proper color mode and settings for either screen or print, and exporting in the desired file format.

LESSON 4: PRACTICING THE PROCESS—BUILDING A WEB PAGE DESIGN

Put the creative process into action. In this lesson, you will construct a Web page. See Figure 8–50.

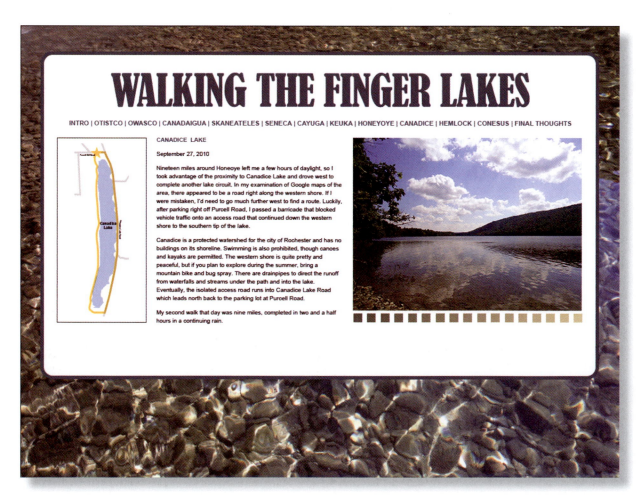

FIGURE | 8–50 |

Completed Web page design.

Setting Up the File

1. In Illustrator, choose File > New.

- ▸ *Name*: **chap8L4_yourname.ai**
- ▸ *Profile*: **Web** (the Color Mode will be automatically set to RGB and the resolution to 72; both settings for images to be viewed online)
- ▸ *Number of Artboards*: 1
- ▸ *Size*: select the 1024 X 768 option
- ▸ *Units*: **Pixels**
- ▸ *Width*: leave as is; it will reflect the size you selected above
- ▸ *Height*: leave as is; it will reflect the size you selected above
- ▸ Orientation: leave as is
- ▸ Bleed: leave as is

Click OK.

2. Choose File > Place and browse for the file **page_template.jpg** in the **chap8_lessons/ assets** folder. Uncheck the link option in the Place dialog box, if necessary, and then click Place.

> Note: *When you uncheck Link, you are choosing to embed the image into the document.*

3. Choose View > Actual Size. This is a premade template based on a grid developed for a site about walking around the Finger Lakes in New York. The content areas are color coded and labeled for easy reference. When you create your own layouts, consider doing something similar.

4. Make sure the Essentials workspace is selected.

5. Open the Layers panel. In the Layers panel options menu, choose Options for "Layer 1."

6. For the layer name, type **page_template**. Select the Template option (see Figure 8–51), and dim the images to 50% (Figure 8-51). Click OK. Notice that, in the Layers panel, in the visibility column, a Template layer is indicated by an outlined rectangle rather than an eye icon, is automatically locked, and the layer name is italicized.

7. Save the file in your lessons folder.

FIGURE | 8–51 |

Select Template, and Dim Images to 50% in Layer Options.

FIGURE | 8–52 |

Add a layer and name it guides.

Creating Guides

1. Click the Create New Layer icon at the bottom of the Layers panel to create a new layer above the template layer.

2. Double-click on the name of the new layer (**Layer 2**) and name the layer **guides**. Click OK. See Figure 8–52.

3. Choose View > Rulers > Show Rulers.

4. Ctrl click (Mac) or right-click (Windows) on the ruler at the top of the document and select Pixels (if it's not already set to this measurement unit).

5. Place the cursor on the top, horizontal ruler, then click and drag down to position a guide. Drop the guide at the top edge of the white box, which will be the container for all the page content.

6. Create two horizontal guides at the top and bottom of the banner area.

> Note: *To move guides, first unlock them, if necessary. Go to View > Guides > Lock Guides to toggle the lock option off. Then, with the Selection tool, click and drag the guide you want to move to select and move it. Remember to relock the guides so that you do not move anything accidentally.*

7. Continue creating horizontal guides along the horizontal edges of each colored rectangle of the template. Be sure to also create a guide at the bottom of the white container. See Figure 8–53.

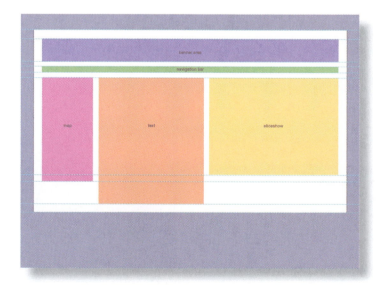

FIGURE | 8–53 |

Position guides at the top and bottom of each content area.

8. Place the cursor over the ruler at the left, and click and drag to create a vertical guide. Place the guide on the left edge of the content area.

9. Create two more vertical guides for the left and right edges of the map area.

10. Place a fourth vertical guide at the left edge of the text area and another at the right edge.

11. Place two more guides at the edges of the slideshow area (see Figure 8–54), and a final one at the right of the content area.

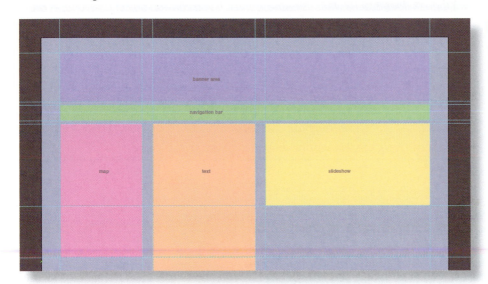

FIGURE | 8–54 |

Position guides to delineate the right and left margins of each content area.

12. Expand the guides layer in the Layers panel by clicking the triangle to the left of the layer's name. Notice that each guide is indicated in this layer. Collapse and lock the layer.

Note: *For precision placement of the guides, zoom in.*

13. Save your file.

Adding the Background

1. Click the Create New Layer icon at the bottom of the Layers panel to create a new layer above the **guides** layer. Double-click its name and rename it water.

2. Use File > Open and locate the background image for this page: **chap08_lessons > assets > water.ai.** Click Open.

3. Click the Layers panel options menu icon and make sure that Paste Remembers Layers is checked. See Figure 8–55.

4. Select the water photo with the Selection tool and copy it: Edit > Copy.

FIGURE | 8–55 |

Use the Layer panel options menu to select Paste Remembers Layers.

5. Click on the first tab at the top of the document window (see Figure 8–56) to flip back to your Web page project and choose Edit > Paste.

6. Zoom out if necessary, position the image exactly within the artboard, lock this layer, and then hide it.

> Note: *Paste Remembers Layers (found under the options menu of the Layers panel) does exactly what its name implies. If you copy an object from a layer and paste it, Illustrator will "remember" what layer that object is from and paste it into a layer with that same name, either in the document or in another document. If you paste into some other document that does not have a layer with the same name, Illustrator will create a new layer with that name. If you deselect Paste Remembers Layers, select several objects in different Layers, and then paste them, all pasted objects will maintain their original stacking order but will end up in the same layer in the original document or any other document.*

FIGURE | 8–56 |

Click on the document title tab at the top of the file to return to your lesson file.

Importing and Creating Content

1. Add a new layer, double-click on its name (Layer 4), and rename it content.

2. Set the fill color to white, and the stroke to a dusty blue. Open the Color panel and, using the Color panel options menu, set the mode to RGB if it isn't already. Note the hexadecimal field at the bottom-right side of the color sliders. The value of this color is 3f5060 (see Figure 8–57).

3. Use the Stroke panel to set the stroke width to 6 pt.

4. Use the Rounded Rectangle tool to draw the content area delineated by the guides you placed. See Figure 8–58.

5. Lock this layer and hide it.

6. Add a new layer and name it banner.

7. Choose File > Place and browse for the file **header.ai** in the **chap08_lessons/assets** folder. Accept the defaults, click Place, accept the defaults, and click OK.

8. Position the image in the area of the template labeled banner. To center it from left to right, make sure that it is still selected and open the Align panel (Window > Align). At the bottom right, select the Align to Artboard option (see Figure 8–59), and then click the Horizontal Align Center icon.

Figure © Cengage Learning 2013

FIGURE | 8–57 |

Use the hexadecimal field to establish the stroke color.

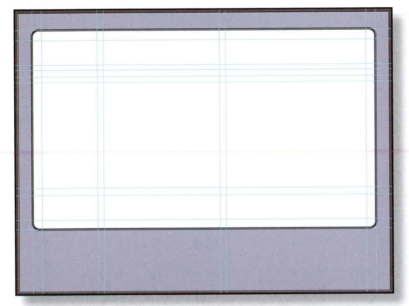

FIGURE | 8–58 |

Create the main content area with the Rounded Rectangle tool.

FIGURE | 8–59 |

Center the header in the page.

If you'd rather, feel free to delete the banner image. Select a typeface you like and use the Type tool to create a new banner directly in Illustrator. Watch the letter spacing—use the Character panel to track and kern where necessary.

9. Lock this layer and then create a new one. Name it navigation.

10. Select the Text tool.

11. Click inside the navigation area with the Text tool and type: intro | otisco | owasco | canandaigua | skaneateles | seneca | cayuga | keuka | honeoye | canadice | hemlock | conesus | final thoughts.

12. Set the fill color to dusty blue. Double-click on the fill box in the Tools panel. In the hexadecimal field of the Color Picker type 3f5060, press the Tab key to update the color. Click OK to exit the Color Picker.

> Note: *The bar character separating each lake name is located at the right of your keyboard above the Enter/Return key.*

13. Select the text with the Selection tool and use the Character panel (Window > Type > Character) to select Arial (or something similar) for the typeface, bold for style, and all caps. Set the size to 11 pt. You may need to choose the Show More Options option from the panel's options menu to access the All Caps icon (TT). See Figure 8–60.

> Note: *If the line of type is too long to fit in the navigation area, decrease the point size as necessary.*

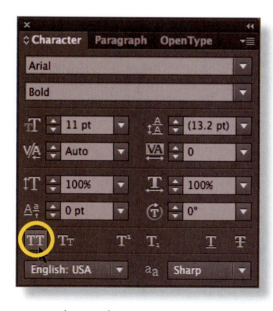

FIGURE | 8–60 |

Specify the typeface, style, and point size for the navigation links.

14. Lock the navigation layer and add a new layer for the lake map. Name it map.

15. Click on the View menu and select the Smart Guides option, if it doesn't already have a check mark next to it.

16. Set the fill color to none and the stroke to black. Use the Stroke panel to set the line width to 0.5 pt. See Figure 8–61.

17. Select the Rectangle tool and then click and drag from the upper-left corner of the map area to the lower-right corner. Note how using Smart Guides helps you to draw and position elements very precisely. When you have Smart Guides turned on, drag objects from a corner guide to the diagonally opposite corner guide to ensure accuracy.

18. Use File > Place to place the **map.ai** file in **chap08_lessons > assets**. Use the Selection tool to position and scale the image to fit in the map area.

> Note: *If you get a warning that the font is missing from your machine, just click OK.*

19. Make sure all the existing layers are locked, and then add a new one for the slideshow. Name it slides.

> Note: *If the template is getting annoying, you can safely hide the page_template layer; you can use the guides to show you where things go.*

20. The slideshow will have buttons to move the slides from one photo to the next. Use the Color panel to set the fill color to a khaki color (5f5d51) and the stroke to none.

21. In the slideshow area, use the Rectangle tool to create a small square (hint: hold down the Shift key to ensure that it's perfect). This will become one of the buttons that control the slideshow. While it's still selected, look at the Control panel. Make sure that the chain icon is not linked, and change the H and W dimensions to 15 px. The reason for not linking the H and W values is in case your square isn't exactly perfect.

22. Use the X and Y fields in the Control panel to position the square approximately at X: 576.5 and Y: 494.5. See Figure 8–62.

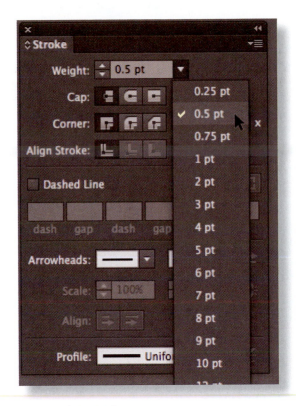

> Note: *If you can't see the H, W, X, and Y fields in the Control panel, use the Transform panel (Window > Transform) instead.*

FIGURE | 8–61 |

Use the Stroke panel to create a hairline border.

23. Deselect the square (Select > Deselect).

24. With the Selection tool active, click and hold down the Option and Shift (Mac) or Alt and Shift (Windows) keys, then click on the square and drag it to the right guide in the slideshow area. Let go of the mouse first, then the modifier keys.

    Holding down the Option/Alt key creates a copy of the object being dragged. Holding the Shift key ensures that it will be dragged perfectly horizontally, vertically, or at a 45° angle (referred to as constrained), depending on where you want to place it.

25. Double-click the Blend tool to open its Options. Set the Spacing to Specified Steps, the Number to 15, and leave the Orientation as is (Align to Page). You could check the Preview box (although the blend hasn't been created yet, so there's nothing to see; see Figure 8–63). Click OK.

FIGURE | 8–62 |

Use the Control panel's X and Y fields to position the button graphic.

Figures © Cengage Learning 2013

FIGURE | 8–63 |

Duplicate the button symbol using the Blend tool.

26. Zoom in on the slideshow area of the Web page, if necessary. With the Blend tool still active, click once on the upper-right corner of the leftmost square, and then click on the upper-right corner of the rightmost square.

27. Select the Direct Selection tool and deselect everything by clicking outside the artboard. Click on the edge of the rightmost square and use the Color panel to set its fill color to a lighter khaki color: d4cba2. Nice, right?

28. To demonstrate how a blend works, use the Direct Selection tool to move that last square around the artboard and see how the button graphics shift accordingly. Double-click the Blend tool again and change the number of steps, and click the preview box to see what that does, then click Cancel to exit without making any changes. When you're done playing, use Edit > Undo until you're back to where you started [Command Z (Mac)/Ctrl Z (Windows)].

29. Choose File > Place and place the **lake.jpg** file from the **chap08_lessons/assets** folder.

30. While the lake image is still selected, use the Control panel to set its size. Make sure that the chain icon is linked this time, and type 390 px in the W box. Because the chain icon is linked, the height is scaled automatically in proportion to the width. Avoid distorting photos (and text) at all costs; it's poor design.

31. Use the Direct Selection tool to position the lake image at the top of the slideshow area, above the buttons. See Figure 8–64.

32. Lock this layer and save your file.

Adding the Text

1. Open the Layers panel if it's not already open. Create another new layer and name it text.

FIGURE | 8–64 |

Position the slideshow image.

2. Select the Text tool and drag a text field from the top-left corner of the text area guides, down to the bottom-right corner of the guides (see Figure 8–65). Make sure the text ibeam is flashing at the top-left side.

3. Use File > Place and locate the **text.doc** file in the **chap08_lessons > assets** folder. Click Place, and then click OK to accept the defaults.

4. Select the type with the Selection tool and use the Character panel to set the typeface to Arial, Regular for style, and 10 pt for size. Read the copy and, if necessary, insert paragraph spacing. See Figure 8–66.

5. In the Character panel, note that the points value indicated for the line spacing (leading) may be in parentheses. This is because Illustrator preferences are set to use 120% of the point size of the type for the line spacing. This would work well for print; for the Web, we need a bit more space. Make sure that the text is selected with the Selection tool, and then change the leading value from 12 to 14 pt.

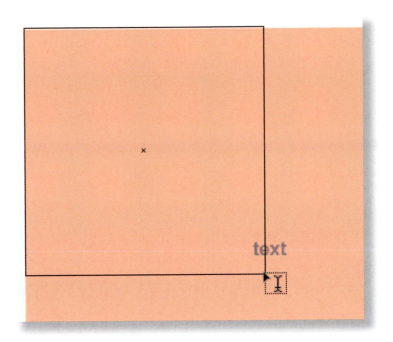

FIGURE | 8–65 |

Use the Text tool to create a text field.

FIGURE | 8–66 |

Format the text and specify the typeface, size, and style.

CANADICE LAKE

September 27, 2010

Nineteen miles around Honeoye left me a few hours of daylight, so I took advantage of the proximity to Canadice Lake and drove west to complete another lake circuit. In my examination of Google maps of the area, there appeared to be a road right along the western shore. If I were mistaken, I'd need to go much further west to find a route. Luckily, after parking right off Purcell Road, I passed a barricade that blocked vehicle traffic onto an access road that continued down the western shore to the southern tip of the lake.

text

Canadice is a protected watershed for the city of Rochester and has no buildings on its shoreline. Swimming is also prohibited, though canoes and kayaks are permitted. The western shore is quite pretty and peaceful, but if you plan to explore during the summer, bring a mountain bike and bug spray. There are drainpipes to direct the runoff from waterfalls and streams under the path and into the lake. Eventually, the isolated access road runs into Canadice Lake Road which leads north back to the parking lot at Purcell Road.

My second walk that day was nine miles, completed in two and a half hours in a continuing rain.

6. With the Text tool, click and drag through the lake name: Canadice Lake. In the Control panel, click on the underlined word Character to open the Character panel, and make Canadice 12 pt, bold, and all caps.

7. Use the Color panel to set the color of CANADICE LAKE to dusty blue: #3f5060.

8. Click and drag the page_template layer to the trash can icon at the bottom of the Layers panel. Do the same with the guides layer.

9. Make sure all the layers are locked and visible and then save your file. See Figure 8–67.

You are finished with the design process. Well done!

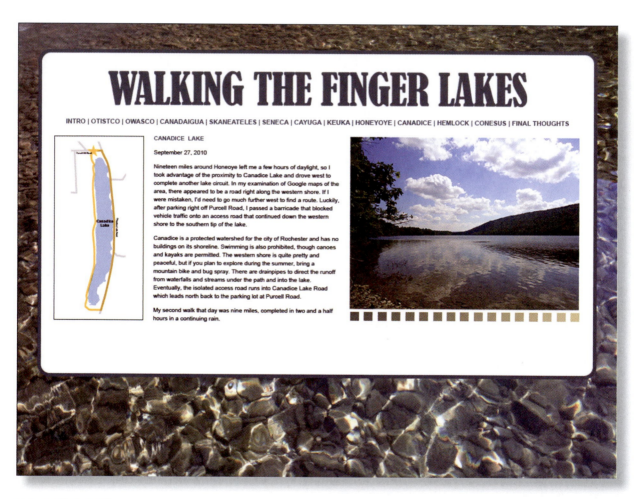

FIGURE | **8–67** |

The final Web page layout.

SUMMARY

After this chapter, hopefully your use of Illustrator has been bumped up to a whole new level. Constructing more complex shapes is no longer a mystery with the use of the Pathfinder panel, grouping, and clipping masks. And suddenly, the not-so-secret steps of producing compositionally complete layouts are within your grasp. Ideas that might have originally been lost can now be put into a tangible form with the importing, organizational, and workflow features of Illustrator.

▶ IN REVIEW

1. What is an important difference between a compound path and a compound shape?

2. What does the Expand command do, and why would you use it?

3. What is the difference between pathfinders in the Pathfinder panel versus the Pathfinder effects (Effects > Pathfinder)?

4. Describe the steps for creating a clipping mask in Illustrator.

5. What tool do you use to select individual parts of a grouped object?

6. Describe the difference between linking and embedding artwork. Where would you go if you wanted to embed a linked file?

7. When you copy something, where does it reside until you are ready to paste it?

8. Explain the EPS format and when it would be useful.

9. Name at least four features of the Layers panel.

10. How do you make ruler guides in Illustrator?

11. Where do you go to make a Template layer?

12. When would you use the Align panel?

▶ EXPLORING ON YOUR OWN

1. Choose Help > Illustrator Help and read the topics Selecting and arranging objects, and Reshaping objects.

2. Explore the Drawing Modes feature. Available at the bottom of the Tools panel, Drawing Modes come in 3 options – Draw Normal, Draw Behind, and Draw Inside (see Figure 8–68). Draw Normal is the default option, allowing you to draw as you have learned thus far in this book. Draw Behind offers a quick way to create a shape just behind a selected art object (see Figure 8–69). Draw Inside allows you to draw inside a selected object by creating a clipping mask of the selected object (see Figure 8–70).

FIGURE | 8–68 |

The Drawing Modes as shown at the bottom of the Tools panel, set to the default one-column view.

FIGURE | 8–69 |

Example of the use of drawing in the Draw Behind mode.

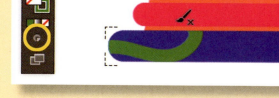

FIGURE | 8–70 |

Example of the use of drawing in the Draw Inside mode.

3. Practice your layout skills by deconstructing a premade design. Cut out a magazine or newspaper article, or print a Web page, and with a pencil and ruler, re-create the grid that was used to position the elements on the page. Label the content areas, such as main copy, logo, header/title, photograph, artwork, etc.

4. For some design inspiration and further instruction on the varied features of Illustrator, explore and bookmark these site locations at adobe.com: http://www.adobe.com/designcenter/ and http://www.adobe.com/designcenter/video_workshop/

5. Scan in a flattened box, import it to an Illustrator file by selecting the Template option in the Place dialog window, and reproduce its design or create your own. Keep in mind that since you are reproducing someone else's design, this project can only be used for educational purposes and should not be presented commercially in any way without prior permission from the copyright holder. The example of student work in Figure 8–68 has been slightly altered for that reason.

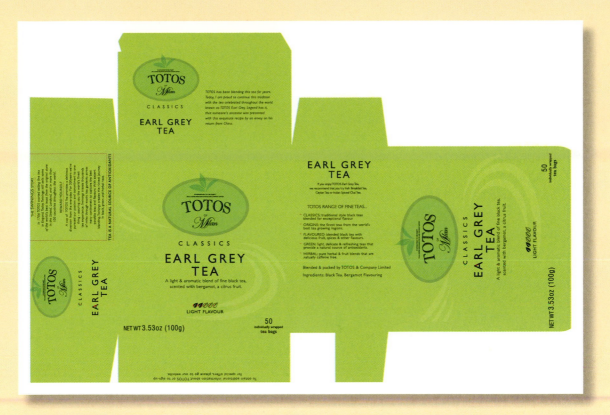

FIGURE | 8–71 |

An example of a design reproduced from a flattened box.

6.   Explore multiple artboards and templates. Illustrator allows you to work with more than one artboard in a single document window. This is helpful if, for example, you want to keep a business card, a letterhead, and envelope artwork all in the same file. See Figure 8–72.

FIGURE | 8–72 |

Use multiple artboards to keep several pieces of a project in the same file.

Try this:

a.　In Illustrator, choose File > New from Template. Go to Templates > Club and open **Stationery.ait**.

b.　Choose View > Fit All in Window to see the business card, handbill, letterhead, and envelope layouts—each layout is on its own artboard. See Figure 8–73.

> Note: *The extension .ait identifies an Illustrator template file. When you choose a template file, it will open a new, untitled document in Illustrator containing the template items that you can then use as a starting point for your designs and layouts. You can also convert Illustrator files that you have created into reusable template files by saving your file under File > Save as Template.*

c.　Choose to view the Letterhead by selecting it in the Artboard Navigation menu in the lower-left corner of the screen. See Figure 8–74.

d.　Select the Artboard tool in the Tools panel to enter the Artboard editing area (see Figure 8–75)—the area around the artboard turns gray, and the artboard itself is surrounded by a dashed border. In this mode you can resize the artboard by dragging on a corner of the dashed border. You can also adjust settings found in the Control panel, such as the artboard's orientation, position,

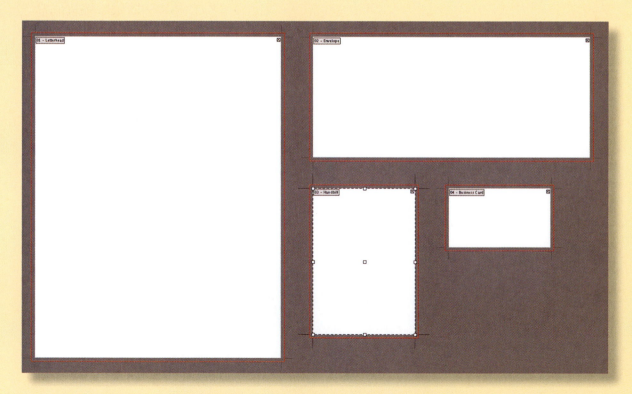

FIGURE | 8–73 |

Sample document layouts using multiple artboards.

FIGURE | 8–74 |

Select an artboard to work on from the Artboard Navigation menu at the lower-left side of the document.

FIGURE | 8–75 |

Select the Artboard tool in the Tools panel.

and display preferences, such as the crosshair, center, mark, and video safe-area identifiers. You can make new artboards by clicking and dragging. Explore these options. See Figure 8–76.

e. To exit the Artboard editing area, choose ESC on the keyboard or another tool in the Tools panel.

FIGURE | 8–76 |

Set options for an artboard in the Control panel.

7. Explore the Shape Builder tool. The Shape Builder tool endeavors to ease a designer's effort to create complex shapes by adding or subtracting regions of overlapping shapes. Try this:

a. In the Tools panel, set black for the Stroke color and None for the Fill color.

b. Create a new Illustrator document and draw an elongated oval shape with the Ellipse tool.

c. Select the Rotate tool in the Tools panel. See Figure 8–77.

d. Hold down the Option/Alt key and click just below the oval. Refer to Figure 8–78. Let go of the key and mouse and the Rotate options box will appear.

e. In the Rotate options box, set the angle to 30 degrees and choose Copy. See Figure 8–79.

f. Continue to make more copies of the oval shape around the registration point by choosing Object > Transform > Transform Again, or Command D (Mac), or Ctrl D (Windows), until enough ovals are duplicated around the center to create a flower shape. See Figure 8–80.

g. Select all the shapes with the Selection tool and select a fill color. You may want to set the stroke to None.

h. Choose the Shape Builder tool in the Tools panel. See Figure 8–81.

i. Roll the cursor over a section of the selected shapes and notice that the area is highlighted with a plaid pattern and a + indicator appears next to the cursor. Click and drag from one section to another to combine them into a single shape. See Figure 8–82.

j. Hold down the Alt/Option key and click on any regions that you would like to remove. See Figure 8–83 for some examples.

Note: *To edit Shape Builder Tool options, double-click on the tool icon in the Tools panel. See Figure 8–84.*

FIGURE | 8–77 |

Select the Rotate tool in the Tools panel.

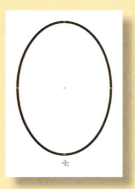

FIGURE | 8–78 |

Set the registration point of the selected object.

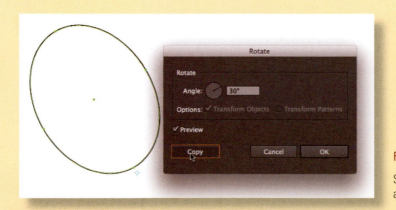

FIGURE | 8–79 |

Set the Rotate options and click Copy, not OK.

FIGURE | 8–80 |

Make copies of the rotating object to create a flower shape.

FIGURE | 8–81 |

Select the Shape Builder tool from the Tools panel.

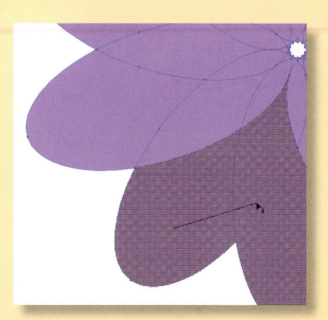

FIGURE | 8–82 |

With the Shape Builder tool, add to overlapping regions to create new shapes. To subtract/delete regions, hold down the Option/Alt key and click.

FIGURE | 8–83 |

Playing with this tool may keep you occupied for hours!

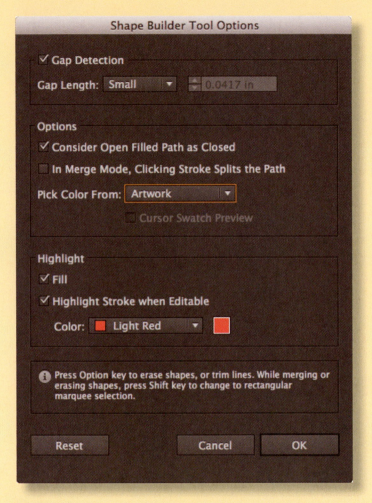

FIGURE | 8–84 |

Options available for the Shape Builder tool.

adventures
IN DESIGN

MAKING A WINE LABEL

In the world of graphic design, Illustrator and Photoshop go hand-in-hand. When working with a project where many elements must come together in a compositionally complete design, often the illustrative and textual elements are created in Illustrator and the more continuous tone elements or effects are created in Photoshop. These separate elements are then combined—layered and arranged in a complete layout—in either Photoshop or Illustrator. Let's look at the development of a five-liter wine box label by Gallo Winery, Modesto, California. (Art direction: Dave Garcez. See Figure D–1.) Then you can apply your own skills to first envision a wine label design and then create parts of it in Illustrator. If you know Photoshop, use that program, too, to reproduce your vision.

Professional Project Example

A five-liter wine box label was created for Gallo Winery using a combination of Photoshop and Illustrator. First, a photograph was taken of a wine glass, a basket, and some grapes. See Figure D–2. Then they were layered together using Photoshop. See Figure D–3. The logo was created in Illustrator. A hand-drawn sketch was scanned and placed as a template into Illustrator. See Figure D–4. Then outlines were created for each letter shape.

The Offset command under the objects menu (Object > Path > Offset Path) was used to create additional outlines around each letter to produce a beveled effect. Colored fill and stroke attributes were then added to the logo. See Figure D–5 and Figure D–6. The final logo design and photographic images were then arranged together in Photoshop, and

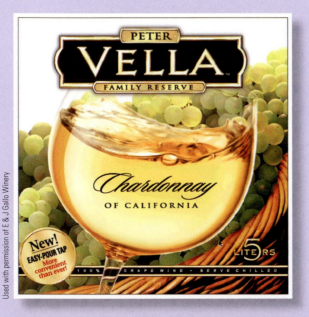

Used with permission of E & J Gallo Winery

FIGURE |D–1|

This 5-liter wine box label was produced using Illustrator and Photoshop.

Used with permission of E & J Gallo Winery

FIGURE |D–2|

Photographs were taken and layered in Photoshop.

Used with permission of E & J Gallo Winery

FIGURE | D–3 |

The photographs arranged in a complete image.

Used with permission of E & J Gallo Winery

FIGURE | D–4 |

A hand-drawn sketch of the logo.

saved and imported into Illustrator, where additional typographic elements were added and the whole file was prepared for print. Refer to Figure D–1.

Your Turn

As you can see from the description of the wine label project, it is a common technique to start with a sketched drawing or template to help you reconstruct an artistic vision (a logo) in Illustrator. In several of the lessons in this book you also used premade templates to aid you in your digital drawing. Now it is your turn to develop an illustrative element using this technique.

Wine Label Project Guidelines

1. With sketchbook in hand, take a stroll through the wine section of your local grocery or liquor store.

2. Take note of the wine labels that catch your eye. What is appealing about the label to you? Its color? Its graphics? Its use of fonts? Its dimensions? Its shape?

3. Sketch your own wine label ideas in the sketchbook. First determine the general size of the label. Make up a name for your wine. Start blocking out content zone areas. (Where will the title, the main graphic element, the copyright, ingredients, and alcohol content information go?) How will the graphics you create for the label reflect the title for the wine you have chosen?

4. Create a final sketch of the wine label in the sketchbook. Be as precise as possible with your drawing—measure the label, use colored pencils or markers to indicate the color scheme, and draw to the best of your ability what you envision the label will look like.

5. Scan a copy of your sketch into a digital format (a TIFF or JPEG image).

6. Import the image into Illustrator and put it on a template layer.

FIGURE | D–5 |

The stages of re-creating the logo drawing using Illustrator.

FIGURE | D–6 |

The final logo design with value and texture.

7. Begin to construct the label, using the tools you have learned in Illustrator.

8. After you have read Chapter 10, you can prepare the label for print.

Things to Consider

It would be ideal to actually get paid for your work, or at least recognized with high praise. Here are some things to consider when working on your wine label or any other professional project:

▶ A design is never finished. Leave time to do revisions.

▶ Save often and back up your work. I suggest also saving different versions of your work, like "mylabel_v1," "mylabel_v2a," etc.

▶ Keep your document organized. In other words, use layers and name them intuitively.

▶ Show your wine label to a few trusted friends or colleagues. Ask them what they think. Is the information clear and easily readable? Are the graphics visually appealing?

▶ Print your design from a desktop printer to get a good idea of the size of the label. Cut out the label and superimpose it over an actual wine bottle to see how it looks.

▶ If you "borrowed" from someone else's work, or used an existing image as a template in the creation of the label, keep copyright issues in mind.

Kevin Hulsey

"The first step in a freelance illustration career is to create a portfolio of 10 or more samples of your best work," Husley said.

"Your abilities will be judged on your worst sample, not your best sample, so make sure that they are all equally high-quality."

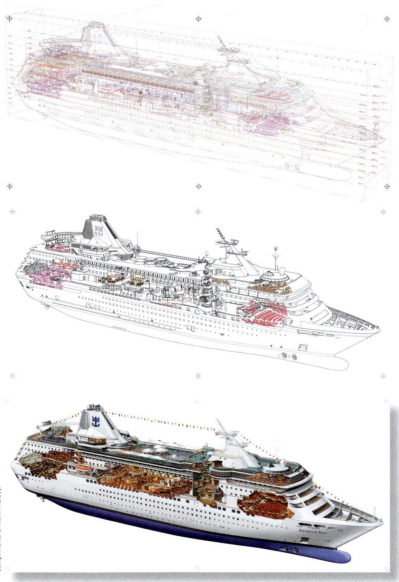

Compliments of Kevin Hulsey.

The well-organized layers in Kevin's Illustrator file are just one part of the process to create accurate and detailed technical illustrations.

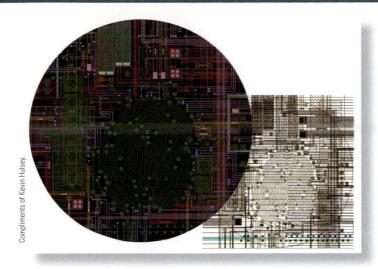

Compliments of Kevin Hulsey.

Rendition of an Intel fingerprint.

About Kevin Hulsey

Kevin Hulsey was born in Los Angeles, California, in 1955. His exposure to both commercial and fine art contributed to his development as an artist and illustrator.

Kevin's early work was heavily influenced by the Pop and Photo-Realist fine art movement of the 1960s. Artists Don Eddy and Richard Estes exerted the greatest influence with their sense of light, shadow, reflection, and realism. By the late 1970s, Kevin was drawn to the commercial art world through his admiration of the work of David Kimble, Richard Leech, Tony Matthews, and Japanese technical illustrators Makoto Ouchi and Yoshihiro Inomoto.

Specializing in automotive and industrial cutaway illustration, Kevin has earned a reputation as one of the world's premier technical illustrators. Since 1980, his talent has been recognized by the advertising industry; he has received numerous awards from Belding, Best in the West, Communication Arts Magazine, and the ADLA. Over the years, Kevin has worked for many of the top Fortune 500 companies.

Although largely self-taught, Kevin has a strong background in architecture, drafting, and design. He works in various media, including oils, acrylics, airbrush, and computer graphics in both fine and commercial art. His studio is located in Carmel, California.

Visit Kevin's informative Web site at http://www.khulsey.com/. The site includes detailed student tutorials and lessons on his technical illustration techniques and processes using Illustrator and Photoshop.

Compliments of Kevin Hulsey.

Digital camera design.

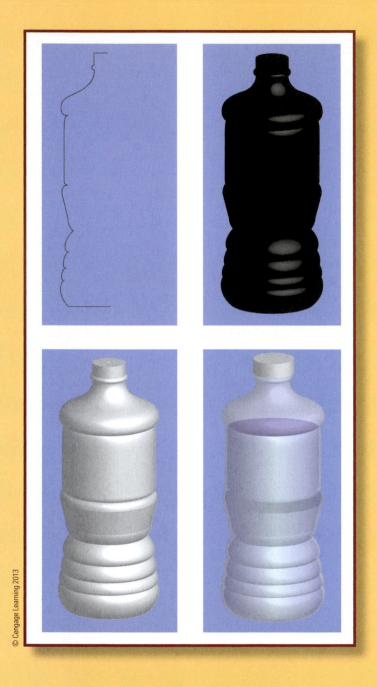

| Spatial Illusions |

charting your course

Our world would be a flat place indeed without the third dimension. And so would your 2D artwork without any means to create spatial illusion. In fact, the arrangement of objects into a whole—the definition of composition from the previous chapter—is really only the surface of what could be a more dimensional visual experience. With a little Illustrator magic, you can create the illusion of three dimensions, organic form, and space in your drawing and design. Obviously, we can't show you all the methods for creating such spatial illusions, but we will cover some Illustrator tools and commands to help you get started. This chapter will explore the use of the blend and mesh commands, the liquify reshaping tools, and 3D effects.

goals

In this chapter you will:

▶ *Integrate new skills with those you have developed in previous chapters*

▶ *Discover the use of blends for producing subtle transitions of color and shape*

▶ *Distort and transform blended objects*

▶ *Reshape and distort objects with the liquify tools*

▶ *Use envelopes to mold objects*

▶ *Precisely control the tonal detail of gradients with gradient meshes*

▶ *Use 3D effects to construct objects in the x, y, and z dimensions, simulating a 3D look*

MAKING SPACE

Establishing a sense of space in 2D artwork involves the skillful application of the fundamental elements of design: line, shape, value, texture, and color. The ways in which these elements might be sized, rearranged, and positioned trick our eyes into seeing and believing the illusion of depth and dimension on flat surfaces. A simple example of this concept is one-point perspective drawing—the convergence of lines and shapes at a distant vanishing point.

> Note: *The one-point perspective example shown in Figure 9–1 is an easy and fun task to re-create and expand in Illustrator. Some suggestions: Turn on View > Smart Guides to snap your lines into place. To identify lines that are in the back of the box shape, use the dotted lines option in the Stroke panel. You will explore the Perspective Grid tool in Chapter 10.*

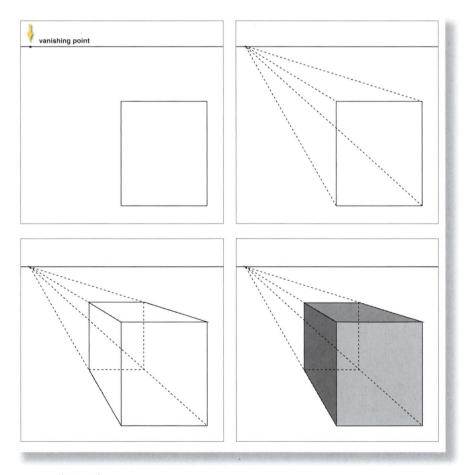

FIGURE | 9–1 |

One-point perspective—placing lines and shapes to create the illusion of three dimensions.

Another example of spatial trickery is the use of light and dark shades of color (or value) to achieve dimensionality. In Figure 9–2, this photo of the Luxor Hotel in Las Vegas has been broken down into light and dark shapes that create the illusion of dimension. Since you are drawing digitally with Illustrator, mastering the art of spatial illusion can be more manageable than doing it by hand. First, you have the luxurious feature of undoing and redoing. Also, as covered in this chapter, you get to use some specific tools and commands, such as blends, envelopes, liquify tools, gradient meshes, and 3D effects.

FIGURE | 9–2 |

The stages of the drawing of the Sphinx at the Luxor Hotel.

BLENDS

With the Blend tool or the Object > Blend > Make command, you can create smooth transitions or distributions of color or shapes. It is a great way to make anything from simple borders to morphed, organic shapes.

In general, you start with creating the shapes or paths you would like to morph. If they have different fill or stroke colors, those will blend too. See Figure 9–3.

FIGURE | 9–3 |

Blend shapes, fill, and stroke colors.

Go to Object > Blend > Blend Options to open the Blend Options window. See Figure 9–4.

FIGURE | 9–4 |

The Blend options.

For Spacing, you can choose Smooth Color to space the blended objects smoothly, like a continuous gradient.

Specified Steps distributes a specified number of morphed objects between the start and end objects.

Specified Distance controls the distance of objects within a blend.

When blends are created, the objects are transformed into steps along a straight path, called a spine, which can be adjusted with Illustrator's editing tools. The Orientation option lets you control how the objects are oriented to the spine, perpendicular either to the x-axis of the page or to the spine itself. You can also edit the straight spine by adding anchor points, or replacing the spine entirely, which you'll be doing in a bit.

Open **chap09_lessons/ch9L1.ai** to begin exploring the blend options in Illustrator.

Blending Colors

The advantage to using blend options to create a gradient, rather than using the Gradient panel, is that a blend is flexible, whereas a gradient is rigid: linear or radial.

1. Hide all but the water layer in your lesson file. There are three paths already created for you.

2. Select the top wavy path on the artboard, click the stroke icon in the Tools panel to make it active, and use the Stroke panel to set the width to 10 pt. Set the stroke color to the light aqua in the Swatches panel, Basic RGB library.

> **Note:** *Scroll down in the Swatches panel to see these colors. If they are not showing at all, use the Swatches panel options menu and select Open Swatch Library > Other Library. Navigate to chap09_lessons > assets and open the* **ch9L1swatches.ai** *file.*

3. Select the middle wavy path on the artboard and set the width to 10 pt and the stroke color to the medium aqua in the Swatches panel.

4. Select the bottom straight path on the artboard and set the width to 10 pt and the stroke color to the darkest aqua in the Swatches panel. See Figure 9–5.

FIGURE | 9–5 |

Set the stroke of each water path to 10 pt, and a different shade of aqua.

5. Double-click the Blend tool in the Tools panel to access the blend options. Make sure that Smooth Color is selected for Spacing (refer to Figure 9–4) and click OK.

6. Click once on the left point of the top path, then once on the left point of the middle path (see Figure 9–6), and then finally on the left point of the bottom path.

   If you have more than one object, the order in which you click on each object will affect the blending pattern.

7. Use Edit > Undo (Command Z in Mac/Ctrl Z in Window) to step backward to the point before you established the smooth color blend in step 6—three 10 point paths with stroke colors applied.

8. With the Blend tool, click on the upper-left point first, then the lower-left point, and finally, the middle-left point. Interesting, right? See Figure 9–7.

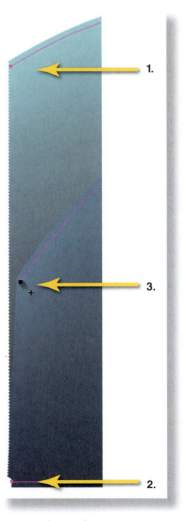

FIGURE | 9–6 |

Click on the left end point of each path to create the water blend.

FIGURE | 9–7 |

Changing the order in which each object is clicked on changes the nature of the blend.

9. Unhide the other layers, click outside the artboard to deselect objects and admire your ocean scene, and then save your file. See Figure 9–8.

10. For fun, let's add some turbulence to the water. Click the target icon in the Layers panel to select the water—you should see the three main paths selected and the blend path (spine) that connects them. See Figure 9–9.

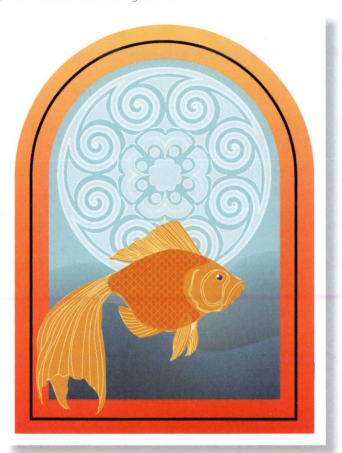

FIGURE | 9–8 |

The fish illustration with water added.

FIGURE | 9–9 |

Use the Selection tool to select the water in its entirety.

11. Go to Effect > Distort & Transform and choose the Roughen option.

12. In the Roughen Options dialog box, set the Size to 5%, the Detail to 30/in, and Points to Smooth (see Figure 9–10), then click OK.

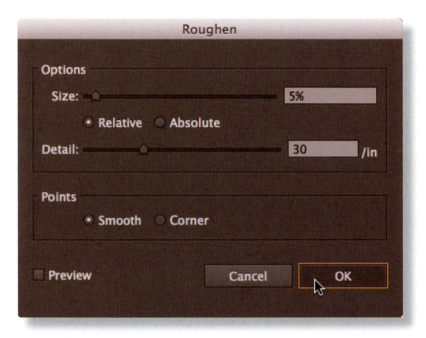

FIGURE | 9–10 |

The Roughen options.

13. Save your file as **blends_yourname.ai**.

> Note: *Be aware that creating blends and then adding effects to them can get memory-intensive. The effect might take a while to render and redraw. This is normal; your computer has to process a lot of data to execute more complex graphics. Save often when things get slow.*

> Note: *If you don't like an effect once it's been applied, edit it using the Appearance panel, not the Effects menu. If you use the Effects menu, you will be applying the effect a second time—which is not necessarily a bad thing, if you are sure that's what you want to do.*

Aside from blending colors in nonlinear/nonradial ways, you can blend objects that can morph in shape, size, color, or just to create an interesting border effect. Blended objects can also be saved as Flash animation files!

Blending Objects

1. Lock the **water** layer and unlock the **starpath** layer. Below the artboard, select the star with the Selection tool.

2. Press Shift Alt (Windows) or Shift Option (Mac) and drag a copy of the star to the right. Holding the Shift key keeps the spine perfectly horizontal. See Figure 9–11.

FIGURE | 9–11 |

Hold down Option/Alt and Shift as you drag to create a copy.

3. Double-click the Blend tool in the Tools panel to open its options.

4. Select Specified Steps and set the number to 30, then click OK.

5. Click with the Blend tool at the top point of the left starfish shape. Then click again on the same point of the starfish at the right to create the blend. Make sure that you click on the same point on each object. See Figure 9–12.

Note: *If you want, go ahead and click on different points of each star (the top of one, and then the bottom right of the other, for instance) to see how the blend evolves, then undo that and create the blend the "right" way.*

FIGURE | 9–12 |

Click on the same point on each star to create the blend.

6. With the Selection tool, click on one of the end stars in the blend and observe the spine that connects them. The spine controls the direction and distance of the blend, along with other attributes, like size, position, and color. If you adjust one of the original objects (the first or last star in this case) in the blend with an editing tool, such as the Scale tool, or change the fill color of one, the blend will update. See Figure 9–13.

FIGURE | 9–13 |

A blended object with 30 steps.

Note: *To remove a blend between objects, choose the blend group with the Selection tool, then choose Object > Blend > Release. To create individual, editable objects from each blend object, choose Object > Blend > Expand.*

In addition to the Blend tool, the Blend menu options offer additional ways to manipulate blends.

1. Select the star blend group if necessary, hold down the Shift key, then also select the starpath.

2. Choose Object > Blend > Replace Spine. Figure 9–14.

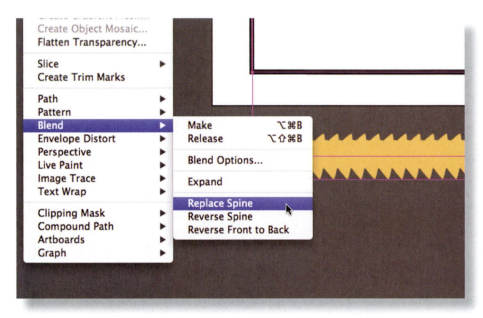

FIGURE | 9–14 |

Use any path to change the shape and direction of blended objects.

3. If you altered one of the original stars in step 6, choose Object > Blend, and select the Reverse Spine option to see what that does.

4. If you didn't alter one of the original stars in step 6, click on this new border with the Selection tool and note which star is also selected. Deselect everything and then use the Direct Selection tool to select this "master" star. Use the Scale tool to make it a bit larger. Watch the blend update. Change the color of the star to see how that changes things.

5. Use Command Z (Mac)/Ctrl Z (Window) several times to revert to the original border blend you made in step 2.

6. On your own, try using other Effects on the star border blend. Remember from your experience creating Graphic Styles that you can add several fills and strokes to a shape using the Appearance panel. Be patient, and save often!

Mop Up

The water seems to be spilling over the edges of the arch.
Cleaning that up is just a matter of creating a mask (which
you did in Chapter 8).

1. Hide all but the water layer so there's nothing blocking the
    layer.

2. Use the Rectangle tool and drag a rectangle that is just a
    bit narrower at the edges than the water and up a bit from
    the bottom. The top of the rectangle should be clear of
    the water. The fill and stroke colors of this rectangle don't
    matter, as they will disappear once the mask is made. See
    Figure 9–15.

3. Select both the water and the rectangle, and then use
    Object > Clipping Mask > Make (the option is down toward
    the bottom of the menu). See Figure 9–16.

4. Unhide all the layers and save your file! Nice job. See
    Figure 9–17.

FIGURE | 9–15 |

A mask object can be
any color to start.

FIGURE | 9–16 |

Use a clipping mask to
hide messy edges.

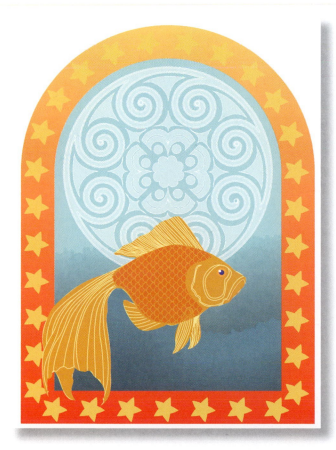

FIGURE | 9–17 |

The completed fish illustration.

The liquify tools.

LIQUIFY TOOLS

Seven playful tools for reshaping and distorting objects (vector or rasterized) are located in the Illustrator Tools panel. See Figure 9–18. These are the liquify tools, with fun names like Warp, Twirl, Pucker, Bloat, Scallop, Crystallize, and Wrinkle. To use a liquify tool, select it from the Tools panel and then click or click and drag the tool over the object you want to reshape. If you double-click on a liquify tool icon in the Tools panel, the options for that tool appear. See Figure 9–19.

An example of what each liquify tool does is provided in Figure 9–20. For you to experience each hands-on, a practice version of this file is located in the folder **chap09_lessons/assets/liquify.ai**.

1. Select a liquify tool in the Tools panel.

2. Click or click and drag the tool over an object you want to reshape or distort.

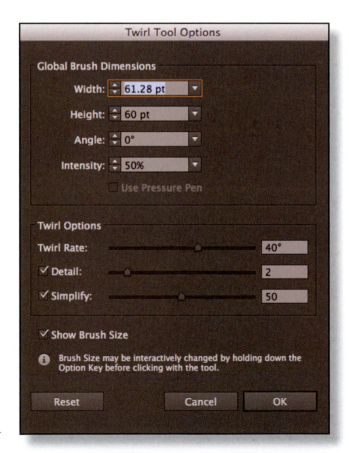

The options for the Twirl tool.

FIGURE | 9–20 |

Examples of what each liquify tool does.

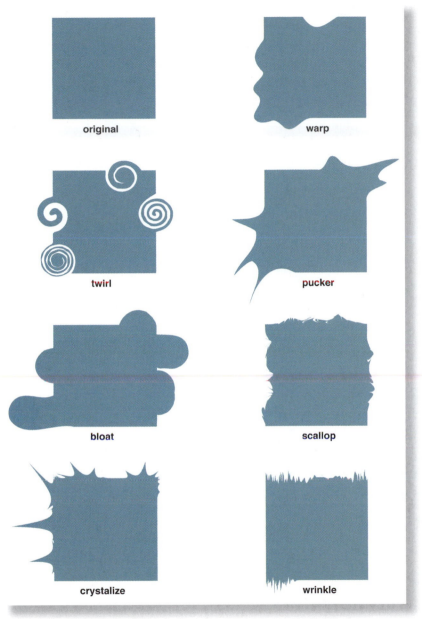

original

warp

twirl

pucker

bloat

scallop

crystalize

wrinkle

> **Note:** *Liquify tools cannot be used on linked files or objects containing text, graphs, or symbols. To work with these objects, first outline the text and ungroup and/or expand the graphs and symbols.*

3. To modify the tool, double-click on the tool's icon in the Tools panel to bring up its options box.

4. To adjust the size and shape of the liquify tool as you draw, hold down Option/Alt. Add the Shift key to constrain the shape into a perfect circle.

ENVELOPES

Like the liquify tools, an envelope allows you to reshape and distort objects. Think of envelopes as molds that wrap around objects, bending them in multiple ways, as shown in Figure 9–21. You can edit an envelope with Illustrator's editing tools, such as the Direct Selection, Transform, and liquify tools. Envelopes can also be created from paths, compound paths, text, meshes, blends, and bitmap images, such as GIF, JPEG, and TIFF.

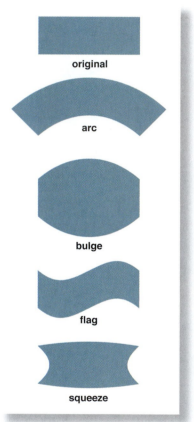

FIGURE | 9–21 |

A few of the Make with Warp options for envelopes.

To make an envelope, select an object, choose Object > Envelope Distort, and choose from one of three envelope types: Make with Warp, Make with Mesh, or Make with Top Object.

Make with Warp

With Make with Warp, you have a variety of choices for creating envelopes. See Figure 9–21.

1.   Select some text, a placed bitmap image, or vector object.

2.   Choose Object > Envelope Distort > Make with Warp.

3.   In the Warp Options dialog box, select Preview.

4. Choose a Style, Bend amount, and a level of horizontal and vertical distortion. See Figure 9–22. Experiment with different settings and see what distortions are possible.

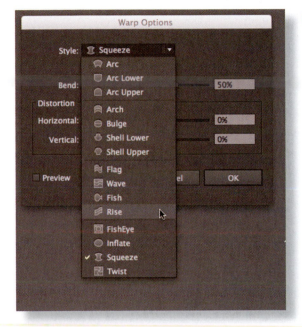

Figures © Cengage Learning 2013

FIGURE | 9–22 |

The Warp Options dialog box—so many warp styles to choose from!

5. Click OK.

6. Modify the scale of the warp using the Scale or Free Transform tool, or individual anchor points with the Direct Selection tool.

Note: *To remove an envelope, choose Object > Envelope Distort > Release. To create individual, editable objects from an enveloped object, choose Object > Envelope Distort > Expand.*

Make with Mesh

A mesh object, shown in Figure 9–23, looks like a grid on graph paper, and in this case, each point at the intersections of the mesh can be modified. New lines and mesh points can also be added.

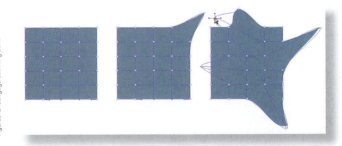

FIGURE | 9–23 |

An example of a 4-by-5 Mesh Grid on a simple rectangle, modified with the Direct Selection tool or the Mesh tool.

1. Select some text, a bitmap, or vector object.

2. Choose Object > Envelope Distort > Make with Mesh.

3. In the Envelope Mesh dialog box, choose the number of rows and columns you would like in the mesh. Click OK.

> Note: *Depending on the shape you are trying to create from the mesh, you might want to experiment with more or fewer rows and columns. Keep in mind, more rows and columns produce more editable anchor points; however, the time it takes to redraw the mesh will increase.*

4. Modify points on the mesh with the Mesh tool. See Figure 9–24.

5. To add more rows and columns to the mesh, click on the grid lines with the Mesh tool.

6. To delete a row or column, press and hold Option/Alt and click with the Mesh tool on a point or grid line.

FIGURE | 9–24 |

The Mesh tool.

Make with Top Object

You can create an envelope of any shape to surround and reshape an object or group by using the Envelope Distort Command. See Figure 9–26.

1. Select the object(s) you want to reshape and the object you want to use as an envelope. Very important: Make sure the object to be used as the envelope is above or in front of the object(s) you want to reshape. If both objects are on the same layer, select the object to be used as the envelope and choose Object > Arrange > Bring to Front. Another option is to place the envelope object on a layer (or sublayer) above the object you want to affect in the Layers panel.

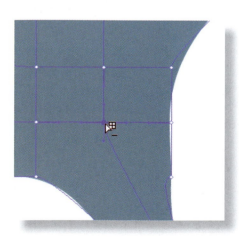

FIGURE | 9–25 |

Hold the Option/Alt key and use the Mesh tool to delete rows, or columns in a mesh object.

FIGURE | 9–26 |

An object stacked above another object (i.e., the transparent yellow shape above the text) can become an envelope for the object below it (i.e., the text).

2. Choose Object > Envelope Distort > Make with Top Object. The two objects are grouped into an envelope.

3. Edit or add a new fill or stroke to the selected envelope using the options in the Appearance panel, or select the envelope and the object and use Object > Envelope Distort > Edit Contents. See Figure 9–27.

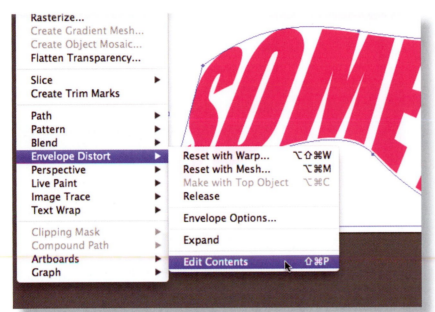

FIGURE | 9–27 |

Edit the contents of an envelope.

4. To adjust the envelope, select it with the Mesh tool and alter the anchor points and direction handles. See Figure 9–28.

5. Depending on what's selected, the editing options for Envelope Distort change. See Figure 9–29.

FIGURE | 9–28 |

Adjust an individual section of the envelope.

FIGURE | 9–29 |

Use Object > Envelop Distort to edit either the contents or the envelope.

FIGURE | 9–30 |

Use gradient meshes to create tonal detail and smooth transitions of color.

GRADIENT MESHES

Gradient meshes allow you to control the application, coloring, and tonal detail of gradient blends. See Figure 9–30. There are two ways to create mesh objects: select the Create Gradient Mesh command (Object > Create Gradient Mesh) or use the Mesh tool. The Create Gradient Mesh command allows you to define a regular pattern of mesh lines and points. To create a customized mesh with a varied pattern of lines and points, use the Mesh tool. Here are some important things to know about mesh objects.

► Once a mesh object is created, it cannot be converted back into a path object. You can, however, Edit > Undo a mesh if you make a mistake. You can also use Object > Path > Offset Path and set the offset amount to 0, which will create an approximate duplicate of the original shape.

► Meshes can be created on simple objects, but not directly on text (see note), compound paths, or linked EPS files.

> **Note:** *Meshes can be created on text if it is first converted to outlines (Type > Create Outlines) and any compound paths within the text shape (or any other shape, like the holes of the scissors in Figure 9–30) are released (Object > Compound Path > Release).*

► Complex mesh objects can affect a computer's performance and the speed at which the graphics refresh on the screen. Keep your mesh objects simple. Breaking complex images into smaller parts—and keeping them on individual layers—can make your work a lot easier.

► Even though you have the Offset Path trick at your disposal, it's a good idea to create a copy of your object before applying a mesh to it, so you have something to go back to should things not work out the first time.

Of course, as with any tool you have been using, the best way to understand how it works is to try it out. Using the **ch9L2.ai** file in the **chap09_lessons** folder, or with your own artwork, practice your mesh-making skills with the following steps:

1. Select a filled object.

2. Choose Object > Create Gradient Mesh

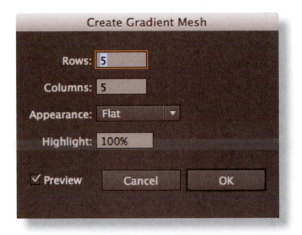

FIGURE | 9–31 |

The Create Gradient Mesh options box.

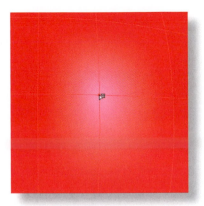

FIGURE | 9–32 |

Select an anchor point with the Mesh tool.

3. Set your gradient options in the Create Gradient Mesh dialog box. Choose Preview to see how each option affects the object. Keep your rows and columns to a minimum. See Figure 9–31. Click OK.

4. Select the Mesh tool (refer back to Figure 9–24) and click on a mesh patch, where an anchor point intersects a row and a column. See Figure 9–32.

5. Open the Swatches panel.

6. Choose a colored swatch to apply to the selected patch area.

7. With the Mesh tool, select another anchor point and apply a different color. Notice how the colors blend. See Figure 9–33.

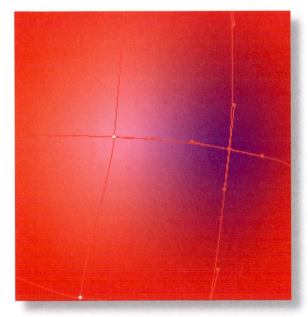

FIGURE | 9–33 |

Apply a color to a mesh object.

8. Click and drag on a mesh point or its handles with the Mesh tool to modify the anchor points and the color blend. See Figure 9–34.

Modify an anchor point of a mesh patch.

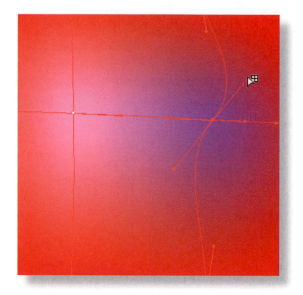

9. Click between two anchor points on the mesh to add another row or column. See Figure 9–35.

Add another column and row using the Mesh tool.

10. To delete a column or row, Option/Alt click on the point with the Mesh tool.

> Note: *Instead of choosing Object > Create Gradient Mesh, you can create a gradient mesh by selecting a filled object and then clicking directly on it with the Mesh tool, adding rows and columns as you like. Remember to use Edit > Undo if you make a mistake.*

Note: *Transparency/Opacity values can be assigned to individual mesh patches. Select one or more mesh patches (the areas between the points) and set the opacity in the Transparency panel, Control panel, or the Appearance panel.*

3D EFFECTS

You can easily get lost—in a good way—using the 3D Effects, where paths and shapes can be extruded, rotated, and revolved around the x-, y-, and z-axes. See Figure 9–36, Figure 9–37, and Figure 9–38. You can also adjust the lighting and shading of the 3D objects, and place artwork on their surfaces (called mapping).

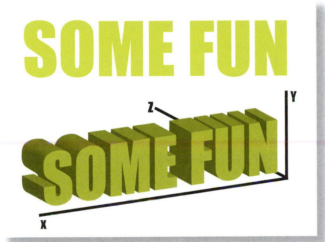

FIGURE | 9–36 |

Extrude and bevel text in three dimensions.

FIGURE | 9–37 |

Rotate and add perspective to text.

3D Effects are located in the Effect menu (Effect > 3D), where you choose from Extrude & Bevel, Revolve, or Rotate. An options dialog box window appears where you choose the direction (x, y, or z) in which you would like your object to move and distort. To do this, click, then drag the cursor on an edge of the cube. See Figure 9–39. The x-axis rotation icon and text box are at the top, the y-axis options are in the middle, and the z-axis options are at the bottom. To adjust the cube and the three axes together, click and drag on a surface, rather than the edge of the cube. See Figure 9–40. Checking the preview box will let you see the effect before you click OK. Even though each alteration takes longer to render with Preview checked it gives you a better idea of the final look.

Expect to spend late nights captivated by the many options in the 3D Effects Options box. To get you started, the following steps describe how to use the 3D Revolve effect. Use the **ch09_L3.ai** file in the **chap09_lessons** folder, or draw your own paths.

1. Draw one side or edge (called a profile) of an object that, when revolved around an axis, will produce a symmetrical shape, such as a water bottle (see Figure 9–41), a chess piece, a pine tree, or an ornament. Use guides to help you align the start and end points of the path.

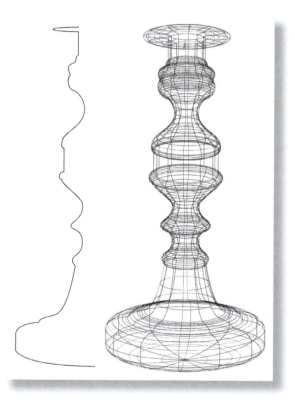

FIGURE | 9–38 |

Revolve the profile of our candlestick from Chapter 4 around the y-axis.

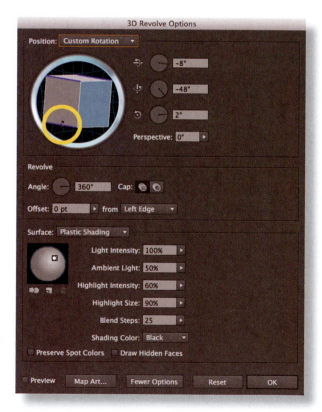

FIGURE | 9–39 |

Adjust the x-axis of the object.

Figures © Cengage Learning 2013

2. Select the profile. Choose Effect > 3D > Revolve.

3. Enter your specifications in the 3D Revolve Options dialog box. See Figure 9–42. Turn on Preview as you make adjustments to see how it looks on your selected path. For the water bottle profile, try the following 3D Revolve options:

- ▶ *Position*: Off-Axis Front
- ▶ *Revolve angle*: 360°
- ▶ *Offset*: 0 pt from Right Edge
- ▶ *Surface*: Plastic Shading

Click OK. See Figure 9–43.

FIGURE | 9–40 |

Adjust the *x*-, *y*-, and *z*-axes of the object at the same time by clicking and dragging on a side of the cube.

FIGURE | 9–41 |

A profile of a water bottle to be revolved around the *y*-axis.

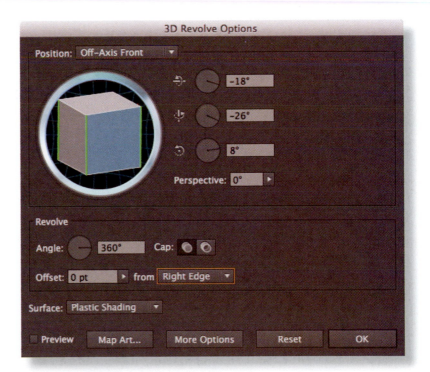

FIGURE | 9–42 |

The 3D Revolve Options dialog box.

4. The color of the completed object is specified by the stroke color of the original path. To alter it select the object's original path and change the stroke color. The stroke in our example is white with an opacity setting of 60% (set in the Appearance panel). See Figure 9–44.

5. To fine-tune, the original path, select and move individual anchor points with the Direct Selection tool. The revolved shape updates with each new adjustment. The adjusted version of the water bottle is shown in Figure 9–45.

6. As with all Illustrator Effects, you must use the Appearance panel of the selected path to edit or remove the effect. Click on the effect name in the panel to open its options and make adjustments. To remove an effect, select it in the panel and choose Clear Appearance at the bottom of the panel. See Figure 9–46. Alternatively, you can drag the effect to the trash icon at the bottom of the panel.

7. Save your file often when using complex effects that require a lot of processing to render.

FIGURE | 9–43 |

The completed Revolve.

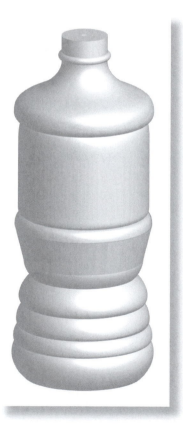

FIGURE | 9–44 |

Set the color and transparency of the original profile—the revolved object is updated.

FIGURE | 9–45 |

The final version of the water bottle.

FIGURE | 9–46 |

Remove the 3D Revolve effect using the Appearance panel.

GRAPHIC STYLE 3D EFFECTS AND THE FREE DISTORT EFFECT

Before you get distracted with these newfound tools and options, there are two more things you should know about: the 3D Effects Graphic Styles Library and the Free Distort effect.

For quick and easy application of a 3D Effect, open the Graphic Styles panel. Then, from the Graphic Styles panel options menu, choose Open Graphic Style Library >

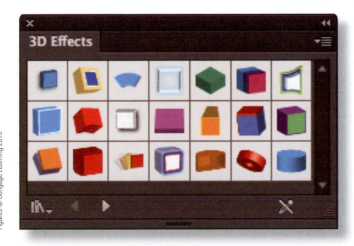

FIGURE | 9–47 |

Open the 3D Effects graphic styles library.

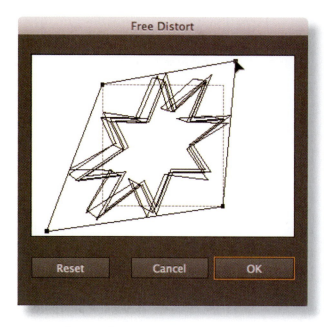

FIGURE | 9–48 |

Use Free Distort to alter the dimensions and shape of an object.

3D Effects. See Figure 9–47. Draw a simple path or geometric shape on the artboard, select it, and then take your pick of any of the predefined dimensional shapes in the 3D Effects Library.

To further modify your 3D effect or any selected path or shape, use the Free Distort effect: choose Effect > Distort & Transform > Free Distort. Free Distort allows you to bend selected artwork within a flexible bounding box. Click and drag on any of the four corners of the box and the artwork is distorted accordingly. See Figure 9–48.

While you're experimenting with these new toys, take a look at the Appearance panel to see how the effects are created. See if you can create some of your own (refer to Chapter 6).

FIGURE | 9–49 |

Examples of 3D graphic effects (left) and Free Distort options (right).

SUMMARY

Perhaps this chapter has transported you to another drawing dimension—one that is not flat, but rather filled with spatial possibilities.

▶ IN REVIEW

1. What are Smart Guides? Why are they so smart?

2. What are the two methods for creating blends?

3. What tool is used to modify individual anchor points of blended, meshed, or warped objects?

4. How do you change the brush size of a liquify tool?

5. When making an envelope with a different object, where must the object that will be used as the envelope be located?

6. How do complex mesh objects affect computer performance?

7. What three options are available when using the 3D Effects feature?

8. How do you change the color of a revolved 3D object?

9. Name four options available in the 3D Effects Options dialog box and describe what they do.

10. To adjust or modify an effect, where do you go?

▶ EXPLORING ON YOUR OWN

1. Access the Help > Illustrator Help option and read up on Reshaping objects.

2. Take a black-and-white photo of yourself and import it into Illustrator, or import a color photo and convert it to grayscale (Edit > Edit Colors > Convert to Grayscale). Use the photo as a template to draw a realistic self-portrait. Identify the light and dark areas of the photo and draw each area with light- and dark-colored filled shapes. Refer to Figure 9–2.

3. Create your own perspective boxes (or other dimensional shapes) as shown in Figure 9–1. Use Smart Guides to place the paths and shapes accurately.

4. Create an abstract design, pattern, or collage using the tools discovered in this chapter. See if you can create a sense of dimension in the artwork.

FROM PAPER TO PIXELS

Be prepared for a special treat! Michael Fleishman, an illustrator extraordinaire, presents a personal account of his creative process and provides guidelines to bring to light your own artistic inspirations.

Originally from Pittsburgh, PA, and now living in Yellow Springs, OH, **Michael Fleishman** earned both his BA in Art Education and an MA in Fine Arts from Indiana University of PA. He teaches at Edison Community College in Piqua, OH, where he was honored to receive a regional SOCHE Excellence in Teaching award (2006), as well as a national teaching excellence award from NISOD (2004).

Mike's illustration clients are numerous, and he's written for a variety of publications. He is the author of two books for North Light (now out of print), as well as *Starting Your Career as a Freelance Illustrator or Graphic Designer* (Allworth Press), *Exploring Illustration* (Cengage), *Drawing Inspiration: Visual Artists at Work* (Cengage) and *How to Grow as an Illustrator* (Allworth Press).

Mike has presented at How Magazine's Design World in 2002, NISOD's annual conference in 2004, and ICON 4 in 2005. He's also been a visiting artist at Kendall College of Art and Design, Savannah College of Art and Design, and Minneapolis College of Art and Design. He served on the board of directors for ICON6, the Illustration Conference in Pasadena, CA, in 2010.

The Fleishman Artistic Process
By Michael Fleishman

I absolutely love drawing and painting digitally. But I also revel in the very act of drawing or painting on a real surface, with actual tools and physical materials. Saying that, I must confess: currently, the balance has shifted for me—the computer has become the critical tool in my creative arsenal.

Working on a computer can't *replace* the little rush you get from the silky flow of watercolors (or the scratch of a great pen) on good paper. In a related issue, I wouldn't want screen time—and I am on my Mac *a lot*— to supplant the sheer fun and thrilling serendipity of the traditional process. There is also something quite intimate and primary about holding (and looking at) the product of that particular labor in both hands.

I mention all this because I seriously *do* love drawing and painting digitally (it bears repeating, folks) and for many of the same reasons I enjoy working with analog materials and supplies. I adore making marks with a *variety* of tools, and when you're in that zoned-out moment, with the perfect instrument in your hands, it just makes beautiful sense (and gorgeous marks).

The computer simply fits right in with my drawing supplies. It comfortably co-exists with the bulk of my art materials, just as my paints sat next to the inks, 140 lb. watercolor paper rubs up against tracing pads, and pencils spoon with my markers. True enough, I won't do that incredibly messy collage work on the same table, obviously, but, duh, that only makes reasonable sense.

The ways and means of digital illustration are as varied as traditional painting styles and techniques (or *any* medium, for that matter). If you paint, you're a *painter*; but this generic label merely places you in that big, metaphorical ballpark where all the "painters" play ball. Likewise, digital style and technique are not fixed classifications. You may work *digitally*, but that doesn't have to typecast you.

You tap into the computer in many different ways—as a fast sketch tool, or for down and dirty color and/or compositional roughs. The computer may be just *part* of the overall process. Many illustrators make every effort to emphasize the digital quality of the medium, while others try just as hard to make the tool anonymous to the process.

Perhaps you'll scan picture elements into the computer, then incorporate or collage this material to produce the art. You process these design components, and literally piece together the digital final.

Obviously, many illustrators work directly—*digita prima*, so to speak —no paper sketch, no scans, no template. It's all done completely on the computer. Of course, line work is often done by hand and scanned into the computer for clean up. Line at this stage may be refined as necessary; color, texture, and pattern then added digitally to create the complete package. I function just this way.

I apply a "kitchen sink" mixed media approach in my work— combining acrylic; marker and ink; white-out; pencil, crayon, and grease pencil on board, or paper, or canvas—*whatever*

works. At some point the piece *may* be scanned into Photoshop and completed digitally. Or a rough or tiny thumbnail provides the perfect template for an Illustrator illustration. Whatever *works*.

So now that you have an idea of my routine, what do you say we get into a more specific demo of that process, so you can try it on your own? Let's begin!

Your Turn

First, get a concept together. My illustration (digital or traditional) always begins with a *drawing*—the line. For my demo here, I was inspired by a selection of roughs I compiled for the chapter on sketches and roughs in my book, *Exploring Illustration*. Certain doodles caught my eye, and I pulled them out as inspiration for the characters I wanted to play with now. Figure E–1 is a scan of my

FIGURE | E–1 |

The quick doodles and spontaneous ramblings for the concept of *Good Buds*. This paper sketch was scanned as is into Photoshop as line art. *Good Buds*—or just *Buds* works too— was as much the concept of the piece as it is the title of the drawing. A selection of roughs compiled for a chapter on sketches in *Exploring Illustration* contained certain doodles that caught my eye, and I pulled them out as inspiration for the characters—fast friends captured in a snapshot of camaraderie.

actual roughs and the little notes I scribbled to myself as I drew and doped out the initial concept.

So begin here, as well—dope out *your* concept, then create your line work. For the sake of this sample project, we're going to mix and match our approach—let's draw the line art traditionally. Thinking about color is important, but comes just a bit later.

The Scan

Scanned pencil sketches can give you some sweet line quality—it all depends on what you're after with your concept; but let's scan an ink (or inked) drawing for this demonstration.

You have other decisions at this point. Your drawing may be very polished or rather rough. While I usually choose to refine my preliminaries—my roughs are seldom very *rough*—I want to draw directly in Illustrator for this demo. So when you nail your rough, scan that puppy right into Photoshop.

Where to Next?

Now you can go a number of ways.

1. The scanned art is cleaned up and finessed, then finished in *Photoshop*. You could keep it as line art pure and simple (or add color, tone, textures, and effects in Photoshop at this juncture). By the way, this grayscale or bitmapped line art should be somewhere in the neighborhood of 300-400 dpi and saved as a TIFF (you could also save it as a PSD).

2. You could convert the scanned drawing into a vector-based illustration. This process often adds its own flavor to your line quality. Learn and explore the pertinent conversion settings that ultimately achieve the tightest fidelity to your work—if that is indeed your goal (maybe you actually want to live on the edge and see what happy accidents this step brings to the party). In any event, once converted, the art is now editable in Illustrator.

3. Or think of your drawing as a **template**. Here, you scan the line art into Photoshop, then create the

actual illustration in Photoshop or Illustrator on top of a dimmed image—sort of like virtual tracing paper (hint: if you use the art as a template in Illustrator, you may want to save the scan as a smaller-sized PICT). This is the method we will use for this demonstration. See Figure E–2.

© Michael Fleishman

FIGURE | E–2 |

I've cropped the rough in Photoshop, and next will place it into Illustrator as a template.

What a Character

There are many ways to create great line quality. You may opt for the tried and true, time-honored method—you do it by hand.

In Photoshop, you might select the Brush tool, open up the brushes palette, and choose a brush. Use as is, or tap into the program's extensive control set to customize that brush.

Illustrator offers some slick brush options. Brushes come in different categories that present a tremendous range of line opportunities. I should clarify: you're not actually drawing a line; you're creating a *stroke*, of course. You're still making a path composed of segments with anchors that have direction lines and points. But you get a stroke that looks remarkably natural and is surprisingly responsive.

You can manipulate that stroke with a wide variety of tools and commands, and *redrawing*—reshaping— is a dream. Literally, it's a snap— you can redraw a stroke by simply dragging another line adjacent to an existing stroke—the initial line magically snaps to the new stroke. You can reshape with the pencil, brush, smooth, and erase tools, as well as the classic pen tools.

Make a mistake? Change your mind? No problem—do a Command Z (undo) until you're back to square one. Want more choices? Go to the brush libraries for other alternatives, or customize existing brushes. You can even create personal brush libraries using your own actual lines.

Ready, Set...

Like my colleague, David Julian (and many other artists), I'm not a "filter hound." It's educational to dabble with all the many bells and whistles a good graphics application has in its repertoire. It is fun to try out all the on-board gizmos. There are various filter, preset, and style packages you can add on, as well.

But as with many illustrators (digital or otherwise), I like to keep things clean and simple. To my eyes, there is frequently an obvious (and often overblown, in the wrong hands) sterile, "computer look" I never cared for, and still scrupulously avoid.

So, let's continue our little clean and simple demo that taps into some basic Illustrator tools.

Go!

Open up a new Illustrator document and place your drawing as a **template**. See Figure E–3. Make sure the template and link boxes are checked in the dialogue box. Once we're back to our document, the Layers window should indicate that the rough came in with a *template* designation. On your screen it will be grayed around 50% (you can lighten the value even further).

Your rough should be the second layer down on the list (under Layer 1). Unlock the layer, so you can size the

template up or down. Size it and lock the template layer again (so you don't move it inadvertently).

Rename Layer 1, if you wish. *Make sure you're working in this layer* (*not the template*). Under Window in the Menu Bar, choose Show Brushes (if the Brush palette isn't up already) and/or choose a brush library from Brush Libraries. Grab a brush. Select the Brush tool from the Tools panel. Make sure you are working with a stroke color, and the Fill is set to none (you could also draw with the Pencil tool and apply the brush to these strokes, but I usually just draw with the Brush tool directly).

Now—trace over your template. It's that simple.

© Michael Fleishman

FIGURE | E–3 |

My rough is now the template for my illustration, renamed and in the right layer—below the actual illustration. Yes, this scan of the original screen shot reveals that, at the time, I was working in an earlier version of Illustrator, probably Illustrator CS or CS2. Once I have the grayed out image to size and position, I'll relock this template layer and start the drawing.

Going on a Line Hunt

That's the beauty of it—it's easy to do. But your control over these lines is quite powerful and extensive. Reshape, resize, and reposition your lines at will; the Tools panel offers so many options to get your drawing exactly the way you want it.

Normally, I shoot for a line of pronounced character, keeping it as close as possible to the line quality I try to achieve with real pen on paper. Outside my digital box, I invariably push my line quality to the full extent of the law: by slowing down my stroke, dragging and/or tilting my pen, and working on an absorbent paper that deliberately bleeds the line (paper towels and napkins are especially wonderful surfaces to draw on). Dried out pens are interesting to play with, too; I don't toss a pen until it's really dead.

Here, there are some fun options we must discuss. Distress your drawing surface: crumple up the napkin or paper before you begin the drawing. See Figure E–4. Consider doing the drawing *small*. Back in the day, I would take the tiny, craggy line art (on that semi-destroyed napkin) and enlarge it on a photocopier about 200-600 percent (my standard equation). The resulting line quality was fantastic! Working on the computer was a game changer, however. And once you go Mac, you can't go

back! I could now scan that little diamond in the rough and blow it up digitally, saving a few trees in the process, with the same wonderful results.

For this demo, I wanted to break from my norm, to challenge myself by doing something rather *different*. My character concept for *Good Buds*—a warm and fuzzy, whimsical, friendly bunch—suggested I explore another line quality. So I went with a clean, thin, but *wiggly* line character. See Figure E–5, A. That was actually part of the exact phrase that popped into my head: draw 'em wiggly squiggly. This clean stroke would work well with the color shapes that I wanted to knock in and out of that line. Working from some initial notes and sketches, I developed my cast as I went along, tweaking characterization many times for each of the crew. And when I had my line work just right, it was time to lay in the color.

Da Color

There are only two layers in this illustration: line and color. (However, as you'll see, there are loads of paths—stay organized, it will definitely help.) I created (and closed) color fields (see Figure E–5, B) with the Pencil tool, but you could select the Pen tool for a more geometric look.

I like doing this, too: juxtaposing geometric, straight-edged "mechanical" color with a more organic line feel. But again, I wanted to make a departure from my norm, so I chose freeform color shapes for this demo. However, the angled style is just as lively and I love that look (see Figure E–5, C).

As you almost "skate around" with the pen tool, you'll see the color field taking shape with each anchor point you put down. Close the shape by bringing the pen point over your starting point. See that small circle right next to the pen symbol? Look for the same tiny icon when closing a shape with the Pencil tool, as well.

© Michael Fleishman

FIGURE | E–4 |

Normally, I shoot for a line of pronounced character, keeping it close as possible to my "analog" line quality. Often, I will push line character as much as possible: by slowing down the stroke, dragging and/or tilting my pen, and working on absorbent (and frequently distressed) paper that deliberately bleeds and bumps the line. *Milhaus* was drawn quite small on a crumpled napkin, scanned and plumbed up some 200-600 percent, then colored in Photoshop.

Draw and redraw your color fields, establish your hierarchy, and manipulate the order of those colors, manipulating hues front to back within the layer (go to Menu Bar > Object > Arrange, or do control—AKA a right—click). Rename to clarify the paths if you choose. You could also work in multiple layers, but I really didn't need to for this basic demo.

Create, size and position, shape, and color all your fields. You could apply blends, gradients, and textures to your color shapes, if you wish.

When you have tweaked your color and line components to taste, put a fork in it, you're done (see Figure E–5, D)!

Noe: *Both final color and line in the completed demo (Figure E–5, D) are a bit different than the original plates of Figure E–5, A and Figure E–5, B. I massaged line quality and color corrected constantly. Right up to the "very end" (and may continue to do so, even after you read this). I was placing, resizing (and repositioning) line, shape, and color until I felt I nailed it (for now). I could have applied blends, gradients, and textures to the color shapes, but chose not to go there on this one.*

In Conclusion

If you are like me and you seriously *love* the sheer joy of drawing and painting, there is not much of a leap to do that traditionally or digitally. Yes, the act of drawing or painting on a real surface with actual tools and physical materials is different by basic definition. But saying that, let's admit it, it's not the *tools* that make the art, it's the *artist*. The computer, the crayons, the pixels, the paper—it doesn't much matter to me. If it's in my artbox (virtual or otherwise), it's a critical tool in my creative arsenal.

I don't want working on the computer to *replace* my acrylics, oils, pens, and inks, and I want screen time to run tandem with my paper trail. It's *all* fun and thrilling—I adore making marks with a *variety* of tools, and hope you do too.

So enough talking already, let's hit it.

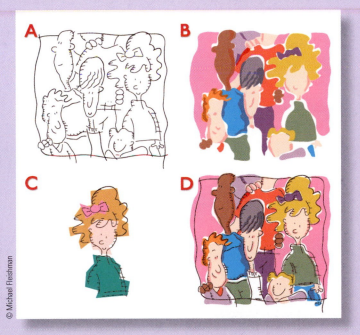

© Michael Fleishman

FIGURE | E–5 |

Figure A: For *Good Buds* I went with a thin line (via the Pencil tool and a clean stroke) with a decided wiggly, squiggly quality. This stroke compliments the color shapes that will knock in and out of that line. The look of the crew was fine-tuned many times as the illustration developed.

Figure B: The color layer for *Good Buds*. Notice the flat color "shading."

Figure C: Geometric, straight-edged, "mechanical" color knocks in and out of the line here. This is the original line plate plus color now created with the Pen tool. The geometric color is a dynamic alternative to the organic shapes produced by the Pencil tool. Here's how to exercise this option: Choose a color. Make sure you are working with the Fill and that your Stroke is set to none. You're going to create colored shapes through a series of clicks and drags.

Figure D: Line and color combined. The final shows the important relationship between the black line, color fields, and white space in this illustration. Check out the hatched line effect working in conjunction with the aforementioned flat color "shading."

Ann Paidrick

Compliments of Ann Paidrick

Magnolia Blossoms. .

About Ann Paidrick

Ann Paidrick grew up in a family of artists. She studied sculpture at Kansas City Art Institute for three years. When she left art school, Ann began to work in fabrics and leathers, creating sculptural pieces, clothing, and illustrations.

Ann and business partner Pat Eby formed Eby-Paidrick Designs in 1977. They produced large-scale architectural textiles, banners, and collages for architects, interior designers, and art directors. Their signature fabric solutions animated spaces in buildings and illustrated ad campaigns, and provided unique environments in theme parks, museum exhibits, and theatrical sets.

In 2000, when the physical demands of building, hauling, and installing projects became onerous, Ann and Pat decided to learn computer graphics to continue working in the creative field. Prior to acquiring two Macintosh G-4s in 2000, their experience with computers was limited to catalog searches at the library.

After a year of twice-weekly tutoring sessions with computer artist Peter Richter, Ann fell in love with Adobe Illustrator. She tolerated Adobe Photoshop and Quark as necessary evils, but Illustrator's reliable vectors spoke to her love of building things. Her sculptor's soul drove her to find ways to make a two-dimensional object appear three dimensional.

Today, her realistic drawings not only push the envelope of the Illustrator software, but they also provide clients with images that can be enlarged to the size of an airplane hangar with no loss of detail and no pixelation. The technique mimics photorealism. The resulting image is rendered flawlessly. Ann's gradient mesh illustrations are especially well suited for food, flowers, glass, metal, and china objects.

To see more of Ann's work, visit *http://www.ebypaidrick.com/*.

About the Work of Ann Paidrick

"I like to start the mesh shapes from a simple rectangle or square," Ann said. "This seems to produce less unruly results. I make my square and place just one set of mesh points in it using Illustrator's Mesh tool. Then I rotate it with an eye toward the final shape. If there's a vein of color down the center of a petal, say, I'll put the center of the square over that. Next, I start 'morphing' the outside points toward the edges of the shape. Finally, I start laying in other points to refine the shape and describe the color changes."

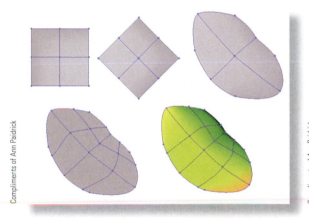

Clockwise from top left, this figure demonstrates the example of stages of Ann's process for building a mesh object from a simple to a more complex form.

Pepper Triplets is a final example of Ann's detailed, mesh-derived work.

Compliments of Ann Paidrick

Compliments of Ann Paidrick

Gold Birthday Bow on Red.

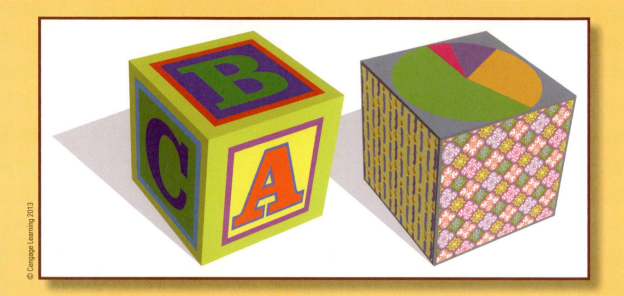

| Getting Technical |

charting your course

As a vector-based program, Illustrator is the perfect place to develop more technical graphics, including package design, architectural and product ideas, interior design, and detailed diagrams and illustrations. It provides charting and graphing tools to develop the graphics that we rely on in scientific and news magazines. Another key process is the new pattern development workflow, which is far more sophisticated in CS6 than in any previous version of Illustrator. Patterns can be applied to such things as packaging, fabrics, and paper, which translates into textiles for clothing and home decor, wrapping paper, wallpaper, party goods, and the list goes on and on.

goals

In this chapter, you will:

▶ *Expand your skills with the 3D Effects options*

▶ *Understand the process for mapping art to 3D surfaces*

▶ *Use the Perspective tool to create 3D objects and scenes*

▶ *Learn the ins and outs of developing charts and graphs, and how to customize them*

▶ *Explore the many ways that patterns are created and applied*

DIMENSIONAL DECORATING

In Chapter 9, you had a cursory introduction to the fascinating options available using Effect > 3D. Extruding, revolving, and rotating objects in space offer a multitude of design possibilities (used with moderation, of course). There is a more practical side to these effects in terms of developing and presenting 3D designs to a client without having to actually construct a box, create a new bottle shape, or manufacture a sign. With skill and patience, this feature can also be used to present 3D ideas, as well as detailed technical illustrations, for products and toys. In addition to the ability to create the illusion of 3D objects, Illustrator provides the option for adding graphics to their surfaces.

This option—mapping artwork—is available in the Revolve and the Bevel & Extrude options windows, which makes it perfect for creating graphic representations of things that will eventually be manufactured as 3D objects. Consider the time and expense saved by being able to present 2D ideas to your client, printed on paper, before proceeding to the prototyping stage of development. See Figure 10–1.

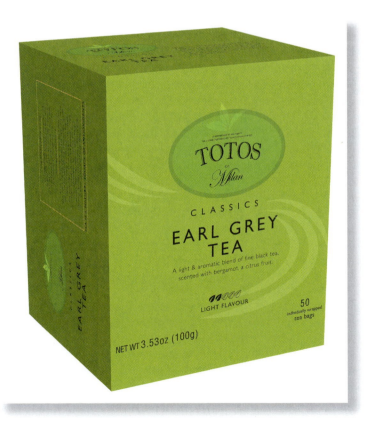

FIGURE | 10–1 |

The Totos Tea package, mapped to a 3D box.

While the perspective applied with these options is good for thinner objects, there is an additional feature within the 3D options that allows you to more accurately indicate the vanishing point for one, two, and three dimensions discussed in Chapter 9. See Figure 10–2.

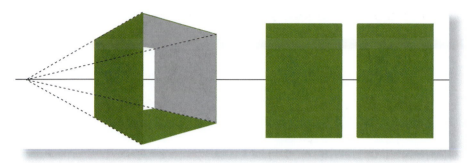

FIGURE | 10–2 |

These green rectangles are identical except for an adjustment in the Perspective field, which makes all the difference between something that creates the illusion of space and something that looks like a couple of 2D rectangles.

One-point perspective is fairly easy to accomplish—just make sure that all the lines converge at a single point. The horizon doesn't even have to be visible for this technique to create a believable 3D object. If a rectangle is turned at somewhat of an angle, as is the left one in Figure 10–2, another of the three dimensions is introduced—a second vanishing point. See Figure 10–3.

> Note: *The point at which all the lines converge is the viewer's eye level. Eye level can be any height, however; consider the difference in the perspective of a room when you're standing on your desk, as opposed to kneeling on the floor.*

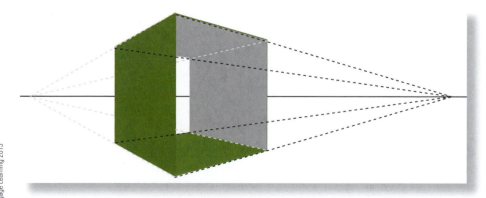

FIGURE | 10–3 |

Turning a cube at an angle introduces a second point of perspective.

In both cases, note that the vertical edges remain straight—perpendicular to the horizon. Without getting too much more technical, there is a third dimension, and that affects the vertical edges. Again, considering vantage point, or eye level, imagine the world from a bird's-eye or worm's-eye view. See Figure 10–4.

FIGURE | 10–4 |

Granted, this is a bit difficult to figure out with all these perspective lines, but if you squint at this cube, you should be able to see that your viewpoint is above the cube; the third vanishing point is actually below ground.

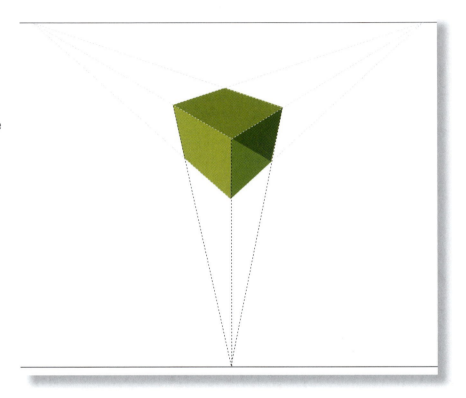

Luckily for us, the fourth dimension (time) is best left to other CS6 applications, like Flash and Premiere.

LESSON 1: BUILDING BLOCKS

Now that you have an idea of how space affects the shapes of things, let's use Illustrator's 3D extrude option to create a baby's building block. Not only will you get some good practice with the extrude options, you'll also get an idea of how mapping graphics to a 3D surface works.

Creating the Block

Since getting started with this exercise is fairly simple, there is no lesson file; we'll start from scratch.

1. Launch Illustrator and create a new print document. Make sure that the unit of measure is set to inches in the New Document window. Accept the other defaults and click OK. If you have already been working in Illustrator, use File > New to create a new document. Reset the workspace to Essentials to clean things up.

2. Set the stroke and fill colors to their default (to do this, just press D on your keyboard).

Figure © Cengage Learning 2013

3. Select the Rectangle tool and click once on the artboard to set dimensions of 2.5 inches by 2.5 inches to create a perfect square.

4. While the square is selected, use Effects > 3D > Extrude & Bevel to access the 3D Extrude & Bevel option.

5. To create a baby's block, we'll use a slight three-point perspective—the eye level of a baby looking down on her toy.

6. Use the following settings to shift the viewpoint:

   ► X axis: –41°
   ► Y axis: –28°
   ► Z axis: 18°
   ► Perspective: 80°
   ► Extrude Depth: 184 pt

   Click the More Options button at the bottom of this dialog box and use these settings:

   Light Intensity: 100%
   Ambient Light: 80%

   Leave the rest of the settings at their defaults (see Figure 10–5) and click OK.

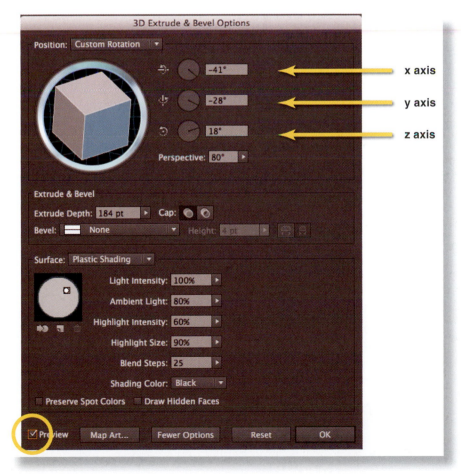

FIGURE | 10–5 |

The Extrude & Bevel settings for a child's building block.

The fill and stroke colors for this rectangle are what determines the coloring of each side of this cube.

6. Select the cube, if it isn't already selected, and experiment with some different fill and stroke colors. We used C: 20, M: 0, Y: 100, and K: 0 (lime green) for both the stroke and fill. See Figure 10–6.

FIGURE | 10–6 |

Choose vibrant fill
and stroke colors.

7. Save your file as **block_yourname.ai** in your lessons folder.

Creating the Alphabet Graphics

To add the letters to the sides of this block requires a few steps. First, we need to create the letters and borders for the visible sides. To apply this art to the cube, we then need to make those elements into symbols; you can only use symbols to map art to a 3D object. Let's go.

1. Lock the block layer (go ahead and name it **block** while you're at it). Then add a new layer and name it **graphics**.

2. Select the Type tool, click the artboard above the blocks, and if you have it, use Clarendon LT Std for the typeface and Bold for the style. Type the point size in the Control panel, rather than using the drop-down menu: **175 pt**. See Figure 10–7.

> Note: *If you don't have the Clarendon LT Std font on your computer, navigate to the* **chap10_lessons > assets** *folder and open* **blockletters.ai**. *Select and copy the outlined letters in this file [Command C (Mac)/Ctrl C (Windows) or Edit > Copy], and then paste them into your own blocks file [Command V (Mac)/ Ctrl V (Windows) or Edit > Paste]. Then skip to step 5.*

FIGURE | 10–7 |

Set the typeface, style, and
size for the letter graphics.

3. Type a capital A, and while it's selected, use Type > Create Outlines to turn it into a vector object so we can manipulate it more easily.

4. Deselect the A and repeat step 3 with a B and a C (or use your own initials, if you'd like). See Figure 10–8.

FIGURE | 10–8 |

Outline the letters so they can be manipulated as vector objects.

5. Select each letter and assign different bright, happy fill and stroke colors to each one. To be sure that the strokes don't interfere with the letterforms, use the Stroke panel to set the stroke to the outside. Increase the weight to 5 pt. See Figure 10–9.

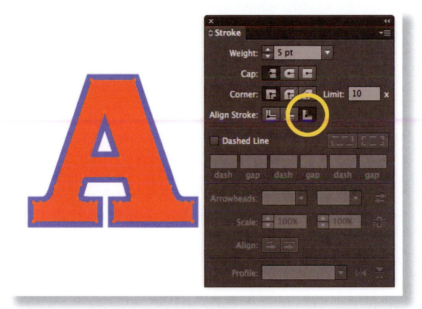

FIGURE | 10–9 |

Set the stroke to the outside to retain the integrity of the letter form.

6. Use the Rectangle tool to create a rectangle that's 2.25 in by 2.25 in—don't worry about the fill and stroke just yet. While it's selected, use the Selection tool to create two copies: click and drag right or left while holding down the Option/Alt key. Hold the Shift key to constrain the drag perfectly horizontally. See Figure 10–10.

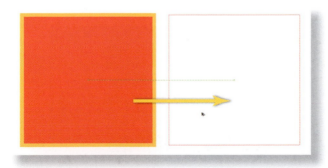

FIGURE | 10–10 |

Hold down the Option/Alt and Shift keys and drag two copies of the rectangle, to create a total of three.

7. As with the letters, select each box and assign a bright fill and a thick, vibrant stroke to each one.

8. Open the Align panel (Window > Align) and select one letter with the Selection tool. Hold down the Shift key and select one of the boxes, so you have one letter and one box highlighted.

9. Click on the Horizontal Align Center icon in the Align panel, and then click on the Vertical Align Center icon (see Figure 10–11). Oops. The letter disappeared; we can fix that easily enough, though.

> Note: *If the box and letter are not aligning properly, use the Align panel options menu to Show Options, and then select Align to Selection from the Align To drop-down menu. Refer to Figure 10–11 again.*

FIGURE | 10–11 |

Use the Align panel to ensure that things are centered with regard to one another left to right and top to bottom.

10. Open the Layers panel and click the triangle next to the **graphics** layer name to reveal the sublayers.

11. Click and drag the letter sublayer above the box sublayer. See Figure 10–12.

12. Repeat steps 8–11 for the other two letters and boxes.

13. Save your file.

FIGURE | 10–12 |

Click and drag the letter sublayer above the box sublayer to rearrange the stacking order.

Making Symbols

You played with symbols briefly way back in Chapter 6, when you created a pattern brush. If you recall, the squares graphic needed to be made into a symbol before it could be applied to the custom brush. In this case, before you can add the letters to the cube, they need to be made into symbols as well.

1. Select one letter and its surrounding box and then open the Symbols panel (Window > Symbols).

2. Click on the New Symbol icon at the bottom of the panel—it looks like a little pad. Alternatively, use the panel's options menu and choose New Symbol. Give it a simple name, like the letter itself (C), and leave the other settings at their defaults. Do the same for the other two letters and boxes. See Figure 10–13.

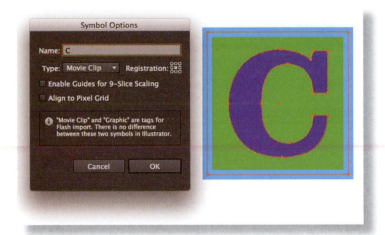

FIGURE | 10–13 |

Select the letter and its box and make them into a symbol.

Mapping the Block

It's time to add the graphics to the block. This is done using the same 3D extrude effect that we applied earlier. Because we don't want to actually extrude the block a second time, we need to edit the original effect rather than choosing Effect > 3D > Extrude & Bevel again. This is true just about every time you apply an effect to an object.

1. Open the Appearance panel. You may want to drag it away from the dock as you're opening this.

2. Unlock the **block** layer and select the cube on the artboard. In the Appearance panel, click 3D Extrude & Bevel to open the 3D Extrude & Bevel option (see Figure 10–14). Don't worry if your cube turns back into a square—that's just because the Preview option isn't checked. Go ahead and check it now, if you like. Checking Preview shows you the cube; then, if you click OK, the dialog box will close and the cube will still be visible. (Doing this is memory-intensive, though, so only use Preview as necessary.)

FIGURE | 10–14 |

To alter an effect, click on it in the Appearance panel.

3. At the bottom of this window is a Map Art button. Click that to open a second window that provides a diagram of the cube, along with the options to select the symbol(s) that you want to apply to the surfaces.

You have to select the surface of the cube that you want to decorate first. In this case, there are three of them: top, left, and front. Make sure that the Preview option in the Map Art dialog box is checked so you can see how this works.

If you click the right-facing triangle to the right of the Surface text box, you can flip through the various interior and exterior surfaces of the cube. As you do so, note that on the artboard, the cube's surfaces are being highlighted in red. Also note the number of the surface in the Map Art dialog box that corresponds to the highlighted surface on the cube. See Figure 10–15.

FIGURE | 10–15 |

The Map Art dialog box with the front of the cube highlighted on the artboard.

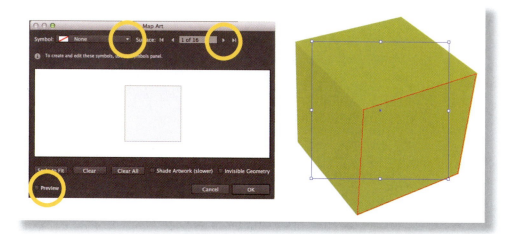

4. Click the arrows to get back to surface 1 if necessary, and then click on the Symbol drop-down menu and select one of your letter symbols. It will be placed in the square map art preview area. You can click and drag it around and use the handles to resize the symbol. Use the handles to reduce it just a bit (hold down the Shift key so it doesn't get distorted!) and center it. See Figure 10–16.

FIGURE | 10–16 |

Use the Map Art dialog box to select the surface, and then the symbol that you want to apply to it.

5. Either click the right arrow to get to surface 9 or type **9** in the Surface field and press the Tab key to update it. Use the Symbol menu to select another letter symbol; then resize and center it.

6. The final surface is 12. Add the third symbol and adjust its size and position. Nice, right?

> **Note:** *When mapping the left surface (surface 12), you'll need to use the graphic's handles to rotate it clockwise, as well as resize and center it. Move the cursor slightly away from a corner to get the curved, double-arrow icon, then click and drag clockwise. Hold the Shift key to rotate the graphic exactly 90°.*

7. Click OK to exit the Map Art dialog box, and OK again to exit the 3D Bevel & Extrude Options dialog box. See Figure 10–17.

8. Save and close your file.

These same principles apply to anything else you might create using the rotate feature as well. Consider decorating a vase or designing a wine label (remember that all graphics need to be symbols for mapping). At this point, you're probably full of 3D ideas. Have fun!

GAINING PERSPECTIVE

While the 3D Extrude & Bevel options are terrific when you're dealing with a single object, they aren't always the most efficient way to create a large 3D scene. That's where the Perspective tool comes in. From illustrating ideas for interior spaces to sophisticated exterior scenes, this tool makes things a lot easier to manage. If you're interested in architecture or interior design, the possibilities with this tool just might captivate your imagination. The perspective grid is a malleable three-point perspective grid that provides the foundation for constructing objects in 3D space from any viewpoint. Setting up the grid to meet the needs of the project is a simple matter of moving the grid controls into place. As they move, the grid proportions and vanishing points change accordingly.

> **Note:** *If you accidentally click on the Perspective tool in the Tools panel (it happens!), use View > Perspective Grid > Hide Grid.*

For an example of an amazing image created using the Perspective tool, take a quick look at *http://blogs.adobe.com/ infiniteresolution/2010/05/drawing_in_perspective_using_a.html.*

FIGURE | 10–17 |

The finished baby block.

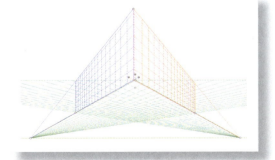

FIGURE | 10–18 |

The grid that appears when you click on the Perspective tool in the Tools panel.

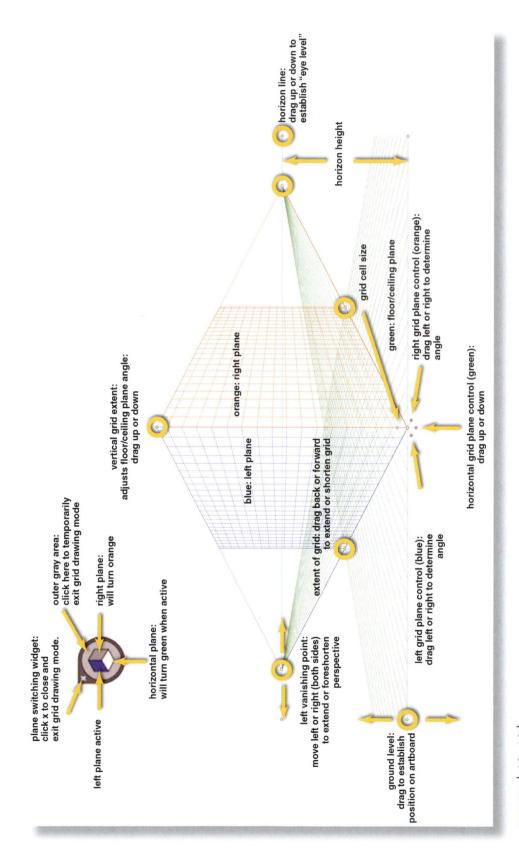

FIGURE | 10–19 |

Once the perspective grid is turned on, there are many ways to manipulate it to suit your purpose.

While the next lesson won't come anywhere near being that complex, you'll get a good taste of how the tool works.

LESSON 2: ARCHITECTURAL RENDERING

The Perspective Grid tool can seem a bit intimidating at first. Work through this lesson to get a better feel for how it functions. You'll be surprised at how easy it really is to create 3-dimensional drawings.

Setting up the Workspace and File

There is only one perspective grid per document, and getting that set up is the first step to drawing something in three dimensions.

1. Open **chap10L2.ai** from the **chap10_lessons** folder. Some things have been created for you to avoid making this exercise too complicated. You'll see that there are several named layers and a sketch of a little Cape Cod house that's been made into a template. There are also a couple of predrawn elements for you to use since creating some of those shapes is not as intuitive when using this feature for the first time. See Figure 10–20.

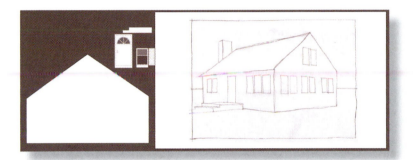

Figures © Cengage Learning 2013

FIGURE | 10–20 |

The file has a few elements already in place for you.

2. Click and hold the Perspective Grid tool in the Tools panel, move your cursor to the right, and click the right-pointing arrow. Drag the Perspective Grid Tool and Perspective Selection Tool group away from the Tools panel so that the group is floating free. Since we'll be using these two tools so much in this exercise, having them readily available will save time. See Figure 10–21. This step will also turn the grid on.

FIGURE | 10–21 |

Click the right-pointing triangle and drag the group to the right to tear the Perspective tools away from the Tools panel and to turn on the grid.

3. This grid has already been adjusted to work with the scan. To see how it all works, study Figure 10–19. Feel free to move the control points around to see how things move and change. When you're ready to move on, reset the grid back to where it was initially by selecting File > Revert.

4. At the bottom of the grid are three wheel-like circles that control the angle of the left, right, and horizontal plane views. If you find the grid cumbersome to work with, click Option (Mac)/Alt click (Windows) on each of these grid plane controls once to turn the

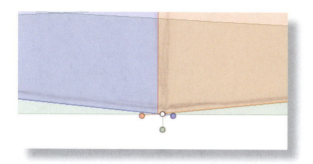

FIGURE | 10–22 |

Click Option (Mac)/Alt click (Windows) the grid plane controls to see translucent planes rather than a grid.

grid into a tinted plane. See Figure 10–22. Click Option (Mac)/Alt click (Windows) each circle again to hide the grid (it's still in effect, just invisible). Click Option (Mac)/Alt click (Windows) them a third time to toggle back to grid view. For this lesson, it's easier to work in plane view, so click Option (Mac)/Alt click (Windows) a fourth time to go there.

5. Click on the double arrow at the very top-right of the panel dock to expand it. That way, you'll have easy access to all the panels all the time, rather than having to open and close them as you work. See Figure 10–23.

6. From the View menu, turn on the Bounding Box and Smart Guides if necessary, and turn off Perspective Grid > Snap to Grid. These settings will make transforming things faster and our work more precise.

> **Note:** *If you lose the grid somehow, click on the Perspective Grid tool, or use View > Perspective Grid > Show Grid to have it reappear. To hide it, you can click on the x in the plane-switching widget with a "grid-savvy" tool, like the Grid Selection tool, or any of the shape tools, or use View > Perspective Grid > Hide Grid.*

FIGURE | 10–23 |

Click the double arrow to expand the panels for easy access.

Raising the Walls

1. Select the target icon in the **walls** layer, then click on the left side of the plane-switching widget (refer back to Figure 10–21) to focus on that side of the house.

2. With the Rectangle tool, click and drag a rectangle over the front of the house. See Figure 10–24.

3. Now highlight the right side in the plane-switching widget.

4. Unlock the **parts** layer and use the Selection tool to select the side of the house shape (the rectangle with a point at the top). Copy it [Command C (Mac)/Ctrl C (Windows), or Edit > Copy].

5. Lock the **parts** layer and highlight the **walls** layer again, and paste the wall [Command V (Mac)/Ctrl V (Windows), or Edit > Paste].

> **Note:** *If Illustrator keeps pasting things on the layer from which they were copied, use the Layer panel options menu to turn off (uncheck) Paste Remembers Layers.*

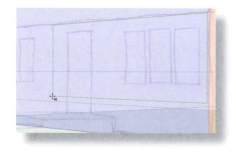

FIGURE | 10–24 |

Click and drag with the Rectangle tool to draw the front of the house.

6. Select the Perspective Selection tool in the Perspective tools group.

7. Use the Perspective Selection tool to drag the side of the house into the grid area at the right and position it to match the template. Isn't it awesome to watch how the shape transforms from straight-ahead into perspective? Drag the shape farther to the right to see how it gets smaller in proportion to how far back it is from the foreground. Drag it back again when you're finished experimenting. See Figure 10–25.

8. Lock the **walls** layer, and highlight the **roof** layer.

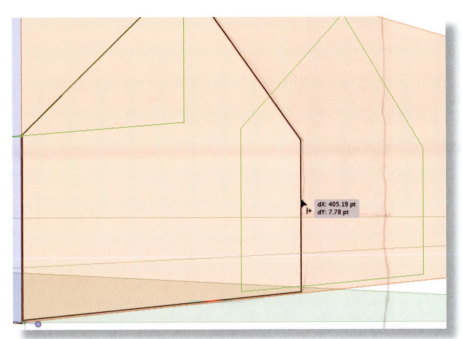

FIGURE | 10–25 |

Drag the side of the house to the right a bit to see how the perspective changes, based on distance.

9. Select the left side of the plane-switching widget. Use the Rectangle tool to click and drag a rectangle above the wall. This will become the roof. Start dragging the rectangle from the bottom left so you can match the eave in the scan. See Figure 10–26.

9. Select the Direct Selection tool and click away from the artboard to deselect everything. Then, click the top edge of the roof rectangle and drag it to the right to match the angle of the roof in the template. See Figure 10–27.

10. Hide the **roof** layer and the **wall** layer, and save your file as **chap10L2_yourname.ai** in your lessons folder.

Now that the sides are in place, let's add some important architectural details.

Letting in Some Light

1. Highlight the **windows** layer. At this point, the left side should be highlighted in the plane-switching widget. If not, select the Perspective Selection tool and click on the left side of the plane-switching widget.

2. Bring the Symbols panel to the front of its group in the dock (see Figure 10–28) and click and drag an instance of the window symbol to the artboard.

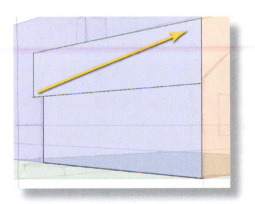

FIGURE | 10–26 |

Draw the plane for the roof with the Rectangle tool from the bottom left to the top right.

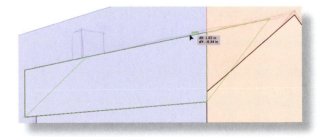

FIGURE | 10–27 |

Use the Direct Selection tool to angle the roof to match the template.

FIGURE | 10–28 |

Click and drag the window symbol to the artboard.

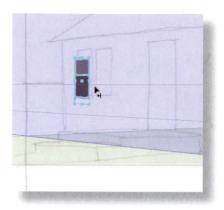

FIGURE | 10–29 |

Drag the window symbol into position on the left side of the house.

3. Use the Perspective Selection tool to drag the window to the far left of the front of the house. As soon as you start to drag, it should snap into perspective. See Figure 10–29.

> Note: *Whenever you think you'll need to use the same graphic more than once, it's smart to make it into a symbol, which keeps the file size smaller.*

4. The Option/Alt drag shortcut to create duplicates works in perspective view as well. You have to use the Perspective Selection tool, though. Add four more windows to the front of the house to match the template. Either click and drag copies (hold down the Shift key so they remain aligned) or drag new instances of the window to the artboard from the Symbols panel.

5. Highlight the right side of the plane-switching widget and add windows there, too. Use the arrow keys to nudge things into place.

> Note: *There is a shutter symbol in the Symbols panel. If you'd like to add shutters to the windows, go right ahead. See Figure 10–30.*

FIGURE | 10–30 |

Add windows to the house, and add some shutters too, if you like.

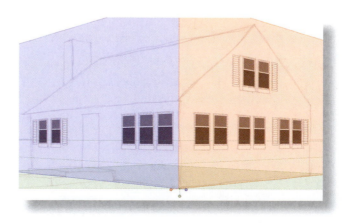

6. Unlock the **parts** layer and select and copy the door [Command C (Mac)/Ctrl C (Windows), or Edit > Copy]. Lock the **parts** layer again.

7. Highlight the left side of the plane-switching widget, select the **windows** layer, and paste the door. Then use the Perspective Selection tool to drag the door into position on the front of the house.

> Note: *To see how your work looks, close the plane-switching widget to hide the grid (see Figure 10–31) while the Perspective Selection tool is active. Then, click on the Perspective Grid tool to continue working.*

8. Lock the **windows** layer and save your file.

Building the Chimney

1. Click on the Perspective Grid tool to show the grid if it is still hidden.

2. Highlight the **chimney** layer, and make sure that the left side of the plane-switching widget is selected.

3. Use the Rectangle tool to draw the left side of the chimney. It's OK to go below the roofline since the **roof** layer will hide that portion.

4. Select the right side in the plane-switching widget and draw the other side of the chimney. See Figure 10–32.

5. Lock the layer and save your file.

6. Show all the layers, and hide the perspective grid to see how your house is coming along. The strokes don't match, do they? Let's fix that.

7. Unlock all the layers except for the parts and **Template_house.jpg** layers, and then use Select > Select All [or Command A (Mac)/Ctrl A (Windows)] to highlight everything we've done so far. Set the stroke to 0.5 pt in the Stroke panel. See Figure 10–33.

8. Turn the grid back on by clicking the Perspective Grid tool and save your file.

Building the Front Steps

We're almost finished! We just need to add some steps up to the front door, and some landscaping once the house is complete.

1. Hide the **walls** layer and lock the roof and **chimney** layers. The stairs will go on the **windows** layer.

2. Click the bottom pane in the plane-switching widget to activate the horizontal pane. See Figure 10–34.

3. Highlight the **windows** layer. Zoom in and use the Rectangle tool to create the top level of the stairs. Set the stroke weight to 0.5 pt. Use

FIGURE | 10–31 |

Hide the grid to view your progress.

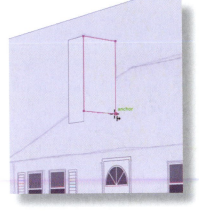

FIGURE | 10–32 |

Add the chimney; the roof will cover the bottom portion.

FIGURE | 10–33 |

Set the stroke of all the elements to 0.5 pt.

FIGURE | 10–34 |

Select the horizontal side in the plane-switching widget to start the stairs on the correct plane.

Figures © Cengage Learning 2013

the Perspective Selection tool and arrow keys to nudge the rectangle into place. See Figure 10–35.

4. Select the left plane in the plane-switching widget and drag a rectangle below the top platform. See Figure 10–36. (This is called a *riser,* in construction-ese.)

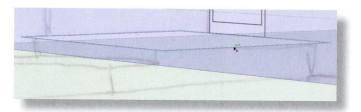

FIGURE | 10–35 |

Draw the top platform for the stairs.

FIGURE | 10–36 |

Start at the left and drag a rectangle for the riser.

5. Now highlight the horizontal side in the widget again to draw a stair.

6. Repeat steps (pardon the pun) 4 and 5 to create another riser and stair. See Figure 10–37.

7. Zoom out and then use the horizontal plane one more time to drag a pathway from the bottom stair to the left edge of the template. You can use the Direct Selection tool to straighten the left edge vertically.

FIGURE | 10–37 |

Create the second riser and the second stair.

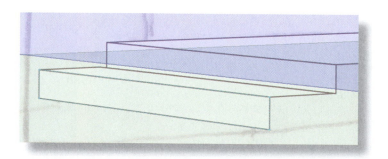

8. Unlock the **parts** layer and use the Selection tool to select the stairs side. See Figure 10–38. Copy and paste the shape, and then drag the Selected Art icon in the Layers panel (the blue square to the right of the layer name) down to the **windows** layer, and then lock the **parts** layer again.

FIGURE | 10–38 |

Copy and paste the stairs, and then drag the Selected Art icon to the **windows** layer.

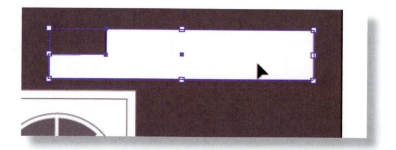

Figures © Cengage Learning 2013

9. Highlight the **windows** layer, if necessary, and make the right pane active in the plane-switching widget. Use the Perspective Selection tool to position the stairs side. It's not going to fit just yet. See Figure 10–39.

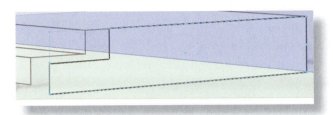

FIGURE | 10–39 |

Use the Perspective Selection tool to place the stair side into position.

10. If the bounding boxes are not showing around your elements, select View > Show Bounding Box.

11. Use the Perspective Selection tool and the bounding box control points to resize the stairs side, and then use the Direct Selection tool to adjust it exactly. See Figure 10–40.

12. Make sure the strokes for the steps objects are all set to 0.5 pt.

13. Take some time to paint the house, shutters, door, and chimney by selecting the elements and adding fill colors. In your imagination, position the sun at the top-right side of the scene. This means that the front parts of the structure will be darker than the side parts. See Figure 10–41.

> **Note:** *If you added shutters and would like to give them a fill color, you must edit the symbol, not the instances in the drawing. Double-click the shutter in the Symbols panel to enter edit mode and make any changes. Don't move the shutter, though, or you will move all the instances of it in the drawing. When you're finished, tap the Esc key to exit edit mode.*

14. Save your file.

FIGURE | 10–40 |

Use the Direct Selection tool to fine-tune the fit of the stairs side.

FIGURE | 10–41 |

Have fun painting the house!

Landscaping

Using the symbols Illustrator provides is all right for people who are just starting out. They are also very handy when working on a project that requires universal symbols, like a map. Once you get more proficient, however, it would be more professional to develop your own. For now, let's use the Nature symbols library to add some foliage and give this house a little curb appeal.

1. Turn off the perspective grid (View > Perspective Grid > Hide Grid) and lock everything but the **backyard** layer.

2. Use the Rectangle tool to create a green lawn below the horizon line in the template and some blue sky above it. Use gradients, if you like. See Figure 10–42.

FIGURE | 10–42 |

Add some grass and the sky.

3. Click on the Symbols Library Menu icon at the bottom-left side of the Symbols panel and select the Nature library.

4. Have fun adding trees, butterflies, and any other elements you want. Use the Scale tool or the Selection tool and bounding box to change the sizes of things, in keeping with the perspective principles (things get smaller as they get farther away).

FIGURE | 10–43 |

The final 3D rendering.

5. Unlock the front **yard** layer to complete the landscaping.

6. Save your file.

GRAPHS

In visual communications, it's often necessary to illustrate data so that the audience has a pictorial reference of a concept. Whether it's a pie chart that shows the breakdown of people in New York City who are vegans or vegetarians, have peanut allergies, or have no diet restrictions, to economic history and forecasts for a major corporation, the percentages or numbers can be difficult to comprehend without some sort of visual representation. In fact, people who rely more on the right side of their brain (the creative side) often must see a visual representation of something before they understand it completely. And left-brain thinkers appreciate the mathematical precision that is the foundation of any chart or graph.

As with learning to use the Perspective Grid tool, using the Graphing tools in Illustrator can be a bit challenging, so we're not going to spend a huge amount of time with them. Just enough, we hope, so that you understand the basics and can use it reasonably well, should the need arise.

GRAPHING BASICS

Illustrator has nine different graphing tools, including bar graphs, column graphs, pie graphs, and line graphs. See Figure 10–44. The first thing you need in order to create any one of these graphs are some statistics that will define the height of a column, the width of a bar, or the wedge of a pie graph. Typically, you need at least two categories in the data—the labels for what you're comparing, and the corresponding numbers or values.

FIGURE | 10–44 |

The many Graphing tools.

Once you have some data, you can use any one of the graph tools to illustrate it using relatively sized graphics. Select any of the graphing tools, and click and drag to create the size of the graph. Once you do that, the Data Input dialog box will open, and you can either type in your data or import it from a TXT (plain-text) file.

Note: *Use the Selection tool to work with the graph as a unit, and the Direct Selection and Group Selection tools to modify specific pieces. Once the graph is complete, you can use Object > Ungroup a few times to delete unnecessary elements—be sure that nothing needs to be edited before doing so, however, since you can't turn it back into a graph later.*

LESSON 3: CLASSIC COLUMN GRAPH

This is one of the most basic graphs, and a good first experience in using these tools.

1. You'll be starting from scratch for this exercise, so once you have Illustrator up and running, choose New from the file menu. Set the document to Letter size, Landscape orientation, Inches for unit of measure, and accept the other default specifications.

2. Select the Column Graph tool from the Tools panel and click once on the top-left area of the artboard. Set the size of the graph to **8.5 in** by **4 in**. in the Graph dialog box.

   Illustrator will create a very basic graph consisting of a solid block, where the numeric data will be placed, and *x* and *y* axes for labels. See Figure 10–45.

3. We're going to compare coffee sales for three significant coffee shop chains in the United States, so in the light gray text field at the top of the Data Input window, type the following (press Enter or Return after each name so they appear on separate lines):

FIGURE | 10–45 |

Click once with the Column Graph tool to enter specific dimensions, or click and drag to establish the size of the graph.

Starbucks
Dunkin' Donuts
Tim Hortons

4. Click on the top cell in column two to switch the focus, and enter these figures (again, pressing Enter or Return after each one):

   10.7
   5.5
   2.5

   If you make a mistake, click in the cell where the error is and correct it in the input field at the top.

   See Figure 10–46.

FIGURE | 10–46 |

The Data Input dialog box.

Figures © Cengage Learning 2013

5. Press Enter or Return, or click the Apply (checkmark) icon at the top-right side of the Data Input window to generate the graph. See Figure 10–47.

Easy enough!

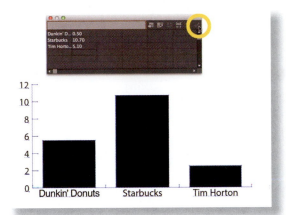

Figures © Cengage Learning 2013

6. Close the Data Input window and save your file as **graphs_yourname.ai** in your lessons folder.

Graphic Columns

As column graphs go, this does the job; however, it's rather plain. There are several ways to dress it up, including using a graphic rather than a solid column to indicate the difference in coffee sales between these three competitors. Let's do it.

1. Open the **coffeecup.ai** file in the **chap10_lessons > assets** folder.

2. Select the coffee cup by dragging a marquee with the Selection tool and copy it [Command C (Mac)/Ctrl C (Windows), or Edit > Copy].

3. Switch back to your graph document and paste the coffee cup image [Command V (Mac)/Ctrl V (Windows), or Edit > Paste]. Move it off the artboard into the canvas area. See Figure 10–48.

4. Keep the coffee cup selected and go to Object > Graph > Design.

5. Click the New Design button and you'll see the coffee cup in the preview window. Nice! Click the Rename button, name this graphic **coffeecup** (see Figure 10–49), and then click OK.

6. Use the Selection tool to select the entire graph, and then go to Object > Graph > Column to open the Graph Column options.

7. Select the coffee cup design. For Column Type, choose Repeating from the drop-down menu. Set Each Design Represents to **3**, and

FIGURE | 10–47 |

Click the Apply (checkmark) icon, or press Enter or Return on your keyboard to update the graph.

FIGURE | 10–48 |

Copy and paste the coffee cup graphic into your graphs document.

FIGURE | 10–49 |

Add the coffee cup graphic to the Graph Design options.

For Fractions, choose either option (see Figure 10–50). Click OK. Click a blank area of the canvas to deselect everything. See Figure 10–51.

8. Let's make the typography a bit more interesting. Select the names of the coffee companies—use the Direct Selection tool and the Shift key to select multiple items.

9. Open the Character panel [Window > Type > Character, or Command T (Mac)/Ctrl T (Windows)] and leave the typeface set to Myriad. Change the style to Black, and the point size to 18.

10. Use the Direct Selection tool to drag a marquee down through the numbers at the left of the graph to select them. Use the Character panel to change the style to Black (Mac)/Bold (Windows), and the point size to 10.

11. With the Type tool, add dollar signs, and the word **Billion** to the numbers. See Figure 10–52.

FIGURE | 10–50 |

Set up the graphic for the column design.

FIGURE | 10–51 |

Look at these results!

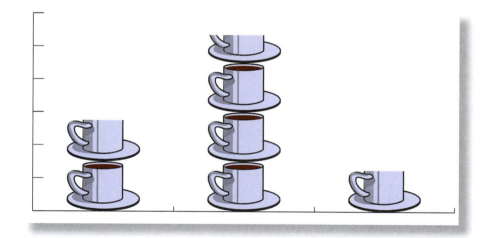

FIGURE | 10–52 |

Add text to the money labels so people understand that this is about dollars, not cups of coffee.

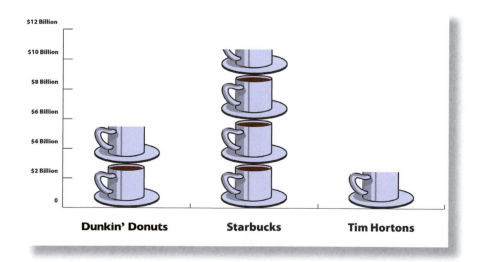

12. Click Select > Deselect, and then, with the Type tool, add **THE COFFEE MOGULS** as a headline above the graph. Select a bold serif typeface to contrast with the sans serif in the graph. Also, select a large point size. See Figure 10–53.

13. Save your file!

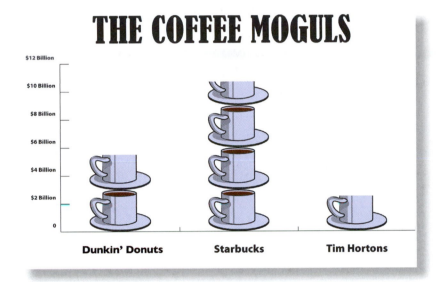

FIGURE | 10–53 |

The final graph.

Pie charts are another great way to compare relationships, and with your new 3D Extrude & Revolve skills, you can make one look much classier than the standard 2D version.

3D Pie Graph

1. Add a new layer to your graphs file, and hide the layer with the column graph that you just finished. Feel free to name each layer while you're at it.

2. We'll use the same data as for the column graph. Select the Pie Graph tool (see Figure 10–54) and click once in the top-left corner of the artboard. Enter dimensions of **7 in** by **7 in** and click OK.

FIGURE | 10–54 |

Select the Pie Graph tool.

3. In the Data Input window, place the names of the coffee moguls along the top row, rather than down the first column, so the chart turns out correctly. (Doing it the other way creates three circles, rather than one with pie wedges.)

Starbucks   Dunkin' Donuts   Tim Hortons

4. Enter the dollar amounts in row two:

10.7   5.5   2.5

See Figure 10–55.

5. Click the Apply (checkmark) icon to generate the graph and close the Data Input window. Press Command Shift A (Mac)/Ctrl Shift A (Windows) to deselect everything. See Figure 10–56.

> Note: *If you make a mistake in the order in which you enter data, click on the second icon from the left, next to the input field, to reverse the data.*

FIGURE | 10–55 |

Enter the labels horizontally this time, to generate a true pie graph.

6. Illustrator uses shades of gray to differentiate the slices. We can do better than that. Use the Direct Selection tool to select each slice of pie and give it a bright color. Change the color of the legend boxes to match. Finally, set the strokes to none for all the objects. See Figure 10–57.

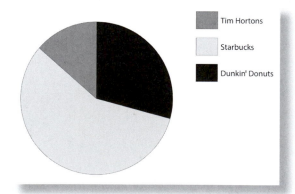

FIGURE | 10–56 |

The initial pie graph.

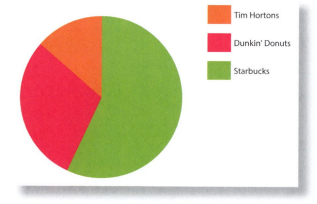

FIGURE | 10–57 |

From boring to bright!

7. Make sure all three slices are selected and choose Effect > 3D > Extrude & Bevel. Set Position to Isometric Top, Extrude Depth to 25 pt, Bevel to Rounded, and Height to 10 pt. If you have Preview checked, don't freak out—we can fix the way this looks now (see Figure 10–58)! Click OK.

8. Given that we are sure our data is correct and we won't have to add any slices or change their sizes, it's all right to ungroup this graph. Use the Selection tool to select it, then click Object > Ungroup [Command Shift G (Mac)/Ctrl Shift G (Windows)] several times. Click Yes when the warning pops up (see Figure 10–59).

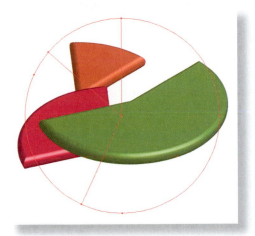

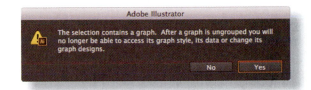

FIGURE | 10–59 |

Click Yes to let Illustrator know that you're aware of the consequences of ungrouping the graph.

FIGURE | 10–58 |

Weird, right?

9. The pie slices need a bit of repositioning. Deselect everything, then select each slice with the Direct Selection tool and use the arrow keys to move it into position. See Figure 10–60.

10. Style the labels by selecting each one and using the Control panel to select a typeface, style, and size, and then move them over their respective slices.

11. Add The Coffee Moguls headline, as you did in the first part of this lesson. See Figure 10–61.

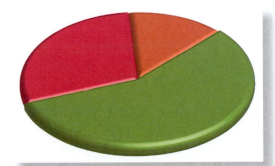

FIGURE | 10–60 |

Rearrange the slices using the Direct Selection tool and the arrow keys.

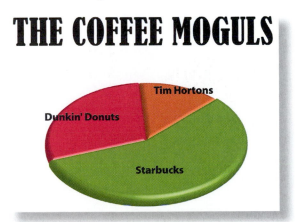

FIGURE | 10–61 |

A 3D pie graph.

12. Save and close your file. You now have a basic understanding of how graphing data works in Illustrator!

> *Note: You can map graphics to an extruded shape. Before ungrouping the graph (as described in step 8 of the last procedure), use the Appearance panel to edit the effect on each slice. Remember that graphics for mapping need to be made into symbols first.*

PATTERNS

Illustrator has had the capacity to create repeating tiles to make an overall pattern or texture for quite a long time now. But this new version, CS6, introduces a terrific new pattern-making process. It offers more options in terms of shaping the tile (previously, they could only be rectangles positioned in a static grid) and endless opportunities to experiment in real time, save your progress along the way, and work with more accuracy.

Surface pattern design is at the heart of the textile industry. If you enjoy doodling in the margins of your notebook, you just might fall in love with this feature.

The basic principle for making a pattern is to work with a shape that can be repeated left, right, up, and down. Think about the tile in a bathroom, or a linoleum floor. The graphics within the tile can be cut off at the edges in a way so that when placed together, they combine to finish the design. See Figure 10–62.

FIGURE | 10–62 |

When four tiles are placed together, the graphics in the four corners of the tile (above) come together to create the flower in the center.

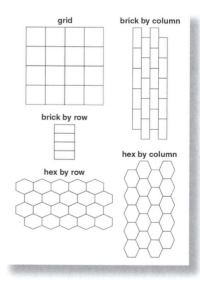

FIGURE | 10–63 |

Along with the original grid tiling, Illustrator now features three additional pattern structures to choose from.

LESSON 4: WRAPPING PAPER

Celebrations of all kinds usually mean gifts, and gifts are generally wrapped in paper or placed in gift bags that have been designed to reflect the occasion. The pattern in Figure 10–62, printed on shiny white paper with a matte white ink (or vice versa) resulting in a subtle color-on-color pattern, could make great paper for a wedding gift or other fancy package. Birthday papers can be richly colored and elegant for grownup gifts, or bright and silly for children. Wrapping paper can be decorative, with an all-over texture, or more illustrative, using actual objects like cupcakes and balloons, or intricate patterns. See Figure 10–64.

Almost everyone celebrates birthdays in one way or another. In the next lesson, you will create a simple pattern that can be used for birthday gift wrapping paper.

FIGURE | 10–64 |

Wrapping paper design can evoke different feelings for different occasions or gift recipients.

Creating the Artwork

1. Launch Illustrator and create a new document—use the Letter preset, and make sure that it's set to Inches for Units.

2. We haven't really played with the Blob Brush yet. Let's use that to draw some candles. Select the Blob Brush in the Tools panel (see Figure 10–65) and use the Control panel or the Color panel to set the fill color to none, using a light blue stroke.

3. Double-click the Blob brush in the Tools panel to open its options. Set the Size to 10 pt. and leave everything else set to the default (see Figure 10–66). Click OK.

FIGURE | 10–65 |

The Blob brush.

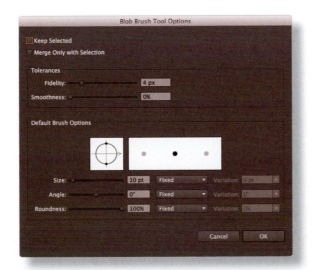

FIGURE | 10–66 |

Set the diameter of the brush to 10 pt.

Note: *You can tap the left bracket key ([ ) to reduce the diameter of the brush, or the right bracket key ( ]) to enlarge it on the fly. These are the same keystroke shortcuts used in Photoshop—how handy!*

4. Click and drag a short vertical line, and don't try to make it perfectly straight. The Blob brush, even though it uses a stroke color, actually creates shapes defined by anchor points. You can use the Direct Selection tool to modify the shape at any time. Add a drip or two at the side. See Figure 10–67.

5. Make the brush a bit smaller and change the stroke color to a bright yellow-orange. Click and drag a flame shape.

6. Make the brush smaller still and change the stroke color to a darker orange. Just click with it at the base of the flame to add a little depth. See Figure 10–67.

7. Create a second candle next to the original using a different color for the candle and the same colors for the flame. Follow steps 3–6. See Figure 10–68.

8. Save your file in your lessons folder. Name it **chap10L3_yourname.ai**.

FIGURE | 10–67 |

Draw a simple candle.

FIGURE | 10–68 |

Create a second candle.

Making the Pattern

1. Select both candles and their flames using the Selection tool to click and drag across them at an angle from the top left to the bottom right (see Figure 10–69), and then choose Object > Pattern > Make. Illustrator will show you a message saying that it's automatically adding this pattern to the Swatches panel, and then you'll enter pattern edit mode. See Figure 10–70.

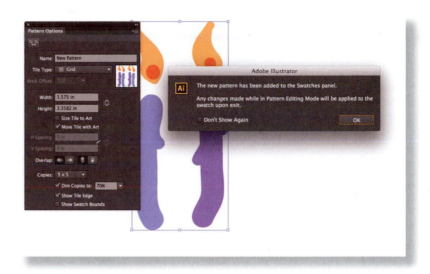

FIGURE | 10–69 |

Click and drag a marquee around both candles with the Selection tool.

FIGURE | 10–70 |

Choosing Object > Pattern > Make adds the pattern to the Swatches panel and puts you in pattern edit mode.

2. Click OK to close the message box. Name the pattern in the Pattern Options panel, and then take some time to explore what the different Tile Types do to the arrangement of the candles. Figure 10–71 is set to Brick by Column. You can also establish the size of the tile, which is the bounding box around the original two candles, to match the size of the artwork, or set dimensions using the Width and Height text boxes. Making the tile larger will space the candles farther apart.

FIGURE | 10–71 |

Experiment with different settings in the Pattern options dialog box.

3. You can edit shapes, their position, color, and size in pattern edit mode. You can also add or delete objects. The surrounding pattern updates on the fly. Very cool.

4. When you have something you like, you can choose to save a copy by clicking on that option at the top-left side of the document window. When you're finished, exit edit mode by tapping the Esc key or clicking on the Exit Pattern Editing Mode icon (which looks like an arrow) at the top-left side of the document window. See Figure 10–72.

FIGURE | 10–72 |

Save a copy, continue working, and then exit edit pattern mode when you're finished.

5. Move the original candles off to the side of the artboard, and draw a large rectangle on the artboard with the Rectangle tool. Make sure that the fill is active in the Tools panel, and then select your new swatch from the Swatches or Control panel. See Figure 10–73.

FIGURE | 10–73 |

Fill a rectangle with your new pattern.

6. If the pattern is too small or too large, you can use Object > Transform > Scale to make changes. In the Scale dialog box, be sure to uncheck the Transform Objects option—you don't want to make changes to the rectangle, just the pattern. To reduce the size, type in a number smaller than 100. To make the pattern larger, use a number greater than 100. In either case, it's usually best to scale uniformly. See Figure 10–74.

FIGURE | 10–74 |

Use Object > Transform > Scale… to make the pattern larger or smaller in relation to the overall document.

7. If you need to edit the pattern, double-click it in the Swatches panel to reenter edit mode. You may want to make a copy of the swatch first using Duplicate Swatch from the Swatches panel options menu, so you keep the original untouched, just in case.

8. If you'd like a colored background, select and copy the rectangle with the pattern in it, and then paste the copy behind the original [Command B (Mac)/Ctrl B (Windows) or Edit > Paste in Back]. While the copy is still selected, set the fill color to something else and see how you like it. See Figure 10–75.

FIGURE | 10–75 |

Different color combinations of the same pattern are called "colorways."

9. Save your file. Nice work!

SUMMARY

▶ IN REVIEW

1. What value do the 3D effects have for designers?

2. What do you have to do to artwork that you want to apply to a 3D object?

3. Name two reasons you should turn a graphic element into a symbol.

4. When using the Perspective Grid tool, how do you select the plane (X, Y, or Z) that you want to work on.

5. How do you edit a symbol?

6. What's the first step in creating a graph?

7. What is a pattern tile?

8. What is a "colorway?"

▶ EXPLORING ON YOUR OWN

1. Use the pattern making feature to create a wallpaper design for a baby's room, or wrapping paper for a wedding gift. Or, create a pattern that could be used as upholstery or curtain fabric.

2. Take a photo of (or sketch and scan) a house in your neighborhood and see if you can recreate it with the Perspective Grid tool. Feel free to simplify areas that are too ornate or complicated.

3. Look through magazines, newspapers, or the web to find examples of charts and graphs. See if you can recreate one using your new Illustrator graphing skills.

| Print Publishing |

11

charting your course

Chapters 11 and 12 are about what you do when you are ready to present your Illustrator artwork to the world. Where will it go? Will it be printed in a magazine, on a CD cover, on the side of a soup can? Will you be able to view it on a Web page, in a TV commercial, or on a multimedia kiosk? In this chapter, you will learn what it takes to prepare your artwork for print. It is not as easy as hitting File > Print and expecting the document to appear on paper exactly as you see it onscreen. There is a host of considerations you should be aware of, such as the types of printing available and the management of color from screen to print. Specific issues unique to the printing process should also be on your output radar—halftoning, color separations, transparency, flattening, and resolution, to name a few. It may be overwhelming to you, and it is beyond the scope of this book to go into great detail here, so this chapter provides a starting place for asking the right questions about the printing process.

goals

In this chapter you will:

▶ *Learn about the different methods of printing*

▶ *Understand the halftone and color separation processes*

▶ *Know what to do about printing transparencies, gradient meshes, complex paths, and fonts*

▶ *Get familiar with the Print dialog box*

▶ *Learn the right questions to ask when consulting a print service bureau*

A FRIENDLY CONVERSION

Have you ever found yourself in a situation where you meet someone who does not speak the same language as you, but you desperately want that person to understand what you are saying?

Donde el baño?

Huh?

Donde el baño?!

It is this type of situation that often occurs when a computer attempts to talk to a printer; they speak different languages, and unless there is an interpreter, the outcome might not be what you intended. Luckily, Illustrator comes equipped with its own translator in the form of a very sophisticated Print dialog box, which will be described later. However, to understand how to use it, you must have an idea of the printing process and the terminology used to prepare artwork for print.

WAYS OF PRINTING

There are several ways to get your artwork onto paper: directly from a desktop printer or digital printing press; from a film negative that is used to create a metal plate for a commercial (mechanical) printing press; or in the Portable Document Format (PDF) or a PostScript file. Let's delve into each option.

Desktop Printing

Without a doubt, you will want to print your work on a desktop printer— if not the final version, at least some paper proofs for layout and revision purposes. All desktop printers are different, made by different companies, with different specifications and different levels of printing capabilities. A low-end inkjet printer, for example, deposits ink onto a page much differently than a high-end laser printer. You should read the specifications for your particular desktop printer, so you can accurately gauge whether a printer issue you may experience is something you can fix in Illustrator or is an unavoidable by-product of your printer.

You should also find out what resolution your printer supports, and what resolution will give you the best quality. It can vary greatly, depending on the type of printer and the paper used. Much of it is trial and error—print it and see what it looks like. In general, laser printers have a resolution of about 600 dots per inch (dpi). Inkjet printers have a resolution of between 300 and 1440 dpi. Dpi is usually the resolution measurement for printers. The resolution measurement for computers is pixels per inch (ppi).

Digital Printing

A digital printing press is a beefed-up version of a desktop printer (often found in the document-processing departments of such places as FedEx Office or Staples). As digital printing technologies improve, digital printing services are becoming a more prevalent alternative to traditional offset printing. Because digital printers rasterize PostScript data—printing directly from a computer file, rather than going through a film and/or metal plate process (see next section)—they can yield quality output with a quick turnaround. Digital printing is ideal for targeted printing jobs and short-run projects that need to be done quickly but at much higher quality than a desktop printer allows. The resolution needed to properly print from a digital printing press should match the resolution of the particular output device. Consult the printing service for the resolution at which your document should be set.

Commercial Printing

The traditional method for getting your virtual work to hard copy is using a commercial or mechanical printing press, the most common being offset printing. A digital file is transferred to a film negative, which is then used to burn a printing plate (or the file is imaged directly to the plate). The plate carries the image, and the press transfers the image to paper. If you are printing a photograph or illustration in more than one or two colors, things get more complicated and expensive. To simulate a full range of colors (four-color process), images need to be broken down into dots of various sizes, called halftones. See Figure 11–1.

To create continuous tone color using the halftone method, each color must be inked and pressed separately to the paper; in short, the colors are separated and then layered back together. To do this, each color must have its own plate (one plate inked with cyan, one with magenta, one with yellow, and one with black), which is produced from separate film negatives. This is the process of color separation.

The individual colors produced by the mixing of cyan, magenta, yellow, and black (CMYK) colors

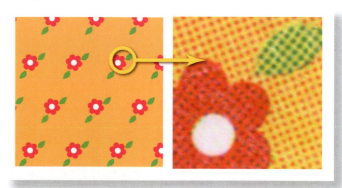

FIGURE | 11–1 |

When you magnify a printed image, the halftone dots become apparent.

are called process colors. You can print with spot colors or custom inks, too. As you learned in Chapter 5, spot colors are special colors composed of premixed inks that require their own printing plate instead of the ones used for four-color process printing.

Illustrator provides options in the Print dialog box for preparing an image for color separation and the subsequent printing process.

PDF or PostScript File

With Illustrator, you can also print your file in the Portable Document Format (PDF)—a PostScript-based file format that can support both vector and bitmapped data. Printing to a PDF is a convenient way to maintain all the attributes of your original Illustrator file in a cross-compatible format. Often print service bureaus will request a PDF version of a file. To set the PDF options, choose a Save command, specify a file name, and choose Adobe PDF as the file format (Mac) or Save as type: (Windows). Click Save and the Save Adobe PDF dialog box appears, where you can indicate general settings and specific presets, such as one specific for [Press Quality]. See Figure 11–2. Check with your print specialist for the settings he or she requires.

> Note: *You can also save a file as a PDF by choosing File > Print, and selecting the Adobe PDF option from the Printer drop-down menu at the top.*

FIGURE | 11–2 |

The Save Adobe PDF dialog box.

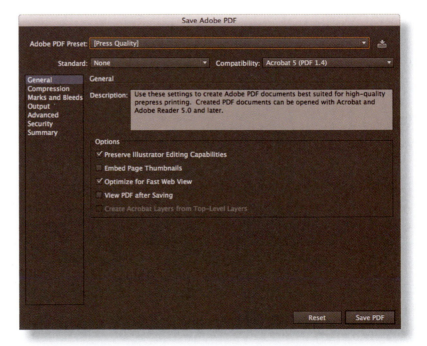

Figure © Cengage Learning 2013

GETTING INTO DETAILS

If you are having your artwork printed professionally, via either a digital or a commercial press, alleviate undue headaches and find yourself a reliable print specialist. A good specialist can identify your printing needs and offer appropriate solutions for getting the best-quality print job for your specific situation. That being said, do not underestimate the necessity of knowing something about printing processes and terminology yourself to facilitate print preparation. Properly setting up your an Illustrator file before handing it to the printer can save you lots of time and possibly money. You should also have an idea of what kind of paper you would like to have the job printed on. For instance, do you envision your creation on porous newsprint or slick, heavy card stock? Different types of paper produce varying color effects and require different prepress specifications.

> **Note:** *A print specialist can provide paper samples and color swatches to aid you in your decision.*

During the final output stages of your document, consult your printing service bureau to find out how best to prepare your file, such as in what format and resolution. Also, consider the artboard setup and be aware that the complexity of your artwork will determine how to prepare it for print. Transparencies, overprints, gradients, fonts, and complex paths, for example, might require extra attention to print properly. Each of these issues is covered in the following sections.

RESOLUTION AND SCREEN RULING

Resolution and screen ruling (or screen frequency) are important for generating the highest-quality artwork possible. For output to printers using halftone dots to render images, you must give consideration to the number of dots to be printed within a given area —the line screen— or in other words, the "resolution." This consideration is like working with the resolution of bitmap images, which, similarly, are composed of a given number of pixels on a bitmapped grid. Halftone dots are deposited on paper based on a screen ruling—the number of lines within a given screen. Screen rulings for halftones and separations are measured in lines per inch (lpi). The frequency and size of dots are determined by the screen ruling. High lpi creates smaller, tighter dots, like those seen in a glossy magazine, slick brochure, or art book. Fewer lpi creates larger, rougher-looking dots that print better on rough paper, like newsprint. A general rule is that the resolution—ppi or dpi when referring to halftone printing—of a given piece of artwork is about 1.5 times and no more than 2.0 times the screen frequency. Come again? OK, imagine, after consulting a print specialist, you discover that the screen ruling for the glossy flyer you want to print is 150 lpi and needs to be in TIFF, an uncompressed bitmap format with a lossless LZW compression option. This information gives you some idea of what resolution your TIFF file should be—between 225 and 300 dpi or ppi (hence, 150 lpi × 1.5 = 225). See Figure 11–3. Keep in mind that the resolution of an image and its screen frequency directly relate to what kind of paper it will be printed on and at what quality: the higher the screen frequency, the better the quality.

► Newspapers or similar highly porous, coarse papers use screens of 85 to 100 lpi. Therefore, artwork resolution should be between 138 and 150 dpi or ppi.

► News magazines or company publications with medium coarseness use screens of 133 to 150 lpi. Therefore, artwork resolution should be between 200 and 225 dpi or ppi.

► Fine-quality brochures and magazines with slick paper surfaces use screens of 150 to 300 lpi. Therefore, artwork resolution should be between 225 and 450 dpi or ppi.

FIGURE | 11–3 |

You can set the resolution of your artwork in the TIFF Options dialog box when you export your document (File > Export or under Effect > Document Raster Effects Settings).

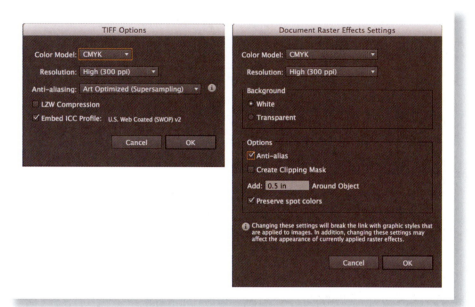

ARTBOARD SETUP

It's important to define the printable areas of your artwork with crop marks. Crop marks indicate where you want the printed paper to be cut. They are also useful for aligning Illustrator artwork that will be exported for use in another application. Crop marks are easy to make using the Artboard tool in the Tools panel. See Figure 11–4. You can also create Crop Marks from the Effect menu (Effect > Crop Marks).

> **Note:** *The Artboard tool offers options for setting up multiple artboards, which is explored in Chapter 8 in the Exploring on Your Own section.*

Try this:

1. Open a document you are working on or choose a premade template by going to File > New From Template.

2. Choose the Artboard tool in the Tools panel (see Figure 11–4). Notice that the document shifts into Artboard mode—a gray area, lighter than the pasteboard, with a bounding box appears around the artwork. Crop marks are automatically identified in this mode and a box appears at the top of each artboard containing the name of the artboard. See Figure 11–5.

FIGURE | 11–4 |

Make crop marks using the Artboard tool.

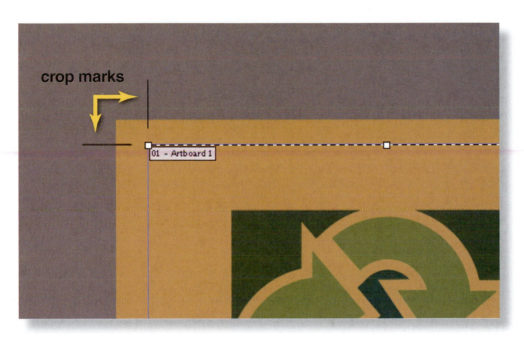

FIGURE | 11–5 |

Example of layout with crop marks indicated.

3. Adjust the handles of the artboard bounding area to where you would like the crop marks identified on the document. See Figure 11–5. You can also have the edges of the artboard fit to the artwork edges by opening the Artboard Options and, under Presets, choosing Fit Artboard to Artwork bounds or Fit Artboard to selected art. See Figure 11–6.

4. Press Esc on the keyboard or select another tool in the Tools panel to exit Artboard mode. Note, the crop marks will disappear, but—no worries—they will be available in the Print dialog box when you get ready to print the document (see About the Print Dialog Box section).

FIGURE | 11–6 |

The Artboard Options window.

TRANSPARENCY

When saving in file formats that do not recognize Illustrator's transparency effects, Illustrator performs a process called flattening. Flattening identifies colored areas that overlap each other and converts the artwork into separate objects that are more easily recognized by other programs and devices. To specify flattening settings, choose Object > Flatten Transparency. To preview how the changes might look when printed, choose Window > Flattener Preview. If you want to make adjustments, do so in the Advanced section of the Print dialog box.

OVERPRINTING

Overprinting relates to transparency: It identifies how overlapping spot or flat colors (i.e., Pantone™) are handled in the printing process. By setting certain conditions in the Overprint options of the Attributes panel (Window > Attributes), you determine whether the top color will appear solid or if it will combine with the color underneath. When you want a color to be pure—that is, not blended with colors below it—the printer must "knock out" or remove the color below. See Figure 11–7. To preview how changes to overprint options might occur when printed, choose View > Overprint Preview.

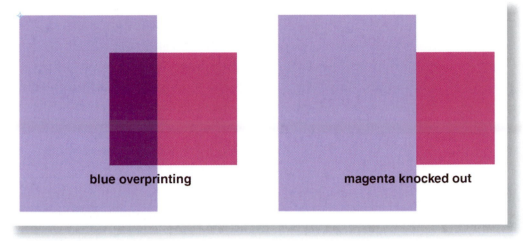

blue overprinting   **magenta knocked out**

Figure © Cengage Learning 2013

FIGURE | 11–7 |

Overprint applies to spot or flat colors, where the bottom color needs to be eliminated—knocked out—in order for the top color to appear "true."

▶ DON'T GO THERE

Do not let the preview (i.e., View > Overprint Preview and the Window > Flattener Preview) be the only indicator of how your work might appear in the printed format. Get an actual print proof of your work before continuing with the full press run.

GRADIENTS

Depending on the type of printer used, gradients, gradient meshes, and blends, particularly with transparency, may produce unwanted results. Gradients and blends contain continuous tones of color, which are difficult for some printers to print, causing distinct bands of color rather than smooth transition. Here are some general guidelines for successfully printing gradients and blends:

▶ Create blends that change at least 50% between two or more process colors.

▶ Use short blends—blends that are longer than 7.5 inches can cause banding when printed.

▶ Use lighter colors if banding occurs between blends.

▶ Use a line screen that supports at least 256 levels of gray.

▶ Adjust the Flatness setting if the curves of the gradient blend or mesh are complex. The Flatness setting (as opposed to the Flatten Transparency setting) is found in the Graphics section of the Print dialog box.

▶ If the gradient or mesh contains transparency, you can work with its resolution (quality of output) setting in the Object > Flatten Transparency options box.

FONTS

As mentioned in Chapter 7, when exporting and printing type, you need the corresponding font files to accurately print the document, or, alternatively, you need to embed the font or font family. Another option is to convert the type into outlines (Type > Create Outlines) to avoid any missing font issues. In either case, it is always a good idea to check the copyright specifications for the fonts used, and, if necessary, get appropriate licensing for their usage. You can set font downloading specifications in the Graphics section of the Print dialog box.

> Note: *Files saved as PDFs embed fonts automatically.*

COMPLEX PATHS

Artwork containing complex paths, particularly curved paths with many line segments, might receive a "limitcheck" error message when trying to print to PostScript printers with limited memory. You can adjust how the complex paths are rendered with the Flatness setting option in the Graphics section of the Print dialog box. A high setting (toward speed) results in the creation of a path with longer, fewer line segments, making it less accurate visually but improving print performance.

ABOUT THE PRINT DIALOG BOX

The Print dialog box sets preferences for how you want your artwork to print. If you have different output options—maybe one specific for desktop printing and another for creating a film negative—you can customize and save your settings in this box. See Figure 11–8.

To open the Print dialog box, choose File > Print. At the top of the Print dialog box, you can choose a Print Preset that you have saved previously, select the default, or create a new custom preset. If you are printing the artwork to a desktop printer or creating an Adobe PostScript File (see Note, page 341), select the appropriate option under Printer. If your output device supports PostScript, you can specify a PostScript Printer Description (PPD). Illustrator uses the information in the PPD file to determine which PostScript information to send to a PostScript printer when printing a document, such as font specifications, optimized screen frequencies, resolution, and color separations and management.

FIGURE | 11–8 |

The Print dialog box is very useful for specifying and saving print options.

> **Note:** *If your desktop printer does not support PostScript (only a few inkjet printers do), and you want to use some of the specifications PostScript offers, like the ability to make color separations, you might consider purchasing Adobe Acrobat. Open the Illustrator file in Adobe Acrobat, set the PostScript Options in the Advanced Print Setup dialog box (File > Print > Advanced button), and then print the file using the inkjet printer.*

In the lower-left corner of the Print dialog box is the artwork preview window. If you have set up multiple artboards in your document, you can choose which artboard you would like to print. Click through the navigation at the bottom of the window preview to choose the desired artboard. See Figure 11–9.

FIGURE | 11–9 |

At the bottom of the preview window choose which artboard you would like to identify for print setup.

Let's briefly go through the print categories found in the list box on the left-hand side of the dialog box: General, Marks and Bleed, Output, Graphics, Color Management, Advanced, and Summary. Keep in mind that the settings in each option area vary depending on the type of printer selected. There is a ton of information in this dialog box, so for more details on each option, choose Help > Illustrator Help > Printing.

GENERAL

In the General category, you specify the number of copies, media size, and orientation. Under Options, you can also adjust the placement of the artwork to best fit on the printed page or film negative. If your artwork is larger than a single page, you can determine how you would like the multiple pages to print by selecting a tiling option.

MARKS AND BLEED

In this category of the Print dialog box, you can set up mark and bleed specifications. If your document is to go through the color separation process, it is important to

FIGURE | 11–10 |

A file with printer's marks applied.

include printer's marks on each separation page. These marks are needed for the printing device to align the separations accurately (called registration) and ensure that the colors are printing properly. See Figure 11–10 for an example of a file with printer marks indicated.

Bleed is when color or artwork extends to the edge of a printed piece. When that is part of the design, you must extend the color or artwork past the edges of the artboard. Consult your printer for how much of a bleed you should indicate on your document to ensure the ink is still printed to the edge of the paper after it is trimmed (usually around 1/32 to 1/8 of an inch). Figure 11–10 shows a file whose color bleeds beyond the crop marks, ensuring an accurate look after trimming.

OUTPUT

The Output category of the Print dialog box lets you control how color separations are generated. You can choose which CMYK and spot colors to separate and, if necessary, convert spot colors to their closest CMYK equivalent.

GRAPHICS

The Graphics category of the Print dialog box makes clearer some of what was discussed in the section Getting Into Details, such as setting the flatness of complex paths and determining how fonts download.

COLOR MANAGEMENT

As discussed in Chapter 5, color matching problems can occur when printing artwork on different printers, as each printer has its own way of managing colors. One solution to alleviate these issues is to use a color management system (CMS), which can translate color accurately between devices. To find out more about CMS, go to Help > Illustrator Help and search for "consistent color." If you are using a CMS for your document, you can specify additional color management settings in the Color Management category of the Print dialog box.

ADVANCED

Specifications for overprinting and transparencies can be found in the Advanced category, along with the option to print artwork as bitmaps (versus vectors) when printing to low-resolution printers. It's important to note that if you want something to overprint, you need to set it in this pane.

SUMMARY

The Summary category summarizes all the settings you indicated in the Print dialog box. It also provides warnings about any special issues you should consider regarding flattening, resolution of raster effects, color mode, spot, and out-of-gamut colors. See Figure 11–11.

Once you have specified the print options, and depending on whether you are printing the file or saving it as a PDF, choose Print or Save. Choosing Done saves the print specifications with the file; it does not print anything.

FIGURE | 11–11 |

The Summary category of the Print dialog box lets you view your specifications and gives you warnings about special print concerns.

SUMMARY

There is a lot to think about when preparing artwork for print, so you should know the right questions to ask of the professionals in the industry. You also learned the importance of understanding what options are available in Illustrator for streamlining the printing process. Finally, it does not hurt to get a proof or two of your final, meticulously edited work before running the full print job.

▶ IN REVIEW

1. Describe halftone printing.

2. What is a PDF? What is so great about printing to PDF?

3. Screen ruling determines what about the halftone process?

4. The resolution of a piece of artwork is usually how many times greater than its screen ruling?

5. What does Flatten Transparency do?

6. What is overprinting?

7. What does the Flatness setting in the Graphics category of the Print dialog box do?

8. How do you create crop marks for your artwork?

9. What is the function of printer marks?

10. What is a bleed?

▶ EXPLORING ON YOUR OWN

1. Access the Help > Illustrator Help menu option and read up on Printing.

2. Find out if your desktop printer supports PostScript and if you have the ability to specify options for color separations in the Print dialog box. If so, try printing separations for a document that has been saved in the CMYK Color document mode (File > Document Color Mode).

3. Open the sample file **printlogo.ai** in the **chap11_lessons folder.** Take a look at the printer marks that have been created around the artwork. Using the Help files, investigate what each printer mark represents. Also, open the Print dialog box (File > Print) and see what print options have been saved for this particular document.

4. Awaken the detective inside you. Call a printing service (or search online) and inquire about what printing services it offers and what file specifications it requires. Be specific with your questions; use the terminology you learned in this chapter.

Suzanne Staud

"When I was young, as I sat deep in thought, my father would ask me: 'What is going on in that little head of yours?' I believe he saw me as his sensitive and contemplative child. No one else in the family had an artistic bent. Years later, when he discovered I wanted to be an artist, he was worried I'd end up like Vincent Van Gogh. He didn't want to squash my ambition, so he suggested I take a typing course (the word "secretary" was mentioned). Happily, typing helped immensely with the coming of computer graphics."

Suzanne's rules:

- ▶ Always do thumbnail sketches before starting a digital illustration.
- ▶ Stay true to your illustrations unless happy accidents occur. Sometimes happy accidents are gifts.
- ▶ Never give up, even when the phone isn't ringing.
- ▶ Don't be afraid to try new techniques, but stay focused.
- ▶ Continually be in pursuit of excellence in art and in life.
- ▶ Aim for the trash can, but reach for the stars.
- ▶ Break the rules in art including your own.
- ▶ Look to unique areas for inspiration.

About Suzanne Staud

Suzanne Staud was born in San Francisco, but raised ninety miles west in Modesto, California. As a fine arts major throughout high school and college, she entered the graphic design world knowing very little about how to design a logo, brochure, or, for that matter, anything printed. After working for several design firms, learning on the job and applying her years of basic design and fine art schooling to her designs, she started STAUDESIGN, a freelance award-winning graphic design/digital illustration/fine art studio, with her husband Randy Alford. She couldn't have managed the practical side of business without him. Suzanne works from her home. Her unique loft office/ studio was featured on HGTV as an eclectic museum of hand-me-downs, estate sale finds, and family antiques, all of which Suzanne draws inspiration from for her art.

She went to Catholic grammar school, where art wasn't a focus. Students copied postcards of the masters. She did great copies. When she entered Modesto High School, back in the late '60s, the art classes were a haven for her. She was encouraged to be creative and discovered the world of design. Teachers submitted her art to competitions, and she started winning awards. She saw this as a sign that art could be a career, plus she was terrible at math. She went to college and studied fine art—hoping to be the next Picasso, but ended up in a print shop inking press plates. Thus, began her career in commercial art and the road of hard knocks.

She has designed corrugated boxes for produce, illustrated a children's book, and designed and illustrated two lines of fabric—in addition to designing hundreds of logos, wine labels, brochures, posters, billboards, and newspaper ads. A few years back, she designed, illustrated, stitched, and installed the display case at the state capitol for Stanislaus County. She

Compliments of Suzanne Staud, STAUDESIGN.
Antique Toyland fabric design.

has won multiple fine art and digital illustration awards, local and national. Her work has been included in the California State Fair's prestigious California Works Fine Art show three times. Her digital illustrations have been peer juried into New York's Society of Illustrators juried show, The San Francisco Society of Illustrator's peer juried show, *Step-By-Step* Magazine (four issues), 1991 Print Magazine Annual of Best Design & Illustration, Seybold digital illustration juried exhibit for MacWorld 2001 and 2002, and featured in the book, *Secrets of Award-Winning Digital Artists*, by Jeremy Sutton and Daryl Wise.

Enjoy more of Suzanne's work at *www.staudesign.com.*

About the Work of Suzanne Staud

Antique Toyland

Before I designed the Antique Toyland fabric design, I watched an old Disney cartoon on television. It dawned on me how creative it was of the person who told stories, or made cartoons, of the little worlds of animals being much like our lives, but doing silly things we couldn't possible do, like riding on top of a blimp, or a duck flying an airplane. However silly, they are the kind of worlds I would love to visit, and Antique Toyland reflects those imaginary places. When the time came to select the palette for Antique Toyland, I used colors that compliment each other in just the right intensity so that outlining the art was unnecessary.

Whistling Trixi

Back in high school I won an award from *Seventeen* magazine for fabric design. I actually received money. It's no wonder I have had this love affair with all things fabric. I started doing fabric sculpture in the '70s and am currently working on art quilts. *Whistling Trixi* was designed and illustrated for a quilt. I've made the quilt and hope to sell it, as a label, to a California winery.

Quilt Artist's Business Card

Freddy Moran is a wonderful quilt artist. Her life and quilts are filled with color . . . her home has more than 30 colors painted on the walls and floors. It was obvious to me that her environment was very inspirational to her, so I designed and illustrated Freddy as a house.

Compliments of Suzanne Staud, STAUDESIGN.

Whistling Trixi.

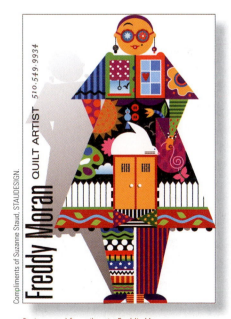

Compliments of Suzanne Staud, STAUDESIGN.

Business card for quilt artist Freddie Moran.

| Web Publishing |

12

charting your course

Today, a good percentage of illustrative artwork is used in digital format for Web pages, multimedia presentations, DVDs, TVs, and handheld devices. Designing graphics for the onscreen space is not the same as designing graphics for print (see Chapter 11 for details about print publishing). Each new version of Illustrator is supplemented with options for saving and preparing artwork and layouts for the growing digital medium, particularly online. In this chapter, you will learn the specifications for working with Web graphics, such as format, size, and color. Also, special attention will be to image slicing, the SVG and SWF vector formats, and reusable graphics called symbols.

goals

In this chapter you will:

► *Become an image optimization master*

► *Get a handle on Web file formats, including SVG and SWF*

► *Learn about Web image color and compression*

► *Discover the reusability of symbols*

► *Slice a Web page*

OPTIMIZATION

When it comes to publishing graphics for the Web, it is all about optimization.

Optimization, when referring to online artwork, is the process of preparing graphics for the Web, which are very different than those destined for print. It is a balancing act between the visual quality of an image and its quantitative file size. There are three interrelated areas to consider in the Web optimization process: image format, image color, and image size—all of which relate to image compression: reducing an image's file size so it looks good on screen and downloads quickly over an Internet connection.

ABOUT COMPRESSION

An image's file size can be reduced by compression. If you compress a bitmap image too much—make it smaller in file size—you lose visual quality. For instance, it might lose its anti-aliased effect, which is the smoothing of pixelated edges through a gradation of color, or it could dither, which is when colors that are lost during the compression are replaced by colors within a reduced palette. See Figure 12–1 and Figure 12–2.

There are two basic types of compression: lossy and lossless (or nonlossy). Lossy compression discards data to make a file smaller. Let's say you are optimizing a line of pixels into the JPEG format, which uses lossy compression. In this scenario, 10 of the pixels are white, followed by a gray pixel, and then 5 white pixels. With lossy compression, the computer reads the line as 16 white pixels; the gray pixel is converted to white.

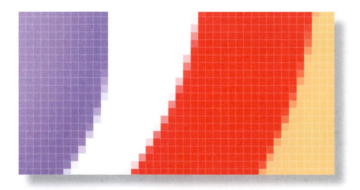

FIGURE | 12–1 |

Anti-aliasing close-up creates a stairstep effect of color gradation. When viewed from a distance, the edge of the object looks smoother.

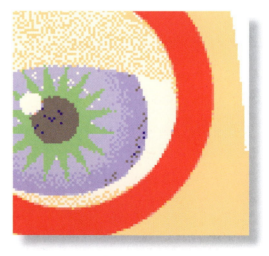

FIGURE | 12–2 |

Dithering (in the light and dark blue areas, for instance) attempts to simulate colors that are lost in the compression process.

Lossless compression, on the other hand, does not eliminate detail or information. Instead it looks for efficient ways to define the image, such as through the use of customized color tables. Ultimately, how compression is applied to images varies, depending on the image's format, color, and size.

IMAGE FORMAT

Traditionally, most Web images are saved in bitmap formats: Graphic Interchange Format (GIF), Joint Photographic Experts Group (JPEG), or Portable Network Graphic (PNG). The resolution and dimensions of a bitmap determine its file size and quality. Because of this, they are generally larger in file size than vector graphics, and when it comes to the Web, that could mean a slower download. Vector-based file formats— including Small Web Format (SWF) and Scalable Vector Graphics (SVG)—allow us to save and view graphics as streamlined paths, shapes, text, and effects in the online environment. Such graphics are scalable in size and easier to download—a wonderful combination for experiencing more interactive and animated imagery on the Web and in content for resource-limited handheld devices, like a personal data assistant (PDA) or mobile phone.

The file format you choose for an optimized image depends on the color, tonal, and graphic characteristics of the original image. In general, continuous-tone bitmap images (images with many shades of color), such as photographs, are best compressed in the JPEG or PNG-24 formats. Illustrations or type with flat color or sharp edges and crisp detail are best as GIF or PNG-8 files. Vector-based graphics or animations are either saved in the SVG or SWF formats. The following is a bulleted rundown of the characteristics of each Web-based graphic format—all of which you can export from Illustrator. Further clarification of these characteristics is presented in the sections Image Color and Image Size.

Graphic Interchange Format

The Graphic Interchange Format (GIF)

- ▶ supports an 8-bit color depth. Bit depth determines the amount and range of color an image can contain. A 1-bit image supports two colors, black and white; an 8-bit image can support up to 256 colors. A customized 256-color palette is referred to as indexed color.
- ▶ works best compressing solid areas of color, such as in line art, logos, or illustrations with type, with no gradients or continuous tones.
- ▶ is supported by the most common Web browsers, such as Windows Internet Explorer, Firefox, Safari, and Google Chrome.
- ▶ can be animated.
- ▶ traditionally uses a lossless compression method. Lossless compression is when no data is discarded during the file optimization process (see previous section, About Compression). You can save a GIF file multiple times without discarding

data. However, because GIF files are 8-bit color, optimizing an original 24-bit image as an 8-bit GIF will degrade image quality.

> **Note:** *You can create a lossy version of a GIF file in Illustrator and Photoshop. The lossy GIF format includes small compression artifacts (similar to those in JPEG files), and yields significantly smaller files.*

- ▸ can be interlaced, so images download in multiple passes, or progressively. The downloading process of interlaced images is visible to the user, assuring the user the download is in progress. Keep in mind, however, that interlacing increases file size.
- ▸ includes dithering options: the process of mixing colors to approximate those not present in the image.
- ▸ supports background transparency and background matting: the ability to blend the edges of an image with a Web page background color.

Joint Photographic Experts Group

The Joint Photographic Experts Group (JPEG) format

- ▸ supports 24-bit color (millions of colors) and preserves the broad range and subtle variations in brightness and hue, such as gradients, found in photographs and other continuous-tone images.
- ▸ is supported by the most common Web browsers.
- ▸ selectively discards data. Because it discards data, JPEG compression is referred to as lossy. The compression is set based on a range between 0% and 100%, or 1 and 10. A higher setting results in less data being discarded. The JPEG compression method tends to degrade sharp detail in an image, particularly in images containing type or vector art. Because of the nature of JPEG compression, you should always edit the original JPEG file, not a newer, "second-generation" version of the file.
- ▸ can be interlaced, so images download in multiple passes.
- ▸ does not support transparency.
- ▸ does not support animation.

Portable Network Graphic-8

The Portable Network Graphic (PNG-8) format

- ▸ uses 8-bit color. PNG-8 compresses solid areas of color while preserving sharp detail, such as that in line art, logos, or illustrations with type.
- ▸ is supported by most common browsers.
- ▸ uses a lossless compression method in which no data is discarded during compression. However, because PNG-8 files are 8-bit color, optimizing an original 24-bit image as a PNG-8 can degrade image quality. PNG-8 files use more advanced compression schemes than GIF, and can be 10–30% smaller than GIF files of the same image, depending on the image's color patterns.
- ▸ can be indexed to a specific 256-color palette, such as adaptive or Web.

- includes dithering options: the process of mixing colors to approximate those not present in the image.

- supports background transparency and background matting: the ability to blend the edges of an image with a Web page background color.

Portable Network Graphic-24

The Portable Network Graphic (PNG-24) format

- supports 24-bit color. PNG-24 preserves the broad range and subtle variations in brightness and hue found in photographs. It also preserves sharp detail, such as that in line art, logos, or illustrations with type.

- uses the same lossless compression method as the PNG-8 format in which no data is discarded. For that reason, PNG-24 files are usually larger than JPEG files of the same image.

- is supported by most common browsers.

- supports background transparency and background matting: the ability to blend the edges of an image with a Web page background color.

- supports multilevel transparency in which you can preserve up to 256 levels of transparency to blend the edges of an image smoothly with any background color. However, multilevel transparency is not supported by all browsers.

Small Web Format

The Small Web Format (SWF)

- supports full-screen, scalable, vector graphics, and animated objects.

- is an Adobe Flash format that must be viewed using Adobe's Shockwave and/ or Flash Player. Any computer equipped with a Flash player can view SWF formatted artwork. This player is free and can be downloaded from the Adobe Web site *http://www.adobe.com*.

- is a cross-compatible file format for exporting from Adobe's Flash program, as well as other Adobe programs.

> Note: *Artwork on Illustrator layers can be converted to vector-based SWF frames for use in Flash.*

- supports the use of reusable vector-based symbol objects (see the section About Symbols later in this chapter).

- uses a sophisticated, lossless compression scheme.

Scalable Vector Graphic

Scalable Vector Graphic (SVG) format

- supports full-screen, scalable, vector graphics, embedded raster graphics, and animated objects.

- is a royalty-free, vendor-neutral, open standard developed by the W3C (World Wide Web Consortium, at *http://www.w3.org/Graphics/SVG/*).

- ▶ utilizes a form of XML microsyntax that helps keep file sizes small. The SVG format was built from the ground up, with many influences.
- ▶ supports the use of JavaScript to create interactive events directly on graphics, such as button rollover actions. This can be done in Illustrator using the SVG Interactivity panel (Window > SVG Interactivity).
- ▶ requires the SVG plug-in, which is normally installed with Illustrator. To download the plug-in, if necessary, go to *http://www.adobe.com/svg*.
- ▶ supports the use of reusable symbol objects (see the section About Symbols).

The Wireless Bitmat Format

The Wireless Bitmap (WBMP) format

- ▶ supports 1-bit color, which means images are reduced to contain only black and white pixels.
- ▶ is the standard format for optimizing images for mobile devices, such as cell phones and PDAs that do not support viewing complex images in color.

IMAGE COLOR

Photographs and artwork to be viewed onscreen, such as on a Web page, must be saved in the RGB color mode. Why? For an answer to that question, review Chapter 5. To convert your artwork to the RGB color mode, choose File > Document Color Mode > RGB Color.

Color Reduction Algorithms

Adobe uses color reduction algorithms to generate a specific color table for an optimized image. You will get a better idea of how color tables work in Lesson 1: Preparing Artwork for the Web. Color reduction algorithms apply only to the GIF and PNG-8 formats. Because these two formats support the 8-bit format, an image with 256 colors or less, the color tables determine how the computer calculates which of the 256 colors of the image to keep.

> Note: *If the original image has less than 256 colors, you can adjust the maximum number of colors that are calculated, further reducing the image's size.*

Each color reduction palette produces slightly different results, so you need to understand how each type works. The descriptions for the following first five color tables were extracted from the Illustrator Help files. In addition, there are more color tables you can choose from the Save for Web settings for the GIF and PNG-8 formats.

Perceptual: Creates a custom color table by giving priority to colors for which the human eye has greater sensitivity.

Selective: Creates a color table similar to the perceptual color table, but it favors broad areas of color and the preservation of Web colors. This color table usually produces images with the greatest color integrity. Selective is the default option.

Adaptive: Creates a custom color table by sampling colors from the spectrum appearing most often in the image. For example, an image with only the colors green and blue produces a color table made primarily of greens and blues. Most images concentrate colors in particular areas of the spectrum.

Restrictive (Web): Uses the standard 216-color table common to the Windows and Mac OS 8-bit (256-color) palettes. This option ensures no browser dither is applied to colors when the image is displayed using 8-bit color. Using the Web palette can create larger files, and is recommended only when avoiding browser dither is a high priority.

Custom: Preserves the current perceptual, selective, or adaptive color table as a fixed palette that does not update with changes to the image.

Black and White: Builds a color table of only two colors—black and white.

Grayscale: Creates a custom table of grays, black, and white.

Mac OS and Windows: Builds an 8-bit palette, capable of displaying 256 colors, using the color table of the system you select.

IMAGE SIZE

Size does matter. However, before we go there, we need to discuss resolution. Remember resolution, the somewhat elusive concept of measuring bitmap images in pixels per inch (ppi)? If you recall from Chapter 11, the resolution of artwork going to print varies depending on where it is being printed and on what kind of paper stock. For online display, an image's resolution is much easier to grasp; it only needs to match the average resolution of images viewed via the Web, which is 72 ppi for Mac and 96 ppi for Windows.

Of course, the concept of resolution does not apply to vector-based graphics, such as those saved in the SWF or SVG formats. These types of images are unique in their application to the Web: They are inherently scalable and compact in size. So keep in mind that much of this information on file size and compression applies to bitmap (or rasterized) images. Until more Web designers use the latest online vector graphic formats, many of the graphics on the Web will be in a bitmap format.

A bitmap image's size is related to its resolution. Image size can be referred to in two ways, and both impact optimization: (1) actual dimensions (i.e., 5-by-5 inches or 400-by-600 pixels) and (2) file size—the image's actual weight, per se, in digital bits. This is measured in bytes, kilobytes (KB), megabytes (MB), or gigabytes (GB). A byte is 8 bits, a kilobyte is 1,024 bytes, a megabyte is 1,024 kilobytes, and a gigabyte is 1,024 megabytes. How big is too big for a Web image? That depends on how many images you have on a single Web page, whether they are bitmap- or vector-based, dimensionally large or small, and of course, the viewer's Internet connection speed.

FIGURE | 12–3 |

The Symbols panel.

FIGURE | 12–4 |

The Symbolism tools available for modifying symbol instances.

It is recommended to keep Web images to 10–50 KB each in file size. In fact, when building Web pages, it is not uncommon to keep the total file size of everything on a Web page under 60 KB to accommodate those viewers with slow Internet connections. The best way to be sure that your images are a good size is to upload your optimized images to the Web and test how long it takes to download them on different Internet connections.

About Symbols

A symbol is a reusable object. You can reuse a symbol in an illustration and, unlike the traditional way of duplicating an object, it produces copies of a much smaller file size. This is great when developing graphics for the bandwidth-dependent, online environment. Imagine you need to create an illustration of a swarm of butterflies. It will eventually go to the Web, so you want to keep the artwork's file size down. First, you draw a butterfly. Then you convert it to a symbol by dragging it into Illustrator's Symbols panel (see Figure 12–3). After you create the symbol, you drag instances of it to the artboard. Each instance is actually defined by the original symbol in the Library, resulting in an overall smaller file size.

When you edit an original symbol or change its attributes, any or all instances of it already present in the artwork will also be redefined. You can modify instances of a symbol with the Symbolism tools in the Tools panel. Modification options include scaling, rotating, moving, coloring, or duplicating instances. See Figure 12–4 and Figure 12–5. To view the options for the

FIGURE | 12–5 |

Examples of modified instances of a butterfly symbol.

Symbolism tools, double-click on the active Symbol tool in the Tools panel. See Figure 12–6. To use a premade symbol, choose Window > Symbol Libraries (you might need to scroll down to the bottom of the Windows panel to see this option) and select a library such as Nature.

Figures © Cengage Learning 2013

FIGURE | 12–6 |

Options for the Symbolism tools.

Using symbols is highly compatible with the SWF and SVG vector-based file formats. A plus is that you can save an Adobe Illustrator symbols library and then import it into an Adobe Flash file's Library. The symbols appear in a folder or folders. They can be placed on a single frame or multiple frames ready to be animated. See Figure 12–7 and Figure 12–8.

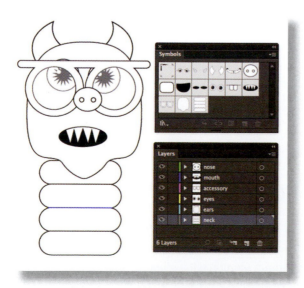

FIGURE | 12–7 |

Symbols located on individual sublayers in Illustrator. To export the symbols; open the Symbols panel options menu, click Save Symbol Library, and then save the Symbols library.

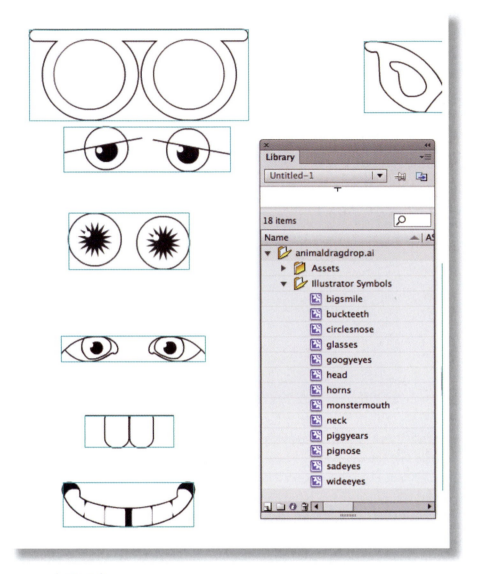

FIGURE | 12–8 |

Symbols created in Illustrator and imported into Flash. To import the symbols; click File > Import > Import to Library, navigate to and select the symbols library that you saved in Illustrator, and then click OK in the Import dialog box. The symbols appear in a folder or folders in Flash's Library panel.

SAVE FOR WEB

Think of the Save for Web feature as a fitness program for artwork destined for the Web. Depending on your image's body mass index (format), you can try various fitness regimes (compression schemes) to produce the best looking, leanest image possible. A two-window view lets you compare and contrast an image's optimization settings to the original file. See Figure 12–9.

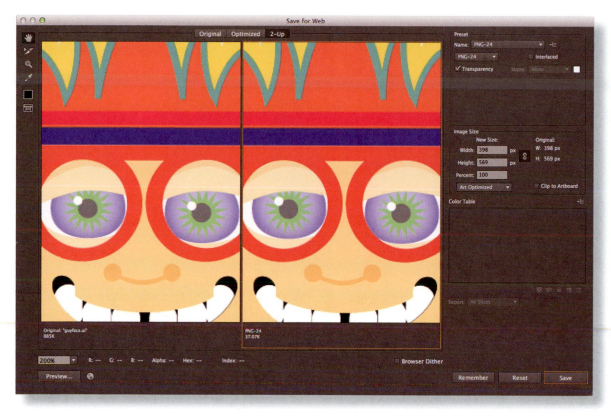

FIGURE | 12–9 |

The Save for Web dialog box is filled with options for optimizing artwork, including two-window viewing for comparing different optimization settings.

There are general guidelines for saving different kinds of artwork in different formats—photos as JPEGs, line art as GIFs. However, the finesse to finding the right size and quality comes from adjusting the options in the Save for Web dialog box. A simple adjustment to the bit depth of a GIF image, for example, can reduce the file size of the image immensely, resulting in a much more efficient Internet download. There are many options to choose from in the Save for Web dialog box, but do not let that overwhelm you. When you are ready to review said options, check the Illustrator Help files. For now, we will concentrate on some of the basics and help make you comfortable trusting your visual instincts when comparing and contrasting settings in the Save for Web dialog box.

LESSON 1: PREPARING ARTWORK FOR THE WEB

In this lesson, you will optimize and save a color logo, originally created in Illustrator, using the settings in Illustrator's Save for Web dialog box.

1. Open Illustrator, and choose File > New. Name the file **THClogo**; profile: **[Custom]**; units: **Pixels**; height: **339 px**, weight: **339 px**. Click OK. See Figure 12–10.

2. Choose File > Place. In the folder **chap12_lessons/assets**, select the **THClogo.ai** file. Uncheck Link (if necessary) and choose Place. In the Place PDF box, choose Bounding Box for the Crop to option and then click OK.

3. Choose Select > Deselect.

4. Choose View > Pixel Preview to view the graphic as it might appear when rasterized into the GIF, JPEG, or PNG format. Magnify an area of the image, and note the difference visually when Pixel Preview is turned off and on. See Figure 12–11 and Figure 12–12. You should turn on Pixel Preview when you want to control the precise placement, anti-aliasing, and size in the final rasterized object.

FIGURE | 12–10 |

Note the different options in a file set up for the Web, as opposed to one going to print.

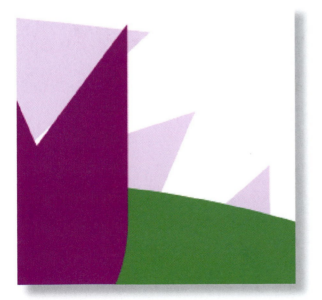

FIGURE | 12–11 |

Example of artwork with Pixel Preview turned off.

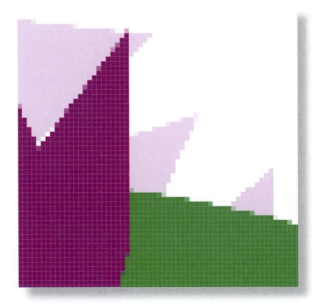

FIGURE | 12–12 |

Example of artwork with Pixel Preview turned on. A grid of pixels appears and anti-aliasing smoothes the edges.

Setting the Save for Web Options

1. Select the logo.

2. Choose File > Save for Web.

3. In the Save for Web dialog box, select the 2-Up tab at the top of the dialog box. A two-window view of the logo becomes available. See Figure 12–13.

FIGURE | 12–13 |

The 2-Up window of the Save for Web dialog box.

4. Click on the left window—a highlighted frame appears around the image. Note this window shows the original image at a file size of about 431 KB. Also, in the information area to the right of the dialog box, notice the preset, Original.

5. Click on the right window—a highlighted frame appears around the image and the optimization settings for the image become available. Notice the viewing annotations at the bottom of the selected window. These provide valuable information about the optimization settings for that particular method, including file format and size.

6. Select the following options:

    ▶ *Optimized file format:* GIF
    ▶ *Color reduction algorithm:* Adaptive
    ▶ *Dither algorithm:* No Dither
    ▶ *Transparency:* Uncheck

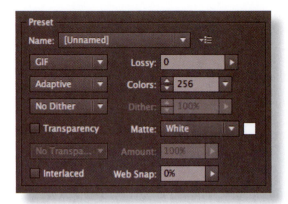

FIGURE | 12–14 |

Settings for the second window.

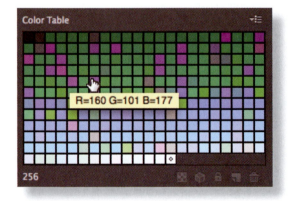

FIGURE | 12–15 |

A color table shows the colors used in an optimized image.

▸ *Interlaced:* Uncheck

▸ *Lossy:* 0

▸ *Colors:* 256

▸ *Matte:* White

▸ *Web Snap:* 0%

Compare your settings to Figure 12-14.

7. The Color Table shows the colors used in the image; this is determined by the color reduction algorithm setting (Adaptive) and the maximum number of colors in the algorithm setting (256). The swatch with a diamond in the middle indicates a Web-safe color (for more on the restrictive Web-safe color table, see the section Color Reduction Algorithms). The other swatches are in the general RGB color space. Point to a swatch to reveal the color's attributes. See Figure 12–15.

8. Now select the original image (on the left) and set the Name option to any GIF format. Adjust the GIF settings as follows:

▸ *Optimized file format:* GIF

▸ *Color reduction algorithm:* Restrictive (Web)

▸ *Dither algorithm:* Pattern

▸ *Transparency:* Uncheck

▸ *Interlaced:* Uncheck

▸ *Lossy:* 0

▸ *Colors:* Auto *(Note: If Auto doesn't appear automatically, type in the word Auto in the Colors field.)*

▸ *Matte:* None

▸ *Web Snap:* 0%

9. In the Color Table for the selected window, notice the swatches with diamond icons in the middle. This means these colors are within the traditional Web-safe color palette. Point to one of the swatches to reveal its hexadecimal color value.

10. Now change the image at the left to the PNG-8 option and adjust the settings to match these:

▸ *Color reduction algorithm:* Perceptual

▸ *Transparency:* Uncheck

▸ *Colors:* 256

▸ *Web Snap:* 0%

Comparing and Contrasting Settings

1. OK. Take a close look at what each optimization setting has done to the artwork. Magnify the image with the Zoom tool

(located on the left side of the Save for Web dialog box), and examine the artifacts of each compression scheme. Use the Hand tool to move the magnified artwork around in the windows.

2. Double-click on the Zoom tool icon to set the view of each window back to the original artwork size. Which version looks best to you?

3. Compare and contrast the viewing annotations at the bottom of both windows. What are the size differences? Is the one you visually like the best a reasonable size for Web display of a logo (under 10 KB, for example)?

4. Click Save to save this version of the file. Name it **weblogo.png**. For format, choose Images Only. Save the file in the folder **chap12_lessons**.

> Note: *If you do not want to save the file right away, choose Done rather than Save. This will close the Save for Web dialog box, and remember the optimization settings.*

IMAGE SLICING

Image slicing is dividing up areas of an image or a complete Web page layout into smaller, independent files. If you are familiar with constructing Web pages and working in HTML, you probably have an understanding of the benefits of slicing. If you are new to Web page design and development, this might seem like a crazy thing to do to your artwork; however, slicing is useful for:

▶ Creating independent files, each containing its own optimization settings
▶ Creating several smaller files, which download independently of one another, for faster download
▶ Creating interactive effects, such as button rollovers

LESSON 2: SLICING A HOME PAGE

In this lesson, you will revisit the Web page layout created in Chapter 8. Using the Illustrator Slice tool, you will slice and optimize areas of the layout for streamlined Web performance.

Setting Up the File

1. Open the file **chap12L2.ai** in the folder **chap12_lessons**.

2. Choose View > Fit All in Window and View > Pixel Preview.

3. Make sure your Workspace is set to Essentials.

4. Open the Layers panel.

5. Hide all the layers, except the layer called **pageTemplate**.

6. Unhide the layer called **guides**. You will use the template and guides to accurately place the slices you create next. See Figure 12–16.

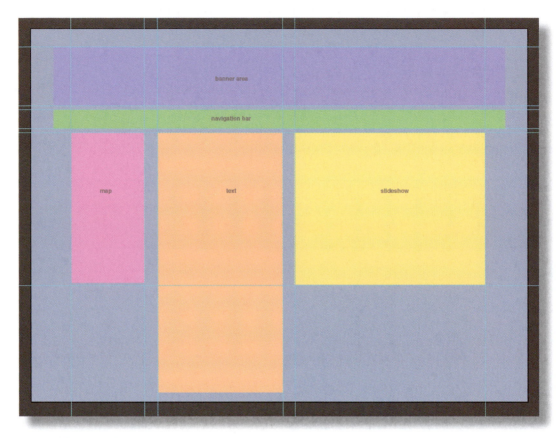

FIGURE | 12–16 |

The Web template and guides are used for accurate placement of slices.

Making Slices

1. Make sure that Object > Slice > Clip to Artboard is checked to keep your slices confined to the artboard area.

2. Create a new layer in the Layers panel and name it slices. The slice areas you define will be saved in this layer.

> Note: *When you make slices, you do not actually "cut up" your artwork, but rather create an overlay of separate areas that determine how the individual files will be created and reassembled when you save the document.*

FIGURE | 12–17 |

The Slice tool.

3. Select the Slice tool in the Tools panel. See Figure 12–17.

4. Place the point end of the Slice tool in the upper-left corner of the banner area of the template and click and drag, defining a box around the **purple**

banner area. See Figure 12–18. Notice that a number for the slice is indicated in the upper-left corner of the box. To show or hide the slice number, choose View > Show/Hide Slices. To change the slice line color, choose Illustrator > Preferences > Slices (Mac) or Edit > Preferences > Slices (Windows).

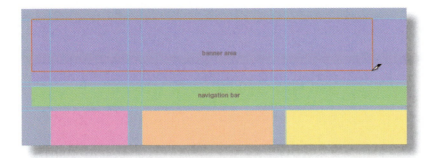

FIGURE | 12–18 |

Click and drag to define a slice area.

5. Create another divided area with the Slice tool, covering the pink **map area**.

6. Slice the **text** area—the light orange rectangle.

7. Define a slice for the slideshow. See Figure 12–19.

Note: *If you make a mistake, choose Edit > Undo and try again. Individual slices can also be deleted in the Layers panel.*

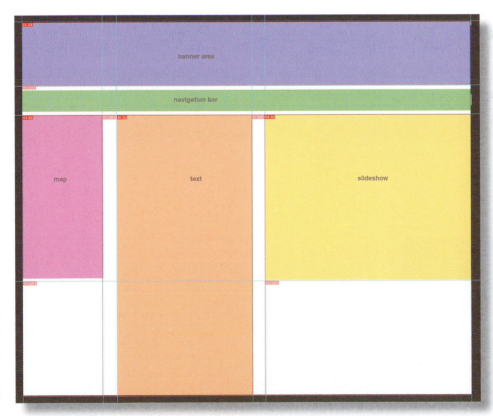

FIGURE | 12–19 |

Divide each section (content zone) with the Slice tool; Illustrator fills in the blank areas with additional slices.

8. Choose View > Actual Size.

9. Save the file **chap12L2_yourname.ai**, and place it in your lessons folder.

10. Unhide all the layers to see how the slices overlay the actual Web page layout.

11. The navigation bar needs to be divided. The name of each lake—will eventually become a button. Hide all layers except for the **slices, navigation**, and **pageTemplate** layers.

12. Select the Slice tool in the Tools panel (if necessary). Be sure that the slices layer is highlighted in the Layers panel, and then place the tool in the upper-left corner of the word intro, which will become the first link.

13. Click and drag, creating a slice around the text INTRO. See Figure 12–20.

FIGURE | 12–20 |

Create a slice for the intro link.

14. Continue creating slices around each link, similar to Figure 12–21. Keep the slices aligned to the top and bottom navigation guides and the pipe characters (|) between links.

> Note: *Slicing always occurs in a gridlike pattern. Even if you do not define a slice in a particular area, Illustrator automatically creates one to maintain the structure necessary for importing into an HTML page.*

INTRO | OTISTCO | OWASCO | CANADAIGUA | SKANEATELES | SENECA | CAYUGA | KEUKA

FIGURE | 12–21 |

Create 13 new slices, defined around each text link in the navigation bar.

15. Hide the **template** and **guide** layers and show all the content layers. Lock all visible layers.

16. Save your file.

FIGURE | 12–22 |

The Slice Select tool.

> Note: *If you need to select and modify individual slices, use the Slice Select tool, hidden under the Slice tool in the Tools panel. See Figure 12–22. To see the options for individually selected slices, choose Object > Slice > Slice Options. Here you can create a name for the sliced area (recommeded to find and edit a slice later, if necessary) or add a link (URL), a message for the browser's status bar, or an Alt tag to it. See Figure 12–23.*

FIGURE | 12–23 |

The Slice Options dialog box.

Optimizing and Saving the Slices

1. Choose File > Save for Web. Select the 2-Up option. On the left side is the original artwork; you will modify the image on the right. Make sure the right side is selected (with a highlighted frame around the window). Drag the image within the window with the Hand tool so that the map slice is visible in the windows.

2. Select the Slice Select tool (located on the left side of the Save for Web dialog box). See Figure 12–24.

3. Select the map slice in the second window to highlight it. Adjust the optimization settings of this sliced area. Since this is a graphic with no continuous tone, try both GIF and PNG and see which works best in terms of quality and file size.

4. Select the slideshow slice. Try the PNG-24 and JPEG options. See Figure 12–25.

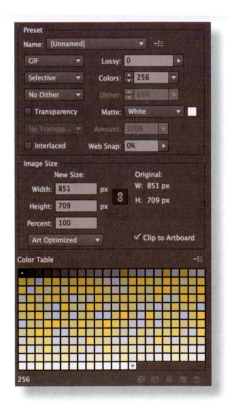

FIGURE | 12–24 |

Select the Slice Select tool.

FIGURE | 12–25 |

Optimization settings for the map.

FIGURE | 12–26 |

Option to turn off slice visibility.

5. Select each of the other slices and optimize them to your liking. Balance the image file size with visual appeal.

6. Turn off the slice view (located in the tools area to the left of the window) to view the final, optimized artwork. See Figure 12–26.

7. Click Save in the Save for Web dialog box.

8. Just below the color table is an Export menu. Choose to export All User Slices. That prevents the export of all the empty slices that Illustrator added to your page.

9. In the Save Optimized As dialog box, enter the following (Figure 12–27):

   ► *Save As:* mywebpage.png

   ► *Where:* chap12_lessons

   ► *Format:* Images Only

9. Click Save to save the individually divided files to an **images** folder that Illustrator will create for you. This folder will be located in your **chap12_lessons** folder. Minimize the Illustrator program and find this folder. Open it and, amazingly, all your sliced images are there! See Figure 12–27.

FIGURE | 12–27 |

Find your saved images.

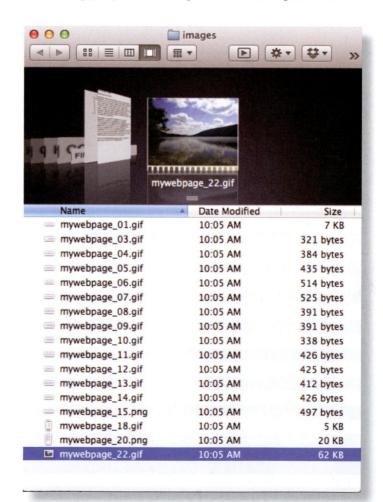

SUMMARY

Illustrator is a resource for exploring the elements of drawing and design, and producing a finished product suitable for print and the World Wide Web.

▶ IN REVIEW

1. Describe image optimization.

2. Photographs are best saved in what format? What about graphics with gradient blends and meshes?

3. To view SVG and SWF formatted graphics, you must have what? And where do you get it?

4. What image formats use color reduction algorithms and why?

5. How many bytes are in a kilobyte? Why is that important to know?

6. What is dithering?

7. How are symbols useful for Web graphics?

8. Name three useful things about slicing images.

9. Where do sliced images go after you save them?

10. Name the five elements of visual design.

▶ EXPLORING ON YOUR OWN

1. For more information about Web graphics in Illustrator, choose Help > Illustrator Help and view the topic Web graphics. Information not covered in this chapter you might want to read is found under Slices and image maps > Create image maps.

2. For more information on using SVG with Illustrator, choose Help > Illustrator Help and view the topic Web graphics > SVG, or visit the World Wide Web Consortium (W3C) site at *http://www.w3.org/Graphics/SVG*. For more information on the SWF format, visit the Adobe site at *http://www.adobe.com*.

3. Using what you have learned about the Save for Web dialog box, decide which optimization settings are best for the example artwork, **guyface.ai**, located in the folder **chap12_lessons/assets**.

INDEX